Scenic Driving

UTAH

Joe Bensen

FALCON®

HELENA, MONTANA

A FALCON GUIDE ®

Falcon® Publishing is continually expanding its list of recreational guidebooks. All books include detailed descriptions, accurate maps, and all the information necessary for enjoyable trips. You can order extra copies of this book and get information and prices for other Falcon® guidebooks by writing Falcon, P.O. Box 1718, Helena, MT 59624 or calling toll-free 1-800-582-2665. Also, please ask for a free copy of our current catalog. Visit our website at www.Falcon.com or contact us by e-mail at falcon@falcon.com.

Cover photo: The Kolob Fingers Scenic Byway.
Back cover photo: View along the Kolob Reservoir Scenic Backway.
All photos by the author.

ISBN 1-56044-486-X

CAUTION

Outdoor recreational activities are by their very nature potentially hazardous. All participants in such activities must assume the responsibility for their own actions and safety. The information contained in this guidebook cannot replace sound judgment and good decision–making skills, which help reduce risk exposure, nor does the scope of this book allow for disclosure of all the potential hazards and risks involved in such activities.

Learn as much as possible about the outdoor recreational activities you participate in, prepare for the unexpected, and be cautious. The reward will be a safer and more enjoyable experience.

 Text pages printed on recycled paper

Contents

Acknowledgments

Many people provided me with useful information, kept me from getting lost, and otherwise showed me great kindness during my months of research. I would like to especially thank Sue Halliday for her background information on the old Marie Ogden colony, and my friend Horea for his input regarding monumental earthworks sculpture in northwestern Utah. A special word of gratitude is due Wayne Decker for rescuing my vehicle from what might have been a very nasty plunge, off that bad back road above Yankee Meadows.

Locator Map

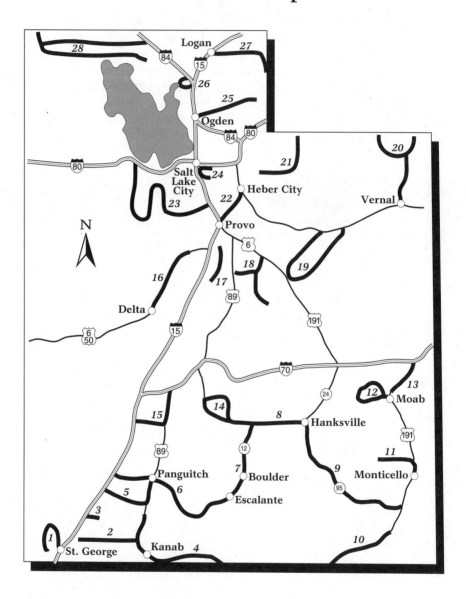

Map Legend

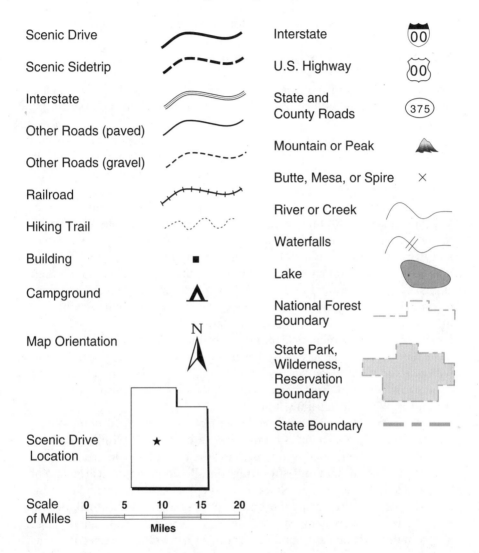

Scenic Drive

Scenic Sidetrip

Interstate

Other Roads (paved)

Other Roads (gravel)

Railroad

Hiking Trail

Building

Campground

Map Orientation

N

Scenic Drive
Location

Scale
of Miles

0   5   10   15   20

Miles

Interstate

U.S. Highway

State and
County Roads

375

Mountain or Peak

Butte, Mesa, or Spire

River or Creek

Waterfalls

Lake

National Forest
Boundary

State Park,
Wilderness,
Reservation
Boundary

State Boundary

Introduction

How many synonyms are there for *spectacular*, anyway? I think by the time I finished this manuscript, I'd used most of them. Utah truly is an extraordinary place, remarkable for its tremendous diversity of scenic grandeur, as well as for the way it stands out as somehow culturally *different* from its neighbors in the American West. Utah is certainly a place apart, topographically and culturally, a place that can sometimes seem, well . . . exotic.

Topographically and geologically, Utah exceeds most of our expectations for natural scenery. This is a photographer's paradise, a rockhound's nirvana, and a geologist's ultimate dreamworld. The entire state is a like a huge open-air geology textbook.

Utah comprises three distinct regions: the Colorado Plateau, the Basin and Range, and the Middle Rocky Mountain regions. The Colorado Plateau includes more than half of Utah, along with parts of Colorado, New Mexico, and Arizona. Composed mainly of sandstone and limestone, the Colorado Plateau has been broken and buckled by dramatic geological faults, then etched by running water into huge and complex canyon systems. The result is some of the most impressive scenery in the world, and Utah certainly got more than its share. The southern and eastern parts of the state are world famous for fantastic rock formations and brilliant colors. These almost unbelievable colors are largely caused by oxidation of iron ores in combination with other minerals. Iron-rich soil oxidizes brilliant red or orange. Without enough oxygen, iron turns green. When iron mixes with oxygen and hydrogen, it turns into deep yellow limonite.

All five of Utah's national parks, four of its six national monuments, and the huge Glen Canyon National Recreation Area lie within the Colorado Plateau region, making this perhaps the nation's single greatest concentration of scenic and touristic attractions. Predominantly an arid land of rock and sky, the lack of reliable water has kept most of this region an uninhabitable desert. The remoteness and emptiness of the land contributes, in many ways, to its great appeal. Yet Utah's portion of the Colorado Plateau also contains spectacular subalpine terrain, with towering, forested plateaus and lush green river valleys. Seventeen of the drives in this guide are devoted to this important region.

Utah's Wasatch and Uinta Mountains, occupying the northeast corner of the state, are Utah's connection to the Intermountain West. Though by far the smallest of the three topographic regions, the Rocky Mountains in Utah are filled with scenic grandeur. The two ranges are distinct from one another, both geologically and visually, and offer different rewards to the visitor. The north-south range of the Wasatch is criss-crossed by numerous good roads, and filled with fertile valleys supporting many mountain communities, farms, and ranches. The Uintas, in contrast, remain an untouched wilderness area through which no roads penetrate and very few skirt closely. Seven of the drives in this guide are located in Utah's mountain wonderland, including two that hopefully will give a glimpse of the remote High Uintas.

Utah's Basin and Range region is, on first impression, a vast wasteland of little commercial importance and dubious interest to tourists. This is a hard, rugged land of treeless vistas, cracked earth, sparse vegetation, and a huge, dead sea. Generally overlooked by visitors, and certainly overshadowed by Utah's mountain and canyon wonders, the Great Basin is hardly "scenic" by conventional standards. But it has a primal power and a distinct personality that must be experienced first-hand. Four of the drives in this book focus directly on Great Basin locales, and two others at least touch on this forbidding yet fascinating region.

Utah is blessed with 79 percent public lands, with individual counties comprised of as much as 97 percent public lands. From the earliest days of Mormon settlement, the issue of community wealth/community good versus individual acquisition was central to everyday life in the Mormon community. This philosophy of communal stewardship of the land exerts its influence on present-day Utah as well—much to the traveler's benefit. With the exception of the few populated and arable valleys, Utah has a somewhat "free and open" demeanor, a feeling that the land is here for us to explore and to enjoy.

Due to the abundance of public lands, there is ample opportunity for camping outside of established campgrounds throughout Utah. When doing so, make every effort to use the numerous established primitive sites, especially if you intend to build a campfire; this will help limit the number of fire rings. When using these sites, the Bureau of Land Management (referred to as BLM in this guide) requires that you use a washable, reusable toilet system.

Regardless of your feelings toward BLM policies on your home turf, they appear to have been very good about overseeing public lands in Utah. In an era of increasing conflict between those who would restrict commercial use of public land and those who view the land as a resource for development, the BLM is generally caught in the middle, stuck in a no-win situation. After many years of admiring Utah's wide, wild, open spaces, I believe we owe the BLM gratitude for their efforts in preserving and sensibly managing these tremendous natural resources.

A relatively small portion of Utah's public land has been set aside as National Park Service areas: five national parks, six national monuments, and two national recreation areas. Each of these renowned sites is highlighted in one of the drives in this book, with the sole exception of remote Rainbow Bridge National Monument, which cannot be reached by vehicle.

In addition to these very important sites, Utah has forty-five state parks—more than any of the lower forty-eight states.

While the majority of the National Park Service areas lie in the southern part of the state, even those within the same geographical regions have their own distinct "personality." Zion is nothing like Bryce, which is nothing like Capitol Reef, which is distinct from Glen Canyon, which looks nothing at all like Canyonlands, and so on through the list. The variety of wilderness scenery in this state is truly outstanding.

Culturally, Utah has managed to maintain its individuality in an ever more homogeneous American West. History and heritage have played upon the look of the land in Utah more than in any other Western state. The state is well known for its unity of heritage and for the distinct social cohesion born of patterns clearly established in pioneer settlement. One hundred fifty years ago Utah began its modern period as a Mormon enclave, and those beginnings are still manifest in the way the state looks and feels today.

Before Utah became the Mormon Zion, it was a sort of paradise for the various waves of native peoples who roamed and settled throughout the Intermountain and Desert West. Flint tools dating back eleven thousand years, left by descendants of the nomadic bands who migrated across the frozen Bering Strait, have been found in caves in Utah. These earliest Utah *Paleo-Indians* were entirely hunter-gatherers. During the *Archaic* period, over thousands of years, these nomadic people gradually settled down. By about the time of Christ, a new culture had evolved. The culture known as Anasazi (*Ancient Ones*) emerged, cultivating the land, weaving baskets, and building stone constructions throughout what is now southern Utah. At about the same time, the Fremont Culture developed to the north of the Anasazi. These two cultures flourished in Utah for over a thousand years, until they suddenly disappeared around 1200 A.D. It is thought that severe drought drove the Anasazi ultimately to abandon their farms and dwellings; it is likely that today's Hopi are their descendants. It is unclear what happened to the Fremont people, though they may have been absorbed by a new incursion of nomadic hunters: the Utes and Shoshone.

The current Native American residents of central and northern Utah are largely descended from these nomadic bands of horse-centered Ute, Paiute, and Shoshone hunters who moved into the well-watered parts of the state in relatively recent times. The Navajo, an Athabascan people from the north, still occupy their traditional lands in the Four-Corners area.

As you travel throughout the state, the pictorial record of Utah's ancient people is a recurring point of interest, a graphic reminder of those who have enjoyed this special place over the centuries. Native American rock art falls into two categories. *Pictographs* are painted, usually in deep red, and always found in caves or under ledges. *Petroglyphs* are incised in stone, often by pecking at the dark patina (sometimes called "desert varnish") that stands out from the lighter surrounding rock. To the long "visitors register" of native peoples were added later the names and dates of the early European-American explorers.

Many of the drives in this guide feature such attractions, and trail hikes throughout the state disclose lesser-known sites. A word of warning and advice is in order regarding Utah's rich variety of historic and prehistoric sites. Much has been lost to vandalism and "souvenir collection" (a.k.a. *theft*). But today an equally dangerous threat is posed by the increasing numbers of visitors to these sites. While the damage caused is largely unintentional, it has been suggested that the public may be "loving to death" its natural resources and historic treasures. It has become ever more important that we practice low-impact strategies when visiting historic sites. Never touch rock art or artifacts. Chalking, tracing, and rubbing all cause damage. We owe this consideration to future generations.

Besides, it's the law. These sites are protected by the Antiquities Act of 1906 and the Archaeological Resources Protection Act of 1979. The ARPA provides penalties up to $250,000 and five years imprisonment for damaging sites or removing artifacts. The BLM maintains a Law Enforcement Hotline, and requests that you report, as quickly as possible, any violations you might observe: 1-800-722-3998. Beyond the legalities, keep in mind that no jail term or fine can replace the loss of these treasures for future generations—once gone, they are lost to all of us, forever.

White exploration of the region began with Spanish expeditions from New Mexico, searching for a route that might connect the New Mexico colonies with Spanish outposts in southern California. The most notable of these efforts took place in 1776, when two Franciscan priests, Francisco Dominguez and Silvestre Velez de Escalante, led a party from Santa Fe to the southwest corner of Utah before turning back in fear of approaching winter. Their route was finally pushed through by the American mountain man and adventurer, Jedediah Smith, in 1826.

For the next twenty years large caravans passed along the Old Spanish Trail, leading mules laden with woolen goods from the sheep-rich hills of New Mexico to the garrisons and ranches of California. The woolens were traded for mules and horses, and as many as two thousand animals were herded back to New Mexico in the spring. The trail was described as "the longest, crookedest, most arduous pack mule trail in in the history of America." Territorial alignments and regional trade patterns were dramatically altered with the Treaty of Guadalupe-Hidalgo in 1848 and Spain's withdrawal from colonial ventures in the American West. With the dissolution of the New Mexico-California relationship, the importance of trade between the two regions declined and the Spanish Trail was no longer of major importance. The trail had, however, established the routes by which later pioneers would travel, and the paths of many of today's modern highways.

The subsequent history of Utah is tied inextricably to the story of the Church of Jesus Christ of Latter Day Saints (LDS). Utah is one of the last places in America to still exhibit a cohesive regional culture, a place where the land and the people are still tied to one another in ways quite different from the rest of American society. This is still very much Mormon country.

On July 24, 1847, a bedridden Brigham Young was carried out to a point above the Salt Lake Valley where, according to legend, he declared "This is the place." Driven from place after place across America, the Mormon leaders were looking for spot on earth no one else wanted, where they could build their modern *Zion*. The Mormon pioneers carved out of the wilderness—first in the Salt Lake Valley, then in remote valleys throughout the region—a true pioneer empire, establishing new colonies of fresh immigrant converts, sent out into the territory's remotest corners by the Church Elders.

There was never in Utah the sense of the wholly independent pioneer, one who made it purely on individual accomplishment. Pioneer life in Utah was first and foremost a *communal* affair, connected by the community stake (church parish) with broader connections to regional temples and the church headquarters in Salt Lake City. Without an understanding of the philosophies and patterns of Mormon settlement, and an appreciation for what it meant to colonize the far-flung desert and mountain corners of this topographically diverse state, it would be difficult to fully comprehend the achievement of the Mormon pioneers. Some advance reading about their fascinating history will enhance your trip, helping explain why the towns are located where they are, and even why they still look the way they do.

One of the visual features that most distinguishes old LDS settlements from their counterparts in other regions of the ranching/farming West is the number of old brick houses. It seems that brick was very much a part of the Mormon village aesthetic, and most of these communities established a brickyard early on. This may have been a heritage transported from their eastern hometowns. With their red brick, white fences, and tidy gardens, some of these towns have an almost back-east look, yet they are very much part of the western frontier—sort of like Norman Rockwell gone "yippee-aye-o-kaiyay."

At any rate, they built their towns to last, which leaves us much to admire today. In most of the larger towns the local chapters of the Daughters of Utah Pioneers (DUP) maintains community museums that give an excellent glimpse into the pioneer past. The standard visiting procedure is to call one of the several numbers displayed on the front door, and a volunteer will come down to not only give you a tour, but tell you everything of note that's ever happened in that part of the county.

Modern Utah ranks as high on the scenery scale as it does low on the excitement scale. With the exception of skiing, river running, and the NBA's

Utah Jazz, manmade excitement is pretty darned scarce in this sector. You have a better chance of finding a good ice-cream parlor in Salt Lake City than a nightclub, and most all other towns are decidedly slow.

But for scenery—especially for *roadside* scenery—this is arguably the best in the West. In fact, Utah appears to have been custom-made for the driving tour. There may be other places on earth that have grander mountains or denser forests or wilder desert country than Utah's, but it's doubtful that any other place encapsulates such spectacular scenic diversity, and certainly none that can be viewed from the family sedan!

Utah has perhaps the best developed tourist infrastructure of any state between the two coasts. Indeed, tourism (including the ski industry) alternates year to year with mining as Utah's number-one industry. Visitors come from all over the world to marvel at Utah's wonders. During the height of the summer tourist season there are more Germans in southern Utah than in Stuttgart. (Well, okay, I just made that up—but there *appear* to be more European visitors here than anywhere else in the American West.) Consequently, Utah is a state of visitor centers and tourist information offices. Between the state and national parks, the various ranger districts, and all of the community, regional, and state travel information offices, Utah has an awful lot of proud, friendly folks eager to help you enjoy your stay. Take advantage of all this assistance; always make the visitor center your first national park stop.

Keep an eye out for rubbernecking tourists whose eyes are on the scenery rather than the road. This is especially a problem in places like Zion Park, where you may actually see drivers with their heads stuck out of the window! (They really need to institute some sort of "designated driver" program in Zion Park.) On some of the narrow canyon and mountain drives, there are few places to pass. If you find a traffic build-up developing behind you—either because you are in a slow-moving vehicle, or simply because you are enjoying the scenery—common courtesy suggests you take advantage of the pullouts to let traffic pass you. Bicyclists are plentiful in Utah, both as day-trippers in the canyons above urban centers (Provo Canyon, the Cottonwood Canyons, Logan, Ogden) and on longer tours—especially on Utah 12 and Utah 95. Keep alert and don't ruin their day.

If you are in a hurry and really need to do the "scenic blitz," most of these roads are fine for speed-limit driving. But you will miss a lot. Use 40-45 miles per hour as an average speed, and allow for plenty of ten-minute stops at viewpoints. While all of these drives can be completed as day trips (a very long day for one or two of them), whole days and more can be spent exploring individual parks and wilderness areas, which you will probably pass through too quickly. A look at the drive locator map will indicate how easy it is to link several drives together as a multi-day excursion. Allow yourself some flexibility in determining precise routes and touring strategies.

Deciding which drives to include as "scenic drives in Utah" presents a real dilemma, since few roads outside the major corridor of Interstate 15 are *not* scenic. There are many drives that deserve mention, in addition to the twenty-eight included here. Utah Highway 20, between Interstate 15 and U.S. Highway 89, is especially attractive. The entire corridor of US 89 is both scenic and culturally interesting. Although U.S. Highway 40, from Heber to Vernal, fails to warrant even a scenic designation on the state road map, the first thing you notice when you head east out of Heber is just how beautiful this drive really is. What is, in Utah, a perfectly normal drive would be a state treasure and showcase drive anywhere else.

The twenty-eight selected drives are representative of the many different kinds of roadside attractions in the state. Some are almost purely scenic, featuring mile after mile of gorgeous or dramatic landscape. Others involve a certain cultural component, featuring picturesque small towns and historic sites. Many of these drives provide access to mountain and canyon hiking trails of extraordinary appeal. Especially with the canyon and alpine drives, there are good opportunities to let your vehicle gain all the elevation you might otherwise have had to work hard for. You may want to plan specifically to combine hikes with these drives.

The drives described in this guide are almost all on good, fast, paved roads, free of any of the extreme grades that might cause problems for any vehicle. The state of Utah has designated Scenic Byway and Scenic Backway drives, and the BLM has named several National Back Country Byway drives in the state. In general, a Scenic Byway is on paved road (usually a major two-lane artery), while Scenic Backways are smaller (usually unpaved) backroads of varying surface quality. A BLM Back Country Byway is usually the same as a Utah Scenic Backway. Most of these twenty-eight drives are essentially the same as the state-designated Byways, sometimes combined with an adjacent Backway of reasonable road quality, and always with recommended sidetrips that sometimes require a more rugged vehicle. If you plan on taking any of these suggested backcountry drives, always inquire locally as to current road conditions. These roads can vary greatly from year to year—even from day to day—depending on weather and level of county maintenance. It is especially important to determine whether these roads are practical for passenger cars, recreational vehicles, or trailers. In some cases you may just have to make a note to return next year in your new 4x4.

In *every* case where you opt to stray from the main routes, be sure your vehicle is in good working order, that you are carrying at least one good spare, that you have plenty of emergency food and water, and that you know where the heck you are going. Vehicles are great for getting us a long way off from civilization; but let's not take lightly the potential dangers. Be prepared, be informed, and enjoy your driving adventure.

With so much topographic diversity, it's no wonder Utah's climate varies so much from north to south and from high elevation to low. The desert country

Capitol Gorge is at the south end of the Capitol Reef Scenic Drive.

can be blistering hot in the daytime, yet chilly at night. Experienced Utah travelers know to keep spare clothes in the car, especially when traveling in the mountain regions. After heavy-snow years or cool springs, many of the higher elevation roads can be closed until late June. And many of the higher campgrounds, even along main roads, may also be snowed in.

The following books may help you to enjoy more fully your travels through this most extraordinary state. Read these books, and Utah's fantastic geological/historical/cultural patchwork will begin to come together as the most fascinating sort of human and topographical quilt.

Chronic, Halka: *Roadside Geology of Utah*. The definitive inside look at a geological wonderland.

Dutton, Clarence: *Report on the Geology of the High Plateaus of Utah*. A classic description by a member of John Wesley Powell's expedition.

Gearey, Edward: *The Proper Edge of the Sky*. This is a must-read for anyone with a real interest in the southern plateauland.

Nelson, Lowry: *The Mormon Village*. This is a fascinating scholarly analysis of the hows and whys of community structure and construction in rural Utah.

Stegner, Wallace: *Mormon Country*. Another classic. A carefully observed and beautifully written set of essays on life in Utah.

Now, get out there and experience it.

Drive 1: Southwest Corner
Scenic Drive
St. George to Littlefield, Arizona Loop

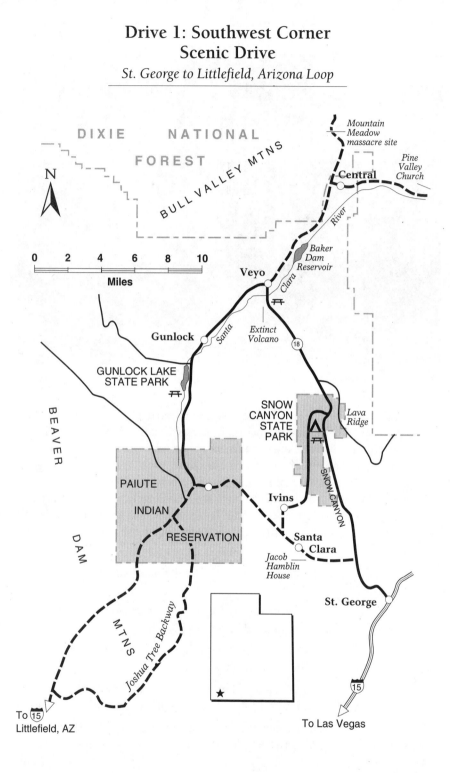

1

Southwest Corner
Scenic Drive

St. George to Littlefield, Arizona Loop

General description: A loop tour, combining redrock canyon and dry Mojave Desert scenery.

Special attractions: Snow Canyon sandstone formations, volcanic cinder cones, Mojave Desert/Joshua Tree Scenic Backway, rock climbing.

Location: The extreme southwest corner of Utah.

Drive route number and name: Utah Highways 18 and 3184, old U.S. Highway 91.

Travel season: Year-round. Fall and spring are the most comfortable. Summers can be hot; start early in the day and carry plenty of water.

Camping: State Park campground at Snow Canyon, commercial campground at St. George.

Services: All services at St. George; limited services at Veyo, Ivins, and Littlefield, Arizona.

Nearby attractions: Mountain Meadows, Pine Valley, Lytle Reserve, gaming in Nevada.

The drive

Mormon pioneers were sent to Utah's southwest corner by the LDS Church in 1861 to investigate the possibility of growing warm-climate crops. The region's southern location, climate, and the success of the cotton crop earned it the nickname "Utah's Dixie."

As you might expect, this is a warm spot, with summer temperatures often exceeding 100 degrees. The landscape tends toward dry, rocky desert, with the exception of the pleasant, narrow valley carved by the little Santa Clara River (through which part of this drive runs). To the north of St. George, the forested Pine Valley and Bull Valley mountains provide a cool, green refuge from the often blistering temperatures down here in Utah's lowest and warmest corner.

The total distance of this drive is approximately 100 miles, depending on which options you choose to follow. The basic St. George to Veyo to Littlefield and back to St. George drive, though relatively short, is packed with enough scenic attractions to warrant spending at least four hours. Add a Snow Canyon hike and a short sidetrip drive or two, and this can easily be stretched into a full day's outing. The short diversion into Snow Canyon should not be considered a mere sidetrip option; along with the Joshua trees to the west of here, the scenery in Snow Canyon is the real *must-do* highlight of this drive.

All roads on this drive are well maintained and driveable in all vehicles. The drive from Veyo south through Gunlock (UT 3184) is extremely beautiful, on narrow, winding roads that pose no problem for any vehicle. The gravel Mojave Desert road through dense stands of Joshua trees is driveable (with care) in all vehicles. If you are concerned about your vehicle (or if weather suggests staying off dirt roads), the paved highway is scenic as well.

This drive begins in St. George, the regional capital of Dixie. St. George is one of the country's fastest-growing urban areas, largely due to the popularity of the weather (and nearby Nevada casinos) among retirees. Given its attractiveness, this location may evolve into another Phoenix. Fortunately, most of the country in this corner of Utah is public land, which should somewhat limit the coming sprawl. St. George was named, incidentally, not for the British saint who killed dragons, but for the Latter Day Saint (and apostle) George Smith, who selected the original families called by the church to settle the region.

Apart from tennis courts, golf courses, and RV parks, there is not a great deal to see in St. George itself—a town that is clearly designed to be *moved to*, rather than visited. Two St. George attractions that really should be seen are the historic (and very beautiful) Mormon Temple and Mormon Tabernacle. The St. George Temple, completed in 1871, is the oldest Mormon Temple still in use, and the first built west of Ohio. The brilliant white building is visible from nearly everywhere in the city. The Tabernacle is one of the finest examples of pioneer-era construction in the entire West. It is open daily to visitors from 9 A.M. to 6 P.M. and is located on the corner of Main Street and Tabernacle Avenue.

Utah Highway 18, north from St. George, is signed for Veyo/Enterprise. About 5 miles north of the Sunset Boulevard turnoff for UT 18, you begin to notice the red walls of Snow Canyon to the west. It is a remarkably pristine 8-mile desert drive from St. George to the turnoff (on the left) for Snow Canyon State Park. It remains to be seen, considering St. George's rapid growth (and the fact that this is mostly privately held land), how long this remains undeveloped.

Snow Canyon is a real gem, a very impressive mix of red and white Navajo sandstone with beds of black lava. This is one of the most convenient places to see, in a small and encapsulated area, the landscape that has made southern Utah world-famous. And what of the snow? While the thought of this redrock wonderland covered in a blanket of winter white is

*Utah Highway 3184 winds along the Santa Clara River
through a gorgeous and rugged desert landscape.*

certainly appealing, this area seldom receives snow. Snow Canyon was named for one of the prominent Mormon families that settled this region.

For the moment, there is no entrance fee for the 4-mile canyon drive, though this is due to change in the near future. There are plenty of scenic pullouts, and several moderate trails leading to overlooks and other canyon features make this an ideal spot to get out of the car to stretch your legs.

It is 2 miles from Snow Canyon's north entrance to the park campground and visitor center. The visitor center has a useful booklet on Snow Canyon geology, as well as guides to some of its popular hiking trails and rock climbs. The modern campground has thirty-four units, electrical hookups, and showers.

Keep an eye open for a distinctive species of heavily built bipeds, which roam freely along the roadside in the park. Ivins, the town at Snow Canyon's southwest entrance, is home to the National Institute of Fitness (a major-league "weight-loss ranch") and has an arrangement for its clients to use the park as an exercise ground. Do be careful of the fitness walkers.

Ivins is hardly worth visiting, unless you are looking for lunch or have a desperate urge to purchase a new condo. In the throes of massive residential subdivision development, this is a fine example of how man and development encroach on the natural beauty of the Desert West. Hardcore Western history buffs might want to make a quick sidetrip, from the Ivins end of Snow Canyon down to Santa Clara, to visit the Jacob Hamblin House. Hamblin was one of the most interesting and dynamic figures in Utah's early pioneer era. He was a missionary, a colonizer, and one of the most effective and respected Indian agents in the entire West. His Santa Clara house is a classic example of a more substantial pioneer home of the 1860s. Located at the north end of town (on the left), it is interesting, attractive—and free!

With or without the Santa Clara diversion, retrace your route through Snow Canyon (hardly a chore, as the scenery is great and the perspectives seem different in either direction) back to the highway. A final note as you retrace the canyon drive: Snow Canyon was the location for some of the filming of Robert Redford's *Jeremiah Johnson*. The filming here of an earlier movie may have been ultimately responsible for the death of The Duke. During the 1956 filming of *The Conqueror* (an excruciatingly bad movie starring John Wayne as Genghis Khan), the government decided to test a nuclear bomb in the Nevada desert, upwind from Snow Canyon. Wayne, director Dick Powell, and several other members of the cast and crew later died of cancer. Perhaps a coincidence, perhaps not. . . .

Continue north on UT 18 for 8 miles to Veyo. Approximately 5 miles north of the Snow Canyon turnoff, notice a prominent steep butte on your left, clearly an extinct cinder cone. Veyo is your last chance for gas and provisions until Santa Clara, Enterprise, or Littlefield, Arizona (depending on your choice of route). This drive hooks back to the south and west here at the only intersection in town, UT 3184, well-marked for Gunlock.

A short sidetrip north from Veyo takes you to the site of the infamous Mountain Meadows massacre, the blackest mark against Utah's Mormon settlers—a wound that took generations to heal. This northern diversion also presents a nice glimpse of the lovely forested hill country of the Pine Valley and Bull Valley mountains.

The incident at Mountain Meadows is one of the most thoroughly discussed and written-about affairs in Utah history, a story well known to every Utahn above the age of three. A brief summary will suffice here. In 1857, ten years after the often-persecuted Latter Day Saints finally found their own Zion in the American West, hostile forces once again threatened their way of life. An expeditionary force was on its way to quell what was perceived as a Mormon rebellion from the Union. Brigham Young declared a state of martial law in the territory, in preparation for what loomed likely as war.

Enter into this tinderbox a large party of emigrants from Arkansas and Missouri, bound for California. Under the circumstances, the Mormon settlers would not have been well disposed to *any* Americans passing through their new land, but the origin of this particular wagon train was perhaps especially significant, given the rough treatment the Mormon pioneers had received in expulsion from their earlier home in Missouri. The emigrants were angered at their inability to secure provisions from the Utahns (either because of the Mormons' preparations for war, or out of simple animosity) and there had reportedly been unpleasant exchanges *before* the party reached the popular camping place at Mountain Meadows, the last well-watered camp before the long haul across the Mojave Desert.

A group of Mormon leaders in Cedar City persuaded a band of Paiutes to attack the wagon train. When the emigrants beat back the Indians, Mormon militia arrived on the scene. They convinced the emigrants to lay down their weapons and accept militia protection and escort out of the territory, then proceded to murder 120 men, women, and children. Eighteen very young children were spared and given over to Mormon families to be raised.

Twenty years after the tragic affair, one man, the important and highly respected Mormon pioneer John D. Lee, was convicted in a trial in Beaver for his part in the massacre. Lee was returned to Mountain Meadows and executed.

It is a disturbing and complex story, and one that much of Mormondom seemed anxious to forget completely until Juanita Brooks published her important book on the subject in 1950.

You can reach this now peaceful site by driving about 12 miles north from Veyo. Watch on the left for the road to the monument. The monument was erected in 1990 by descendants of both the victims and their murderers as an expression of closure to an incident painful to both sides. It was a nice gesture, but many who visit here wonder why there is still no straightforward acknowledgment of the crime.

From Mountain Meadows you might continue this attractive hill-country drive another 8.5 miles north to the community of Enterprise, or else return to Veyo. The mountains between Mountain Meadows and Enterprise are rough and wild, with occasional vistas across lovely green valleys. Beyond Enterprise, the Legacy Loop Highway, which loops east to Cedar City, is fairly uninspiring unless you are into alfalfa farms and ranches.

On your return to Veyo, you may want to take a 7-mile sidetrip up to the forest hamlet of Pine Valley, with its very pretty old LDS chapel. Watch for the road on the left at the town of Central. The forests around Pine Valley supplied timber for the early settlers of the region, and this became a popular early-summer retreat. The Pine Valley Chapel was built in 1868 by Ebenezer Bryce, who later moved farther east and herded cattle in what is now Bryce Canyon National Park. There is a small campground a few miles past Pine Valley.

From Veyo, continue our loop by heading southwest on UT 3184. Just at the bottom of a steep descent, 2.5 miles from town, note the BLM marker on the right for the Old Spanish Trail (see description in Introduction). This

Joshua trees grace the rough Mojave Desert of the extreme southwest corner of Utah.

descent brings the road down into the narrow gorge cut by the Santa Clara River, a lush and pleasant valley. A few miles farther is the extremely picturesque Eagle Mountain Ranch, with what seems like miles of perfect white fences.

The quiet little village of Gunlock has just about everything a small Mormon ranching community could need: a post office, an LDS church, one of the cutest little tree-shaded rodeo arenas you'll see anywhere, and not much else. Gunlock was named after Jacob Hamblin's brother, William "Gunlock" Hamblin. Evidently, he was extremely conscientious in the care of his firearms. There are *no* services in Gunlock—not even a gunsmith.

The road south of Gunlock follows closely the Santa Clara River until the valley opens up at Gunlock Reservoir, 2 miles south of town. Gunlock State Beach has picnic areas, camping sites, and outhouses, but no drinking water. There are nicer camping spots (undeveloped, with no facilities) another mile or so farther south alongside the river and better protected by trees from the wind that whips across the reservoir. South of Gunlock Beach the road passes through more glorious Utah redrock. Five miles south of Gunlock, you enter the small Shivwits (Paiute) Indian Reservation.

A little more than 7 miles south of Gunlock, watch for a "dangerous intersection" sign, then a good paved road that angles sharply back to the right. This is old US 91, formerly the main route west from St. George. Though unmarked, the road is unmistakable—the first paved road to intersect UT 3184. This is the access to the final segment of this drive: the Mojave Desert/Joshua Tree Scenic Backway.

If you choose to skip the Joshua Tree tour and return to St. George, continue south and east on UT 3184. The road runs through an attractive narrow valley and past several ruined cabins, one or two of which are quite picturesque. Two miles south of the US 91 turnoff is the small cluster of reservation housing that constitutes the community of Shivwits, and 8 miles farther is the turnoff (on the left) well marked for Ivins and Snow Canyon.

For the highly recommended Joshua Tree Backway, take the hard right turn on US 91. The old highway climbs out of the Santa Clara River Valley and winds through the desert hills. Just at the top of the first hill, where the road turns back slightly to the left, is a good dirt road on the right, signed for Motoqua. A little more than a mile farther is another dirt road on the left: this is the northern entrance to the Mojave Desert/Joshua Tree Scenic Backway.

Named by the early Mormon pioneers, who were reminded of "Joshua in the wilderness" with arms upraised to heaven, these distinctive plants that look like a cross between a cactus and a tree are actually members of the lily family. This is the northernmost point that Joshua trees grow.

The Mojave Desert/Joshua Tree Backway is a 16-mile loop on maintained gravel and dirt road that comes back out on old US 91 about 2 miles north of the Arizona state line. The road is passable for most vehicles when dry but should be driven slowly. In addition to the interesting plant life, the views of the Mojave Desert to the south and west are superb. The Joshua trees get more abundant the farther along the backway you go.

If you do not care to drive the slow 16 miles of gravel road (it will take an hour or so), the Joshua viewing is fine from the paved highway as well. There are also numerous dirt roads down below on the desert floor that pass through denser stands of the plants. If you prefer to stay on old US 91, you will begin to encounter the Joshua trees after approximately 9 miles. In fact, you can simply pick a likely road and drive around this region to your heart's content.

If you descend onto the desert floor and continue south on old US 91 for about 10 miles, watch on the left for the BLM sign for "Woodbury Desert Study Area." This is also the southern access to the Joshua Tree Backway. This end of the backway is a tad rough and a little narrow, but easy for all but large RVs and trailers. A few miles up and back should suffice to get you in the midst of plenty of Joshua trees.

From here you can either retrace old US 91 back to St. George via Santa Clara, or continue south for 10 miles on fast, straight road across the flat desert to join I-15 at Littlefield, Arizona. The I-15 option is faster and (though the best part is not in Utah) gives the opportunity to drive through the Virgin River Gorge—perhaps the most dramatic 8 miles or so of interstate driving in America.

From Littlefield, you may also opt for the 9-mile drive southwest to the Nevada casino town of Mesquite for a little of the sort of entertainment and recreation you really will *not* find in Utah.

2

Zion Park Scenic Byway

Hurricane to Mt. Carmel Junction

General description: A 60-mile drive highlighted by Zion National Park, one of the Southwest's landscape showcases.

Special attractions: Zion National Park, Grafton ghost town.

Location: Southwestern Utah.

Drive route number and name: Utah Highway 9, Zion Park Scenic Byway.

Travel season: Year-round.

Camping: Limited. Two national park campgrounds at Zion; commercial campgrounds (mainly RV parks with few tent sites) at Hurricane/ LaVerkin (5), Springdale (1), Mt. Carmel Junction (2). Tenters with backpacking equipment can camp in the backcountry of Zion Park (at least 1 mile from roads) with a free overnight permit from the visitor center.

Services: Most services at Hurricane/LaVerkin, Springdale, and Mt. Carmel Junction.

Nearby attractions: Kolob Reservoir Scenic Backway/Lava Point, Smithsonian Butte Scenic Backway, Coral Pink Sand Dunes State Park, Kane County Scenic Drive.

The drive

This route follows UT 9 from its western terminus at exit 16 on Interstate 15 to its eastern junction with U.S. Highway 89 at Mt. Carmel Junction. The most important scenic features of this drive center on the dramatic landscape within the confines of Zion National Park, although the scenery along the length of UT 9 is consistently of a high standard.

In addition to the 6.2-mile Zion Park Scenic Drive, there are two other notable scenic backways departing from UT 9: Smithsonian Butte Scenic Backway and Kolob Reservoir Scenic Backway. Both are highly recommended sidetrips.

You reach the twin towns of Hurricane and LaVerkin 9 miles from the interstate along UT 9. (An alternate approach for this drive, if coming from the north, is via Utah Highway 17 from I-15 exit 27.) Follow UT 9 right through Hurricane, cross the Virgin River, and you are in LaVerkin (Hurricane and LaVerkin are sort of like the Hungarian towns of Buda and Pest, except they are considerably smaller and the food is definitely not as good.)

Just beneath the Virgin River bridge is the small commercial spa called Pah Tempe Hot Springs. There are seven hot mineral pools (100° F), a swimming pool, a campground, and a bed-and-breakfast.

East of LaVerkin, the scenery along the drive becomes increasingly more attractive. The highway climbs to the top of the Hurricane Cliffs, with a fine view back to the west of the Pine Valley Mountains. At the wide spot in the road called Virgin, watch for the well-marked turnoff on the left for the Kolob Reservoir Road. This 45-mile backway drive links UT 9 with Utah Highway 14, east of Cedar City, and provides exceptional views of the west side of Zion Park. The road is paved and suitable for all vehicles as far as Lava Point (22 miles from UT 9) at the northern tip of the park. The backway runs in and out of the park through forests and lovely meadows. There is a beautiful primitive campground (free) at Lava Point, with tables, toilets, and fire grates, but no water. This makes a good place to overnight if you want to spend a full day in Zion Park. If you arrive at Lava Point in the early evening, you will more than likely see large numbers of deer in the open areas near the turnoff to the campground.

It is 9 miles from Virgin to the tidy little community of Rockville. At Rockville, you might want to take half an hour to visit the site of old Grafton or an hour or so to drive the 9-mile Smithsonian Butte Scenic Backway.

The peaceful little ghost town of Grafton, first settled in 1859, is semi-famous as the filming location for many of the scenes in the classic Newman/

The Kolob Reservoir Road traverses the well-watered highlands to the west of Zion National Park.

Drive 2: Zion Park Scenic Byway
Hurricane to Mt. Carmel Junction

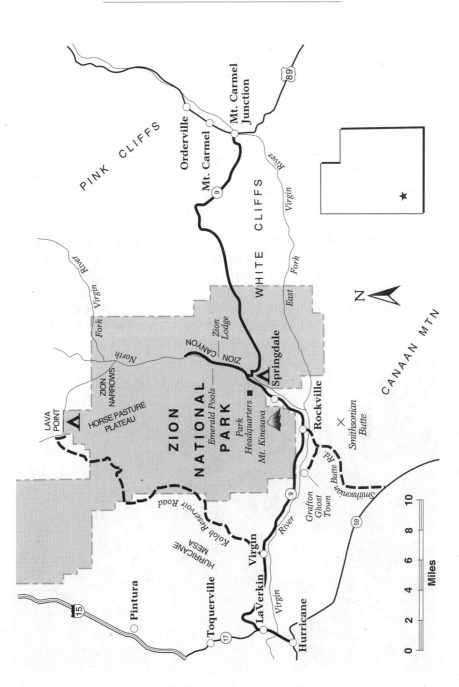

Redford film, *Butch Cassidy and the Sundance Kid*. Today it makes a nice picnic spot. There is no sign for Grafton, so watch for Bridge Road on the right. Cross the narrow bridge over the Virgin River. The road takes a jog to the right and runs 3.5 miles to the old townsite. Note the interesting old cemetery, about 0.5 mile before the town, where people keep swiping the grave markers for the colorfully named Indians in the back row.

This same road, across the Virgin River bridge, is the start to the Smithsonian Butte Scenic Backway. This drive offers spectacular panoramas of Zion Park, a short distance to the north, as well as closer encounters with Smithsonian Butte and Canaan Mountain. It is recommended that you drive the 9-mile-long backway in both directions, as the views change from either direction. The entire drive should take an hour. The well-marked, well-maintained, two-lane dirt road is suitable for most vehicles, although one short, steep section might pose problems for larger vehicles. Inquire in Virgin or Rockville about current road conditions.

One mile east of Rockville is the start of 3 miles of fairly hideous commercial development at Springdale, the west entrance to Zion. Just outside of the park entrance, at the Cinemax Theater in Springdale, is an hourly show about Zion called *Treasure of the Gods* on a six-story screen. At the Obert Tanner Amphitheater, *The Grand Circle* gives a nice overview to the dramatic grandeur of Southern Utah. Springdale has an abundance of

Visitors enjoy the view from Zion Overlook.

bed-and-breakfasts and motels, all of which fill up early during the tourist season.

At Springdale you enter Zion, and the world begins to look a little different. The evocative names of some of the more famous landmarks—the Great White Throne, Angels Landing, Temple of Sinawava, Mountain of the Sun—suggest something of the grandeur of the place. But Zion really must be seen to be believed.

Anasazi and Paiute Indians probably used the canyon as a year-round refuge, as did some of the early white settlers. Among the first homesteaders here was Isaac Behunin, in 1861, who remarked: "A man can worship God among these great cathedrals as well as in any manmade church—this is Zion."

The park was established in 1909 by President William Howard Taft, though it took roughly 250 million years to create. After millions of years of tilting, cracking, and layering, the little Virgin River did most of the fine finish-work in carving the rocky canyon—but it did take her a little while. What you see today is the product of more than 13 million years of persistent erosion.

On calm, blue-sky days it is hard to imagine how this peaceful stream could have had such a profound effect on the rocky landscape. But if you have the opportunity to see the Virgin in a wilder mood, swollen to flash-flood by thunderstorm and spring snowmelt, sweeping full-grown trees and massive boulders along in its torrent, the geology here begins to make sense.

The weather is almost always moderate in Zion Park, with warm days and pleasantly cool nights in summer. Afternoon thunderstorms are common in July and August. There is little winter snow in the canyon itself, though the higher plateaus usually receive a fair accumulation, making winter an especially scenic (and crowd-free) time to visit.

Summer crowds are, in fact, the only drawback to a Zion visit. This is one of the single greatest tourist attractions in the American West, on everyone's *must-see* list. Park traffic can be very busy, sometimes to the point of intensity and irritation. Take your time, observe the 35 mph speed limit and DO NOT STOP ON THE ROAD, except at designated pullouts. A new plan for managing the park's congestion and overuse awaits enactment in the near future. Among the several strategies considered is to completely close Zion Canyon Road to private vehicles; visitors would board shuttle buses to tour the canyon.

One other note on driving in Zion Park: Many recreational vehicles and trailers are too big to pass safely in two-way traffic through the mile-long Zion-Mt. Carmel Tunnel. For vehicles wider than 94 inches (including mirrors) or higher than 11 feet 4 inches, an escort (required) is provided for a small fee ($10 in 1995). You must arrange for the escort in advance at a park entrance or at the visitor center. During the height of the summer

The Zion-Mt. Carmel highway passes through stunning sandstone grandeur.

tourist season, large vehicles may face parking restrictions within the park. Be sure to check on this at the visitor center.

The visitor center is just under 1 mile from the Springdale entrance. Close to the visitor center are the two park campgrounds (no hookups and no showers), one of which is open year-round. Campsites are available on a first-come, first-served basis; they will generally all be taken well before noon in the summer season, so check in early if you want to camp in the park. For those with overnight backpacking gear, a free backcountry permit, obtainable at the visitor center, allows you to camp in primitive campsites along the many trails in the park as long as you are at least 1 mile from the road.

Just east of the visitor center is the turnoff (on the left) for Zion Canyon. Sheer cliffs of brilliant hue tower 2,000 to 3,000 feet above the canyon floor, giving this remarkable 6.2-mile tour along the North Fork of the Virgin River its well-deserved reputation as perhaps the most dramatic of all National Park drives. Along the river, stands of cottonwood, willow, and ash provide shady spots to stretch your legs and picnic. Where the water runs, Zion is a fairly lush place, with almost eight hundred native plant species and a tremendous variety of fauna.

The park has an abundance of hiking paths of varying lengths and degrees of difficulty. Inquire for detailed trail information at the visitor center. Two highly recommended (easy) hikes are the Middle Emerald Pool Loop and Canyon Overlook. Remote primitive campsites allow for several fine overnight backpacking trips in the park, and technical rock climbing has increased in popularity here. From late March until November, there are regularly-scheduled hikes with park naturalists as well as especially-informative evening programs. There are also commercially-run horsepacking tours and an excellent open-air bus tour (inquire at Zion Lodge for both). Zion Lodge provides motel units, cabins, a restaurant, and other amenities and is open year-round. Room reservations are highly advised; call 801-772-3967.

The road east from Zion to Mt. Carmel Junction was completed in 1930 and was considered one of the great road-building accomplishments of its time. As you climb from the canyon floor to the two high plateaus to the east, passing through two narrow tunnels blasted through the cliffs, you will probably understand why it created such a sensation. When you exit the second of these tunnels, you will find yourself in a very different sort of landscape. No longer amidst towering sandstone cliffs, you are now in classic Utah "slickrock" country—a strange moonscape of rounded, molded, weather-sculpted rock. This multi-colored sandstone, eroded and etched with grooves and cracks, presents a fantastic aspect of geologic complexity. Checkerboard Mesa, near the east entrance to the park, is particularly impressive, with its almost surreal cross-bedding of grooves.

Happily, nothing like the commercial development at Springdale awaits you outside the park's east entrance. Thirteen miles east of Zion, at Mt. Carmel Junction, is a small cluster of travelers' facilities, including a well-maintained golf course.

From Mt. Carmel Junction you have several options: turn right, left, or back to Hurricane and I-15. The end of this drive leaves you in the heart of some very scenic country. A left at the intersection with US 89 takes you north into scenic Long Valley. Right takes you south to Kanab, along the start of Drive #4.

3

Kolob Fingers Scenic Byway
Kolob Canyon section of Zion National Park

General description: A 5-mile mini-tour of dramatic, colorful cliffs and deep-cut gorges.
Special attractions: Redrock cliffs, hiking trails.
Location: Southwestern Utah, in the northwest corner of Zion National Park.
Drive route number and name: Kolob Fingers Scenic Byway.
Travel season: Year-round.
Camping: None in this section of the park, except by backcountry permit; BLM campground at Leeds/Red Cliff; commercial campground (with teepee rental!) at Kanarraville.
Services: All services at Cedar City, limited services at Kanarraville.
Nearby attractions: Markagunt Scenic Byway.

The drive

Kolob Canyon, the northwestern section of Zion National Park, features the same dramatic landscape associated with the main section of the park: towering colored cliffs, narrow winding canyons, forested plateaus, and wooded trails along twisting side canyons. What you probably will *not* find here are the crowds of visitors for which Zion is also famous. This place is a real find, and somewhat off the well-worn tourist tracks of southern Utah.

The Kolob Fingers scenic drive is only 10 miles round-trip, and can be done in 40 minutes. As short as it is, this excursion may not be long enough or substantial enough to warrant a special trip, but if you are passing through this part of Utah it would be a huge mistake to overlook this gem. Combined with a short trail walk, and perhaps lunch at the upper picnic area, this is a very pleasant afternoon project.

This is definitely best done as a late afternoon/early evening drive. In the morning you will generally be looking directly into the light, and the steep canyon walls and narrow ravines (mostly viewed from the west) lose all their visual impact. The morning views can seem very ordinary, and the light very dull; in the late afternoon this place is completely spectacular, with the sharply-defined orange cliffs contrasting dramatically with the green of the forest. Sunset from the upper parking area is sublime.

Kolob Canyon is about 18 miles south of Cedar City, conveniently located just off Interstate 15. Whether you are coming from south or north, watch for exit 40. Cross under the interstate, and immediately on the right is the Kolob Canyon visitor center, which should be your first stop (open daily, 8 A.M. to 5 P.M.). Though this is officially part of Zion National Park, there are no entrance fees. There are few facilities and no camping. All you will find here, beyond the visitor center, are a couple of picnic areas (without water or much shade), a few trailheads, and plenty of scenic pullouts. As described elsewhere, a clever camping gambit for backpacking-equipped visitors is to secure an overnight backcountry permit (free) from the visitor center, leave your vehicle at a trailhead, and camp at one of the designated trailside sites. Check with the ranger at the visitor center for specific rules and site recommendations.

The well-maintained paved road climbs steeply from the visitor center, ascending 1100 feet in 5 miles, with fairly steep grades and many curves. Pulling a trailer will probably not be practical on this road, and larger RVs may wheeze a bit on the long climb.

On the lower part of the drive there are fine Zion-like views—the same "we're down here, looking up" sort of perspective as in the main part of Zion. Taylor Creek trailhead, at just under mile 2, is the start of the moderate hike along Taylor Creek to Double Arch Alcove. The trail passes two

The Kolob Fingers Road climbs more than 1,000
in just 5 miles beneath dramatic, deep-orange cliffs.

Drive 3: Kolob Fingers Scenic Byway
Kolob Canyon section of Zion National Park

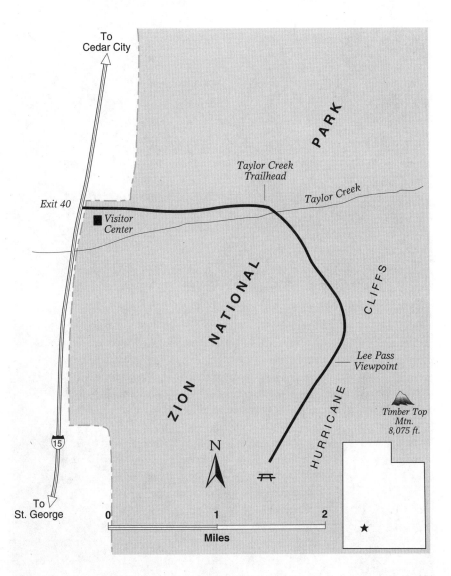

To
Cedar City

PARK

Taylor Creek
Trailhead

Taylor Creek

Exit 40

Visitor
Center

ZION NATIONAL

CLIFFS

Lee Pass
Viewpoint

HURRICANE

Timber Top
Mtn.
8,075 ft.

N

15

To
St. George

0   1   2

Miles

★

*Sheer sandstone cliffs tower over deep-cut canyons in the
Kolob Canyon section of Zion National Park.*

ruined settler cabins en route to the extremely beautiful, mossy alcove. This highly recommended hike is 5.4 miles round-trip and takes approximately four hours.

Just past mile 3 is a large parking area with excellent views of the narrow canyon ahead, and here it really starts to look *Zionesque*. Lee Pass trailhead and viewpoint are at mile 3.7. This is the departure point for the long and fairly strenuous hike to Kolob Arch. Spanning 310 feet, Kolob Arch is thought to be perhaps the largest freestanding arch in the world. This is a serious walk, sometimes done as an overnight; the round-trip is 14.4 miles.

The views from the upper end of the drive are outstanding, and you get a real sense of the complex little wonderland that lies among these narrow canyons and spires. Directly across from the observation point is a perfect example of a hanging valley: a small green cove isolated from the rest of the forested terrain by cliffs on all sides, above and below, creating its own micro-environment.

These canyons are also home to much wildlife. A wide range of high desert and alpine creatures inhabit the area, and eagles can often be seen riding the wind currents above the canyons.

This must have seemed the perfect environment for the earliest human inhabitants of this region: a paradise of cool, protected canyons, running water, and abundant game. The Anasazi, or "ancient ones," hunted and farmed here until their general disappearance from Utah around 1300 A.D. The Paiute Indians were well-established here at the time of the earliest expeditions by white explorers. In 1776, the Dominquez-Escalante party, having just decided to abort their attempt at finding a route to California, passed just to the west of the canyon mouth, following the approximate line of the interstate on their way south. Fifty years later, Jedediah Smith passed the Kolob on what proved to be the first successful traverse of the Old Spanish Trail.

During the 1850s, Mormon settlers spread south from the Cedar City area. They found these canyons a good source of timber and water and useful for raising livestock. Though it may sound like an Indian name, Kolob was named by the early Mormon settlers for the star closest to Heaven in the Book of Mormon—a most appropriate name.

There is not much to say about this drive, other than suggesting it is one of the best short scenic drives in the American West, and probably the most convenient national park visit in the country. There is no finer scenery in Utah than Kolob's, and none so easily reached from the interstate.

4

Kane County Drive-About

Long Valley Junction to Glen Canyon Dam

General description: Mostly a desert and canyon drive, offering glimpses of various area features along the southern part of U.S. Highway 89.

Special attractions: Coral Pink Sand Dunes State Park, Moqui Cavern, Kanab, Vermilion Cliffs.

Location: Extreme southern edge of Utah, between Zion and Glen Canyon.

Drive route number and name: US 89.

Travel season: Year-round.

Camping: One state park campground, two BLM campgrounds, commercial campgrounds at Kanab and Big Water.

Services: All services at Orderville, Kanab, Big Water, and Page, Arizona; basic services at Glendale and Mt. Carmel Junction; gas at Long Valley Junction.

Nearby attractions: Johnson Canyon/Alton Amphitheater Scenic Backway, Paria River Valley Scenic Backway, Paria Canyon hikes, Cottonwood Canyon Scenic Backway, Glen Canyon National Recreation Area, Lake Powell excursions.

The drive

This 115-mile drive is perhaps more notable for its several important and highly recommended sidetrips than for the scenery along the drive itself. It isn't that there's anything wrong with the scenery along US 89. In fact, the first 40-mile stretch, from Long Valley Junction to Kanab, is part of a designated state scenic byway. The stretch of US 89 between Kanab and Big Water City is characterized by sagebrush flats and expansive views across a seemingly limitless desert landscape, broken only by dramatic sandstone cliffs. This is definitely a rough wasteland, appealing to folks who like wide-open spaces. Like so many other scenery-rich Utah drives, this would be considered a premier driving attraction if it were anywhere else. Beyond Big Water City is the dramatic country of Glen Canyon Recreation Area and Lake Powell.

In order to catch some of the most interesting sights and most beautiful landscapes in this part of Utah, you need to explore beyond the highway.

Drive 4: Kane County Drive-About
Long Valley Junction to Glen Canyon Dam

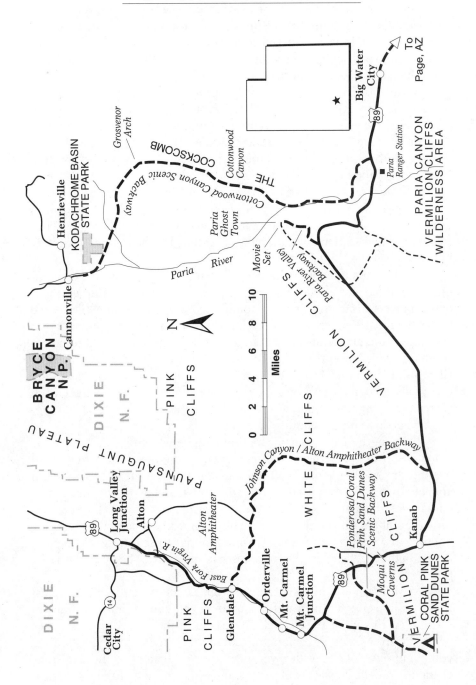

Take advantage of the highlighted sidetrips appropriate for your vehicle. The two main attractions accessed from this drive are the extraordinary landscapes at Coral Pink Sand Dunes State Park and the very interesting sidetrip up to "Old Paria," an old settlement (now vanished) and more recent film set, spectacularly set along the Paria River. It would be a real shame to do this drive and *not* visit these sites.

Begin this drive either at Mount Carmel Junction, for those coming out of Zion's east exit, or at Long Valley Junction, for those driving south on US 89. Either start puts you above the first of this drive's main attractions.

From Long Valley Junction the road descends along the east fork of the Virgin River in one of Utah's prettiest valleys. Thirteen miles south of Long Valley Junction is Glendale, a quiet farm hamlet settled in 1871 by a group of Mormons who had lost their western Nevada farms when they couldn't pay their taxes. Three years later, members of the settlement at Glendale eastablished a new community a few miles down the valley. They called their new settlement Orderville, after the movement then-underway in Utah called the United Order.

The United Order was a system of Christian communism and community self-sufficiency practiced in various parts of Utah during the latter part of the nineteenth century. Brigham Young encouraged the start of the United Order here in 1874, where it lasted until the mid 1880s. All property was communal and all members worked toward what was perceived to be the common good. The entire village awoke to a bugle call at 5 A.M. and shared all meals in a communal hall. Polygamy was the familial norm. The townsfolk eventually tired of the strict regimen, and of the bickering that ensued from such close living, ultimately reverting to more traditional patterns of property ownership and community life.

Today nothing but its name hints at Orderville's unique history. To the casual visitor it is a perfectly ordinary town whose most interesting *visual* feature is probably the odd roadside souvenir shop on the left at the south end of town. Worth a visit is the DUP Museum, with mementoes of Orderville's intriguing past. As with most DUP museums, call one of the phone numbers on the door and a volunteer will be happy to open the building and show you around. The museum is housed in the old schoolhouse on the left, just past the large western-motif curio shop called Apache Fort.

At Mt. Carmel Junction (13 miles from Zion's east entrance) is a cluster of facilities, including a well-maintained golf course, but not much of interest. At this point the road climbs up out of the Virgin River drainage while the river flows west along the southern boundary of Zion Park. As you climb out of Long Valley, you may notice the color of the sandstone changing to delicate shades of orange and pink, hinting at the visual treat just over the next rise.

Fine, brightly colored sand and rich desert plant life make
Coral Pink Sand Dunes State Park a Utah treasure.

Four miles southeast of Mt. Carmel Junction, watch for a turnoff on the right, signed for Coral Pink Sand Dunes State Park. This is a *must-do* sidetrip, and one you will not forget. The 12-mile drive to the park is on a paved but narrow road, suitable for all vehicles.

The dunes at Coral Pink have been created (the process is on-going) by millions of years of high winds blowing through a notch between Moquith and Mocassin mountains. A Venturi effect increases the wind velocity through this notch. The wind deposits grains of eroded, iron-rich Navajo sandstone on the plain. At an elevation of 6,000 feet, Coral Pink receives enough moisture to support stands of ponderosa pine, dune grasses, and many beautiful wildflowers, making its appearance hardly desertlike.

Were these delicately colored dunes in any other state, they would be hugely famous. As it is, this place gets somewhat lost among all of southern Utah's more renowned natural wonders. Still, those who have been here will list Coral Pink among their favorite "surprise finds" in Utah. The park was established in 1963 to preserve the unique environment—the most significant dune area on the Colorado Plateau. There are hundreds of miles of ATV trails, along with a more limited choice of hiking trails. Backdrops of juniper/pinyon, steep red cliffs, and dramatic rock outcroppings make Coral Pink a visual treat.

The wide expanses of dunes hold many trails open to off-road enthusiasts: dune buggies, ATVs, and dirt bikes go wild here. There is also excellent hiking in the Moquith Mountains, which form the east boundary of the park, with views as far as the North Rim of the Grand Canyon. Four miles northeast of the park is the trailhead for South Fork Indian Canyon, where there are interesting pictographs. Park facilities include a twenty-two-unit campground with hot showers (open April to November), an easy boardwalk overlook trail, a half-mile nature trail, and a small visitor center with information on area walks. There is a primitive camping area at Ponderosa Grove, just north of the park, although dune-buggy enthusiasts can make it noisy here, especially on the weekend.

The fastest way to return to US 89 is to take the right turn just to the north of the park, called the Hancock Road. This is also the Ponderosa/Coral Pink Sand Dunes Scenic Backway, and there is a primitive camping site in the ponderosa pine grove on the left as you climb the hill. This 12-mile backway connects the highway with the main road to the park and is meant for those who want an even better view of the dunes and surrounding country. This paved road is suitable for all vehicles and comes out on US 89 well south of the main road to the park.

Just south of Coral Pink, you might want to visit Moqui Caverns, a roadside attraction 5 miles north of Kanab. This *is*, of course, a tourist trap and not an authentic Indian cave at all, but it's enough beyond simple to make it worth seeing. Assembled in this cleaned-up ancient cave are various exhibits of general interest, *mostly* relating to the region. There are dinosaur tracks, a huge (and quite impressive) display of fluorescent minerals, a large display of Native American artifacts, and a replica of nearby cliff dwellings. There are no two-headed calves, no snake pit, and no Elvis wax replicas. But it's worth a stop anyway. Their ad proclaims: "The coolest stop on Highway 89—Never over 70° on the hottest days."

Kanab was first settled in the mid-1860s, abandoned during the Black Hawk Indian War, then resettled for keeps in 1870. Its geographic position, ideal for the burgeoning tourism industry of the 1920s, and Wild-West landscapes, perfect for the booming Hollywood film industry, brought Kanab to its current status as one of the premier tourist towns of the Desert West.

In 1922, Tom Mix starred in *Deadwood Coach*, the first in a string of ninety-two films (and hundreds of TV programs) that gave Kanab the nickname "Little Hollywood." The first outdoor talkie, *In Old Arizona*, was filmed here. Other films made near Kanab, in Johnson Canyon and at Paria, were: *Billy the Kid*, *The Bad Man of Brimstone*, *How the West Was Won*, *Mackenna's Gold*, *The Outlaw Josie Wales*, *Buffalo Bill*, and *Fort Yuma*. And it hasn't all been westerns. Other films that used locations in this part of Utah were: *The Arabian Nights*, *Ali Baba and the Forty Thieves*, the Burt Lancaster/Katherine Hepburn classic *The Rainmaker*, as well as episodes of the television shows *Lassie* and *Route 66*.

In many ways, Kanab defines the classic southwestern tourist town, with its rows of "Indian Trading Post" souvenir shops, tour buses, and steady streams of tourist traffic. And yet, this place still manages to retain a sense of character. Before tourism became the driving force in the local economy, Kanab grew as a service community for the ranches of southern Kane County. Every month during the summer, the Tri-Valley Livestock Association hosts a rodeo either in Kanab or in one of the nearby communities of Orderville or Fredonia, Arizona. These present a great opportunity to see a traditional smalltown rodeo.

So, back to Kanab and on to the main section of this drive, heading east on US 89.

It is about 8.5 miles across sagebrush desert flats to the well-marked paved road on the left, signed for Johnson Canyon. This is the start of the Johnson Canyon/Alton Amphitheater Scenic Backway, a 32-mile drive that loops back north to join US 89, 28 miles north of Kanab. This scenic drive traverses the very colorful country of the Vermilion and White cliffs and provides fine views to the north of the Pink Cliffs, marking the southern edge of Bryce Canyon. The first 15 miles of this backway are paved; the rest is well-maintained gravel, suitable for passenger vehicles.

If the scenery along the Paria River Valley Scenic Backway looks familiar, it's because you've probably seen it in one of the many Westerns filmed here.

Six miles up Johnson Canyon, on the right, is the famous movie set that was featured regularly on the television series *Gunsmoke*. There are twelve buildings on the set, including many familiar from the small-screen representation of Dodge City: the Longbranch Saloon, Doc's office, the livery stable, and blacksmith shop. Other television series that filmed here regularly were: *Have Gun Will Travel*, *Death Valley Days*, and *Wagon Train*. There is also a telegraph and pony express station from the 1953 Chuck Heston movie *Pony Express*.

The landscape east of Kanab is pristine, wide-open, and scenic, though unspectacular: mostly sagebrush flats and grazing land. About 20 miles east of Kanab the landscape begins to get more dramatic, with striking redrock cliffs ahead and the very rugged Vermilion Cliffs to the left.

At mile 32 is the turnoff on the left for "Old Paria" and the start of the Paria River Valley Scenic Backway. This highly-recommended 5-mile backway is really the highlight of this Kane County drive. The well-maintained gravel road is suitable for all vehicles—even larger RVs and trailers, if driven slowly. As always, stay off of it when wet unless you have a dependable four-wheel-drive vehicle.

The short drive to the townsite passes some truly remarkable geological formations: sandstone cliffs banded in the most lovely and delicate hues.

This "pioneer town" in the Paria Valley was built in 1963 for the movie Sergeants Three.

Just before the final descent into the Paria River Valley is a fine view of a cluster of deserted buildings. If the scene looks like something right out of the movies, well, it is.

This extremely scenic site has been an important filming location for more than fifty years. While *not* the original townsite, the buildings you see below were part of a set built in 1963 for the movie *Sergeants Three*, later used for some of the final scenes of Clint Eastwood's *The Outlaw Josie Wales*. Next to the old film set is a small but nicely maintained BLM campground with outhouses, tables, grills, and firepits, but no water.

The original town of Paria (also called "Pahreah Town") was established in 1870 as an agricultural community of some substance. As many as forty-seven families lived here during the town's one-decade existence. Severe flooding of the Paria River washed away most of the farmland, and the town gradually dwindled and died.

The remnants of the actual town are on the west bank of the Paria River. While you may not opt to cross the river to visit the old townsite, the short drive beyond the movie set is very nice, on easy dirt road that presents no problems when dry. A memorial about 0.3 mile past the movie set indicates the site of the town cemetery (no headstones remain). It's about a mile farther to the bank of the Paria River. To find the townsite, cross the river on foot (it's usually ankle-deep at most) heading toward the rough corrals, then climb the bank wherever you can. After all that, about all you'll find is one old chimney stack and a couple of stone foundations—unless you're a hardcore archaeo-tourist, hardly worth the effort.

Continuing east on US 89, you pass through a short stretch of red and gray sandstone, a fascinating jumble of shapes and colors known as the Carmel formation, which suggests a sort of *mini-Canyonlands* zone. Ten miles past the Paria turnoff, on the right, is a very nice ranger station and BLM visitor center where you can find information on the many hikes and bike trails in the nearby Paria Canyon Wilderness Area. The ranger station is also the best place to check on the current status of the Cottonwood Canyon Scenic Backway, which departs US 89 just past the BLM office, on the left.

The Cottonwood Canyon drive runs 46 miles north to Kodachrome Basin and Utah Highway 12, making this the most direct route to Bryce Canyon and the many sights along UT 12 (see Drive #6 and #7). The road is passable for most vehicles when it's dry (though in extremely dry periods it can also be very dusty). The lower part of this drive, along the Paria River and Cottonwood Creek, provides excellent views of wildly eroded sandstone formations.

The Paria Canyon Wilderness Area, south of the highway, was one of the country's very first designated primitive areas. The full 35-mile length of Paria Canyon is one of the premier hikes in the Desert Southwest, a three-to five-day excursion through the most incredible canyon country imaginable—some of it far *beyond* imagination. While this hike is not to be taken lightly, or undertaken without detailed trail (and weather) information, there are numerous less-demanding hikes in the wilderness area. The BLM office has full information and helpful brochures.

East of the BLM office, the landscape along US 89 reverts to scenic but unspectacular sagebrush flats with desert hills and sandstone formations. Thirteen miles east of the office you will reach Big Water City, a 1-mile scattering of services along the highway. It's not much of a town (and hardly picturesque!), but you will find gas, motels, and a few convenience stores here. (You will have to continue on to Page, Arizona, to find a real town.)

Even if you plan to return to Kanab, you might want first to continue on to the Glen Canyon Dam, a very interesting manmade attraction. Other options are available if you don't want to retrace US 89 back to Kanab; the most obvious would be to complete a large southern loop from Page back to Kanab via Marble Canyon, Jacob Lake, and Fredonia, an extremely attractive drive on the Arizona side of the line.

Past Big Water City the views open up over the southern region of Glen Canyon Recreation Area. The landscape here looks more like the Monument Valley area of southeastern Utah: flat desert dotted with eroded mesas and spires. It is really quite scenic, and much different from the narrow, twisting canyons to the west. After 3 or 4 miles you will see the very blue water of Lake Powell off to the left. The Arizona state line is 6 miles beyond Big Water City; 2.5 miles farther is Wahweap Marina, the largest marina and lodging facility in Glen Canyon Recreation Area. Most services are available here (including laundry and showers). Wahweap is also the most active center for boat excursions on Lake Powell, including the popular trip to Rainbow Bridge National Monument. These are half-day excursions at the least, so you might want to check on details here, then head into Page for the night.

It is 5 miles from Wahweap to the Glen Canyon Dam visitor center, next to the dam and the Glen Canyon Bridge. The visitor center is open daily except December 25 and January 1. Free dam tours are offered daily.

At 710 feet, this is the fourth highest dam in the world. The story behind the building of the dam and creation of Lake Powell is one of the more interesting examples of Man's attempts at controlling Nature. Construction began in 1959 and was completed in 1964 (it took three years of round-the-clock work just to pour the concrete). Two years later the power plant began generating electricity.

Above the dam is the much-widened 200-mile stretch of the Colorado River, now known as Lake Powell. This is the second-largest manmade lake in America after Lake Mead, which is just downstream. Lake Powell reached its current level by 1980. The lake was named for Major John Wesley Powell, the most important explorer of the Colorado River Basin, who had named this rough stretch of the Colorado Glen Canyon.

The town of Page was built as a service center during the construction of the Glen Canyon Dam. Today Page is the headquarters for tour companies offering air and boat excursions to the many sights along the shores of Lake Powell, including the popular trip to Rainbow Bridge. A good place to orient yourself on Glen Canyon attractions and the dam construction story is the very fine Powell Memorial Museum, at the corner of North Lake Powell Boulevard and Navajo Drive.

For more details on the fascinating story of Glen Canyon/Lake Powell, see the description under Drive #9.

5

Markagunt Plateau
Scenic Drive
Cedar City to Parowan

General description: A high-elevation mountain and plateau drive, this loop is composed of three separate designated scenic byways, giving two major options to complete either a short or long loop. The scenery is a terrific combination of alpine forest, aspen groves, and Southwestern sandstone.

Special attractions: Cedar City, Cedar Canyon, Cedar Breaks National Monument, lava fields, wildflowers, Panguitch Lake, Brian Head Ski Resort, old Parowan.

Location: Southwest Utah, mostly in the Dixie National Forest. This drive traverses the Markagunt Plateau from west to east, then back from east to west.

Drive route number and name: Utah Highways 14, 148, and 143, and U.S. Highway 89. Markagunt Scenic Byway (UT 14, Cedar City to US 89), Cedar Breaks Scenic Byway (UT 148), Brian Head-Panguitch Lake Scenic Byway (UT 143, Panguitch to Parowan).

Travel season: Mostly year-round. The Cedar Breaks Scenic Byway is closed by snow from mid-October until early summer (depending on snowpack). All parts of this high-elevation drive are subject to winter-driving hazards and temporary snow closures. The Markagunt Plateau presents fine opportunities for viewing autumn colors, especially at the lower elevations just above the Sevier River Valley.

Camping: One national park campground (Cedar Breaks), ten national forest campgrounds on or near the route.

Services: All services in Cedar City, Panguitch, and Parowan; basic services at Duck Creek Village, Long Valley Junction, Hatch, and Panguitch Lake.

Nearby attractions: Kolob Reservoir Scenic Backway (Zion National Park/Lava Point), Red Canyon, Highway 12 Scenic Byway, Dry Lakes/Summit Canyon Scenic Backway, old Paragonah, Parowan Gap pictographs.

The drive

This can be either a very long drive or just a short outing, depending on which option you choose. The full circuit is a 123-mile loop, including

Drive 5: Markagunt Plateau Scenic Drive
Cedar City to Parowan

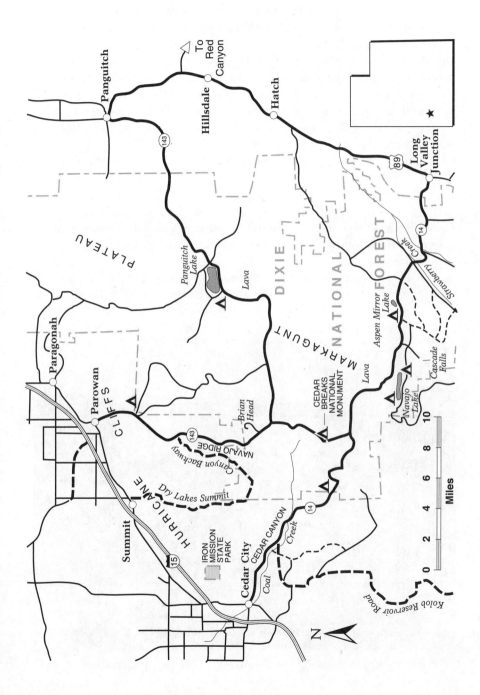

Cedar City - Cedar Breaks - Long Valley Junction - Panguitch - Panguitch Lake - Parowan. The short loop of Cedar City - Cedar Breaks - Parowan is just 39 miles. In either case, this drive should give a good introduction to the fascinating high country of the Markagunt Plateau.

The Markagunt Plateau is the chief water source for southwestern Utah, the birthplace of the Virgin and Sevier Rivers. Indeed, the name "markagunt" means "highland of trees" in Paiute. Here alpine terrain combines with Southwestern sandstone to give the traveler the best mix of Utah's most famous scenic offerings. This drive is highlighted by the fantastic eroded sandstone of Cedar Breaks; this sculpted sandstone jewel is placed within a lush setting of evergreen forest and aspen groves.

The drive's four main roads are paved and suitable for all vehicles. Traffic is generally moderate, except for the road between Parowan and Brian Head during ski season. The Markagunt Plateau receives ample snowfall, making parts of this drive sometimes difficult in winter, and closing the Cedar Breaks Byway (UT 148) from the first major snowfalls until as late as the end of June. Definitely carry chains in winter and check on current road conditions.

A special danger to the long version of this drive must be pointed out: As long as it is, and with so many attractions warranting frequent stops,

The high, open amphitheater of Cedar Breaks, with 11,300-foot Brian Head to the north.

what may have started as a day trip might end up an overnighter. If you plan to do this entire drive in one day, get an early start from Cedar City . . . or else bring your toothbrush.

The drive starts in Cedar City. Coal from the canyons to the east of town and iron ore from the mountains to the west were responsible for the marginally successful Iron Mission smelting enterprise established here at the suggestion of Brigham Young. While the industrial basis for the town was only partly successful, the community endured and is today second only to St. George in regional importance.

Today Cedar City is a pleasant community of nearly 15,000. The town has a small university (Southern Utah University) and is well known for its summer Shakespeare theater. Higher and much colder in winter than nearby St. George, Cedar City has not experienced the much-too-rapid growth that has transformed its southern neighbor into a sprawling mini-metropolis of apartment complexes, trailer parks, and subdivisions. Cedar City, while growing faster than many of its residents care to see, still clings to its small-town look and sense of community.

Utah Highway 14 (Center Street) leaves Cedar City from its intersection with Main Street. Turn east and note immediately on the left the extremely attractive LDS church in an interesting Tudor style. Just a few blocks past the church you will be out of town and in the mountains.

The mouth of Cedar Canyon is one of the few breaks in the geologic formation called the Hurricane Cliffs, which run from north of Parowan all the way south into Arizona. The Hurricane Fault caused the terrain to the east to lift thousands of feet above the flat desert floor to the west. Like other Utah towns to the north that lie at the base of the west slope of the Wasatch Mountains, Cedar City has rugged alpine terrain to the east and rough, dry, Great Basin desert and scrub-covered hills to the west. Thus the area offers a broad diversity of recreational and scenic possibilities. The Hurricane Fault also exposed the colorful layers of sandstone and elaborate formations you see as you ascend Cedar Canyon.

The highway gains elevation quickly, with Coal Creek flowing swiftly on the right. The first few miles up the canyon may seem like a grunt in an RV or dragging a trailer. It's about 5 miles to the turnoff on the right for the Kolob Reservoir Scenic Backway. A sign here describes the first coal mines, established in 1851. Mines in this area operated until the 1960s.

The 45-mile Kolob Reservoir Scenic Backway runs from here to the town of Virgin, near the west entrance of Zion Park. The first 22 miles, to Kolob Reservoir, are the steepest and most difficult, though passable in most passenger cars in dry conditions. Beyond the reservoir, views into Zion Park become most impressive, with an especially fine view from Lava Point. From Lava Point to Virgin the road is paved. This backway is closed in winter.

The old ranching community of Panguitch is a great place to catch a rodeo.

About 7 miles from Cedar City the canyon opens up a little and the views, especially to the left, become extremely dramatic. During the spring and early summer this canyon is alive with waterfalls. You should begin to see the first examples of the black lava that will become common along this highway as well as on the return route from Panguitch. It is assumed that about 30 million years ago the upthrusting action that created the Hurricane Cliffs also created vents through which molten volcanic rock escaped. The lava from that activity is hundreds of feet thick. But most of the surface lava flows and cider cones you will see on this drive are from a very recent era, when small vents spat molten rock and rose to form cones just 1,000 to 5,000 years ago.

At around mile 10 you pass the Southern Utah University Mountain Center, and a mile or so later Cedar Canyon Campground and the entrance to Dixie National Forest. Half a mile farther, the road rises up above the end of the canyon, quite steeply for about 2 miles. There are many nice pullouts, with an especially attractive view from Zion Overlook. From here the views to the south, toward Zion National Park, have opened up splendidly.

At just under mile 18 (from Cedar City) is the intersection (on the left) with UT 148, the Cedar Breaks Scenic Byway. At this point, you may choose to shorten this long loop by driving north, past Cedar Breaks National Monument, to join UT 143 above Brian Head and the descent to Parowan. The total drive from Cedar City to Parowan is 39 miles. Regardless of which version you choose, you really should drive up to the national monument visitor center. I recommend doing a quick round-trip from here of the 6-mile Cedar Breaks Backway, then continuing east along UT 14 to Long Valley Junction and around to Parowan via Panguitch.

Because of heavy snows, the Cedar Breaks road doesn't open until late spring and sometimes remains closed right through June. It generally closes in mid-October. It is 3.5 miles to the Cedar Breaks visitor center. Note that the speed limit within the monument boundary is 30 mph.

Cedar Breaks is highly reminiscent of its more famous relative, Bryce Canyon: it contains a huge amphitheater, over 3 miles in diameter and more than 2,000 feet deep, filled with the most exquisitely formed hoodoos, spires, and twisting canyons. Less expansive, intricate, and complex than Bryce, at 10,350 feet it is higher, airier, and has a sort of *deeper* look. The panorama to the west stretches out across the Great Basin, while the view to the north is defined by Brian Head, at 11,307 feet the highest point on the Markagunt Plateau.

As with Bryce, Cedar Breaks is best viewed from above; you must park and walk out to overlooks to really get a view. The very nice, easy, 2-mile Wasatch Ramparts Trail departs from the visitor center. Essentially a rim overlook walk, the trail offers fine views into the amphitheater. The terminus of the walk is Spectra Point, a small stand of ancient bristlecone pines.

Perhaps the most attractive thing about Cedar Breaks is the relative absence of crowds. This is a much-overlooked attraction.

The rock colors vary greatly here, depending on the oxidation of the various combinations of iron and manganese present. There are pale tans and yellows, a dull salmon pink, various shades of brick red, and even some extraordinary shades of purple. Early Indian visitors named this place "Circle of Painted Cliffs." The name "Cedar Breaks" comes from the regional use of "cedar" for the juniper tree, and the common term "breaks" for eroded badlands at the top of a watershed (remember that great old Nicholson/Brando film, *The Missouri Breaks*?).

A basic campground (open June through September) and picnic area are close to the visitor center. Keep in mind that nighttime temperatures, even in summer, are brisk at this elevation.

From the visitor center at Cedar Breaks, you have a major route decision to make. For the long version, you will return to the intersection with UT 14, turn left, and continue the loop through Long Junction and Panguitch. To make a short trip of it, continue along US 148 to the intersection with UT 143 just above Brian Head, then descend to Parowan.

In either case, the 3 miles to the north end of UT 148 is an extremely pleasant and beautiful drive. You gain most of your elevation en route to the visitors center, so this is mostly level driving through gorgeous high meadowland (road elevation is approximately 10,500 feet).

Continuing north from the visitor center, UT 148 takes you past three terrific overlooks before intersecting with UT 143. Each overlook (all pullouts on the left), spaced about 1 mile apart, gives a slightly different perspective of the Cedar Breaks amphitheater. The rock up here is very crumbly, so stay behind the viewpoint fences and keep a close eye on the kids. Due to frequent lightning strikes, it is best to avoid the overlooks during thunderstorms.

The third overlook is also the trailhead for the 2-mile Alpine Pond Loop, a very pleasant trail that leads to a picturesque pond in a lovely grove of Engelmann spruce, fir, and aspen, with commanding views of the amphitheater. About 1 mile past this overlook is the intersection with UT 143, which comes in on your right. Continue straight here to Brian Head and Parowan, skipping ahead in this route description.

So, back to the long loop. The junction with UT 148 marks the high point of the UT 14 drive, so the drive is mostly downhill from here to Long Valley Junction. About 3 miles from the Cedar Breaks road is a great example of the region's recent volcanic activity, where you can see both a recent lava flow and cinder cone.

The extensive meadow area called Deer Valley is ablaze with wildflowers from late July until the middle of August. The cool, clean air, abundant water, bright sunlight, and good soil of the Markagunt make this plateau

Fremont-Culture rock art at Parowan Gap dates back one thousand years.

land a terrific place to view wildflowers: mountain bluebell, larkspur, lupine, penstemon, columbine, and Indian paintbrush all flourish here in great abundance.

About a mile beyond the meadows is the Navajo Lake Overlook. Navajo Lake has no surface outlet; it drains subterraneously through lava tubes and percolation through porous limestone to resurface later as springs. A mile or so below the lake is a dirt road on the right (Forest Road 053) providing access to Navajo Lake trails and three national forest campgrounds. A branch to the left of FR 053, just after the turnoff, takes you to Cascade Falls, one of the major drainages from Navajo Lake. Here the water gushes forth from a rocky cavern, seemingly out of nowhere, then drops down the falls. A half-mile, self-guided trail leads to the waterfall.

The road continues to descend, past some very interesting lava flows, to pretty Aspen Mirror Lake with its campground, pleasant trails, and prime picnic sites. One mile farther is the private enterprise called Duck Creek Village, which will strike you as either an eyesore or a welcome return to civilization and amenities, including gas, lodging, food, and other basic services. Duck Creek occupies a small island of private land within the public confines of Dixie National Forest. Once past this development you return to the most lovely mountain drive, immediately passing through another wide meadow alive with beautiful ponds and streams.

On your right, just after reentering Dixie National Forest, is the turn-off to Strawberry Point (on Forest Road 058), where the views of the Pink Cliffs and south toward Zion Park are very fine, and the meadows along the way are filled with wildflowers.

As you continue the descent from the Markagunt Plateau, you should begin to see, straight ahead on the eastern horizon, the pink sandstone cliffs of the Paunsaugunt Plateau, site of Bryce Canyon. Twenty-two miles past the turnoff for Cedar Breaks you reach the junction with US 89 at Long Valley Junction, which is just a gas station and convenience store.

While no longer a spectacular mountain drive, the 26-mile drive north through the valley of the Sevier River (pronounced *severe*) is a real scenic pleasure. As you drive north through Long Valley you will just see on your right the little stream that marks the headwater of the Sevier River. The stream meanders lazily through this valley, picking up more volume from flows off the Markagunt and Paunsaugunt plateaus until it turns into a proper river. The valley formed by the Sevier is one of the prettiest in the entire state, and a great place to see farms and ranchland of unrivaled bucolic beauty. The Sevier eventually tires of running north, makes a pronounced direction change to the southwest, then flows out into the desert wastes of the Great Basin, where it runs out of energy and dies.

It's 11 miles to Hatch, where you will find most basic services. Note the splendid pink souvenir shop on the left as you pass through this other-wise nondescript town. The rustic beauty of Long Valley is somewhat di-minished by the garrish billboards just north of Hatch. Eight miles north of Hatch is the intersection with UT 12, on the right, where you may be tempted to jump ahead to Scenic Drive #6, one of the truly great scenic drives in the entire nation. You can get a hint of UT 12's wonders by making a short diversion here to visit the mouth of Red Canyon, about 3 miles east. This sidetrip is especially recommended if you reach this point late in the after-noon, when the late light gives the red rock a brilliant, almost surreal glow.

Panguitch means "big fish," which is what the Paiutes called nearby Panguitch Lake. The first white settlers came here from Beaver and Parowan in 1864. Like most of the other towns in this valley, Panguitch was aban-doned during the Blackhawk War (1865–68), then resettled in 1871. Early residents worked together in the community brick factory, where they were paid in bricks—most were able to build their homes of brick, many of which survive today.

Panguitch is the largest community and the county seat of Garfield County. There is a very nice DUP museum and a new Paunsaugunt Wildlife Museum. Both are on Center Street just as you come into town. Today

Panguitch is a real cowboy town and hosts many rodeos throughout the summer.

UT 143, signed for Parowan, is the left turn at the only real intersection in town. Just as the road leaves Panguitch, climbing back up into the foothills of the Markagunt Plateau, note the prominent sign on the right indicating that you are *not* on US 89 (which continues north in the valley of the Sevier River).

Once out of the valley, as you climb through pinyon-juniper growth, the character of the landscape changes dramatically. This becomes, once again, a mountain drive. Thirteen miles from Panguitch is White Bridge campground, the first of three in the vicinity of Panguitch Lake. The campground sits among the cottonwoods along Panguitch Creek, giving it a slightly different character from the facilities close to the west edge of the lake. It's about 2.5 miles farther to the lake.

Panguitch Lake was a popular summer place for the Paiutes centuries ago. Early Mormon settlers established dairies and ranches here, taking advantage of the cool mountain air. Toward the end of the century this became a popular recreation spot for miners who worked the diggings in the desert west of here, with saloons, gambling halls, and even a racetrack. By the 1890s there were also lodges and dance pavillions for more genteel entertainment. Unfortunately, all of these nineteenth-century attractions have disappeared, though the lake remains the major recreational draw for Panguitch area residents.

UT 143 follows the south edge of the big lake for about 2 miles. There are gas, lodging, and two national forest campgrounds at the west end of the lake. Once past the lake, keep your eyes peeled for the large golden marmot that abound in the meadows up here.

About 3 miles past the lake, watch on the left for Forest Road 069 (signed for Birch Spring Knoll). Here you can drive (or hike, if the road conditions are too rough for your vehicle) through a large lava field. A mile or so farther along the byway, a somewhat better road, also on the left (Forest Road 068, signed for Mammoth Creek), offers terrific scenic views and more interesting geological encounters with Markagunt's volcanic past. At this point (about 5 miles west of Lake Panguitch), UT 143 climbs through aspen groves and lava flows, which you may recognize as a northward continuation of those encountered along UT 14 in the vicinity of Navajo Lake.

About 14 miles west of the lake you reach an obvious "T", with the left branch (UT 148) leading back to Cedar Breaks, the right continuing on to Brian Head and Parowan. Turn right, then watch immediately on the left for the large parking area at the terrific viewpoint that looks east toward Cedar Breaks.

One-and-a-half miles from the intersection with UT 148 you will reach the high point of this drive at 10,400 feet. From here the drive is all in descent—some of it rather steep. If you are towing a large trailer and feel nervous about the hairpin turns, your other option is to drive back south past Cedar Breaks on UT 148, then back down Cedar Canyon to Cedar City.

On the UT 143 descent you will soon pass about 2 miles of Brian Head Ski Resort development (not so bad, actually). In addition to fine skiing in the winter, Brian Head is a good place to rent bicycles for trail rides—an excellent way to explore the ins and outs of this beautiful area. When the snows have all disappeared, you may be able to drive to the 11,315-foot summit for spectacular views of the Markagunt, the nearby Cedar Breaks, and to the west across the Great Basin all the way to Nevada.

About 4 miles below the lowest limit of the Brian Head development, watch for a scenic backways sign on the left for Dry Lakes. This 19-mile backway winds through lovely meadows below Navajo Ridge and gradually snakes its way down the Hurricane Cliffs to the hamlet of Summit. The panoramic views of Ashdown Gorge, Cedar Breaks, and the Summit-Parowan Valley are well worth the hour-long descent. The unpaved road is generally passable by passenger cars in dry conditions, though steep and narrow in places. Check first at Brian Head.

This drive ends at the old Mormon settlement of Parowan. The Parowan Valley was inhabited early on by the people of the Fremont Culture from A.D. 750 to 1250. The Dominguez-Escalante expedition came through here in 1776, but it was another fifty years before the next white visitor, Jedediah Smith, arrived. In January of 1851 Brigham Young sent settlers who established Parowan as the mother colony for the southern frontier. Parowan was passed by, commercially, unlike Cedar City and St. George. Partly for this reason, Parowan retains the look and feel of a pioneer Mormon settlement. The old stone LDS church is a beautiful example of early church architecture. No longer used for services, the church now houses a DUP museum. Check the front door for the phone numbers of the ladies who maintain this facility; they will be happy to give you a tour. And, yes, the separate, identical front doors were originally meant as separate entrances for men and women.

If all the scenery and attractions haven't worn you out, an interesting short sidetrip from Parowan is the 12-mile drive to Parowan Gap, where extensive rock art dates from both the Desert Archaic and Fremont periods. Drive west on 400 North, pass under Interstate 15, and continue out onto the desert.

From Parowan, Cedar City is 18 miles south on I-15; Salt Lake City is 232 miles north.

6

Utah Highway 12 Scenic Byway
Section 1: Red Canyon to Escalante

General description: A 62-mile high plateau and canyon drive, featuring the redrock country of the Paunsaugunt Plateau and the high desert canyonlands south of the Aquarius Plateau.
Special attractions: Red Canyon, Bryce Canyon National Park, Kodachrome Basin State Park, Escalante Petrified Forest State Park.
Location: Southwest Utah, in western Garfield County.
Drive route number and name: Utah Highway 12, Utah Highway 12 Scenic Byway.
Travel season: Year-round. Though winter is quite cold and snowy, Bryce National Park can be extremely beautiful in snow.
Camping: National forest campground at Red Canyon, two national park campgrounds at Bryce, state park campgrounds at Kodachrome Basin and Escalante Petrified Forest, commercial campgrounds at Bryce and Escalante.
Services: Most services at Panguitch and Escalante; limited services at Red Canyon, Bryce Canyon, Tropic, Cannonville, and Henrieville.
Nearby attractions: Sevier River Valley, East Fork of the Sevier Scenic Backway, Cottonwood Canyon Scenic Backway (Grosvenor Arch), Smokey Mountain Scenic Backway, Escalante backcountry drives and hikes.

The drive

The most scenic highway in a state well known for its scenic drives, UT 12 is arguably the most attractive drive in the *nation*, and certainly one of the most diverse. From Red Canyon in the west to its eastern terminus at Utah Highway 24, just west of the entrance to Capitol Reef National Park, UT 12 traverses a little more than 120 miles of ruggedly beautiful landscape. The constant succession of towering redrock, remote slickrock canyons, heavily-forested alpine mountains, and rustic rural villages contribute to the uniqueness and diversity of the drive, which is split into Drives #6 and #7 in this guide.

UT 12 traverses Garfield County, the home of two national parks, three state parks, and one national recreation area. The entire length of this road has been designated a Utah Scenic Byway, and is nearly always described from west to east. Considering Red Canyon, Bryce's pink sandstone, Kodachrome Basin, and the landform just east of Henrieville called "The Blues," this first 62-mile section of UT 12 is a colorful drive indeed.

UT 12 is one of the American West's most important tourist corridors. Expect the road to be well maintained throughout with moderate traffic, sometimes heavy from the Bryce Canyon turnoff and all through the park. This drive is suitable for all vehicles and is generally driveable year-round.

From its western terminus at U.S. Highway 89, 7 miles south of Panguitch, UT 12 immediately cuts through the dramatic redrock formations of Dixie National Forest's Red Canyon. Gorgeous (and almost unbelievably brilliant) vermilion-colored formations and stands of ponderosa pines make the canyon a true gem of roadside beauty. Red Canyon is Mother Nature's original of all those "painted deserts" seen in amusement parks and old Warner Brothers cartoons. Here you will find perhaps the best scenery *from the car* of any drive in the entire country. Definitely try to time your trip so that you drive *with* the light, or at least not against it. That means starting this drive no earlier than about noon.

Once past Red Canyon the highway crosses the top edge of the Paunsaugunt Plateau, through the northern part of Bryce National Park. Just outside the national forest, where the road crosses the East Fork of the Sevier River, is the turnoff on the right for the East Fork of the Sevier Scenic Backway (Forest Road 087). You might wonder why the heck you would need scenic sidetrips on this outstanding drive, and you are probably eager to get to Bryce, the region's top attraction. But you should consider driving at least the top part of this 30-mile scenic backway. The drive offers fine panoramas in all directions and plenty of interesting and beautiful redrock formations. At the backway's southern terminus is the old Podunk forest guard station, built in 1928, with its unique pyramidal roof. Tropic Reservoir, about 8 miles south of the highway, has a very basic national forest campground that makes a most convenient camping spot for Bryce visitors. The entire backway is well-maintained gravel (two-lane until the reservoir) with no steep grades and is suitable for all vehicles.

Bryce Canyon National Park is acknowledged as having the most stunning sandstone scenery in the American West, and is especially famous for its pink and orange spires and hoodoos. A visitor center, campgrounds, scenic overlooks, hiking trails, and the most extraordinarily sculpted landscape on earth are a short drive south of the highway.

Theodore Roosevelt recognized the importance of protecting the unspoiled character of the Bryce amphitheater, and he established a national forest there in 1905. Shortly after, a road was pushed through and Bryce Canyon began to develop as a touristic attraction. Ruben "Ruby" Syrett built a homestead near the present entrance to the park and, in 1920, built his original lodge and cabins at the site of the present Bryce Lodge. As word spread of the scenic wonders here, Bryce was declared a national monument in 1923 and was elevated to national park status in 1928.

Drive 6: Utah Highway 12 Scenic Byway

Section 1: Red Canyon to Escalante

ESCALANTE PETRIFIED FOREST STATE PARK

Escalante

Smokey Mountain Road

Grosvenor Arch

DIXIE

NATIONAL

FOREST

TABLE CLIFF PLATEAU

TABLE CLIFF

12

Henrieville

KODACHROME BASIN STATE PARK

Cottonwood Canyon Road

Paria River

Sevier River

East Fork

Coyote Hollow

Cannonville

BRYCE CANYON N.P.

Lodge

Tropic

Sunset Point

Bryce Point

Visitor Center

Tropic Res.

Yovimpa Point

Rainbow Point 9,095 ft.

N

Miles

0 2 4 6 8 10

DIXIE

NATIONAL

FOREST

RED CANYON

PAUNSAUGUNT PLATEAU

E. Fork of the Sevier Backway

Hillsdale

89

To Panguitch

The cluster of commercial facilities at the intersection of UT 12 and the park road (U.S. Highway 63) are the descendants of Ruben Syrett's pioneer tourist development. Here you will find food, lodging, and RV facilities as well as concessions for park trail rides and helicopter flights. There is also a nightly rodeo at 7:30 (Monday through Saturday, Memorial Day to Labor Day). The park entrance is 3.5 miles south of Ruby's Inn.

Just after passing the park boundary (and *before* the entrance/fee station) watch on your left for the road to Fairyland Canyon. Many visitors, in their eagerness to enter the park, miss this extremely interesting viewpoint, just 1 mile off the main road. The fantastic "hoodoos" you see below you here, and for which Bryce is so famous, were explained by the Paiutes as "legend people" who had been turned to stone. As you study the twisted maze of canyons below, consider the words of early Mormon pioneer (and park namesake) Ebenezer Bryce, who described it as "a hell of a place to lose a cow."

As always, your first park stop should be the visitor center, where you will find a wealth of information on both the park in general and special daily programs. The park brochure describes in fair detail the many overlooks and trails along the park scenic drive. This is also where you must apply for backcountry permits (free) for all overnight trail hikes. The facility is open daily from 8 A.M. to 4 P.M., except on Thanksgiving, December 25, and January 1; hours are extended during the summer tourist season.

Bryce's famous "hoodoos" resemble rows of fantastic cathedral spires.

Due to congestion on the park road, trailers are not allowed beyond Sunset Campground, and vehicles longer than 25 feet are not allowed at Bryce Point or Paria View. You may leave your trailer in the visitor center. During the summer of 1995 the southern end of the park road underwent some major changes to better accommodate the predictable crush of summer traffic. All of the overlooks lie to the east of the park road (left, as you drive south). To avoid cutting across traffic, it is recommended that you drive all the way south, then stop at the overlooks on your way back. As always on these popular drives, park *only* in designated areas and stop *only* at pullouts.

Actually, this is less of a problem at Bryce, as the park cannot really be seen from inside the car. Unlike Red Canyon, Zion, and Capitol Reef, where you drive along the bottoms of steep canyons mostly looking out and *up*, and unlike the northern entrance to Canyonlands National Park, where tremendous pullouts allow you to overlook the canyons right from your car, the Bryce road is up on the mostly forested rim of a great amphitheater, with no clear views of the dramatic scenery below. Here (as with smaller-scaled Cedar Breaks) you use the 18-mile park road to reach parking areas that access overlooks and elaborate trail systems that descend into the fantastic jumble of pink and orange sandstone formations. If you never leave your car in Bryce, you will see a lot of nice trees . . . and not much else.

I recommend stopping *soon* after the visitor center, at the Sunrise Point parking area, to hike the very easy and pleasant Rim Trail at least from Sunrise Point to Inspiration Point. If your party has two cars, you can leave one at the far end of the walk, so you only have to walk the trail in one direction. Otherwise, Bryce Canyon Lodge makes a good starting point, walking in either direction, to Sunrise or Sunset Points. These trails are designed for easy strolls: well-maintained, handicap accessible, and paved, with lots of beautiful overlooks and plenty of benches. Views here are especially impressive to the east and north. Table Cliff Plateau (the southwestern tip of the grand Aquarius Plateau), seen to the northeast of Bryce, was described by Clarence Dutton as "a vast Acropolis crowned with a Parthenon." For a more strenuous hike, numerous trails (50 miles in all) descend into the amphitheater or follow just beneath the rim.

Bryce has most amenities, including a coin-operated laundry and showers (at the general store near Sunrise Point parking area). The two park campgrounds are first-come, first-served and fill quickly in season. Your other camping options are at commercial campgrounds near the UT 12/US 63 intersection or hiking (with free backcountry permit) to one of several primitive sites in the park.

Bryce Canyon Lodge is definitely worth a look. Built in 1924-25 of local stone and timber, it is one of those classic, timeless artifacts of rustic elegance from the early days of automobile tourism in America. Rooms and cabins are available from mid-April until mid-October (call 801-586-7686 for reservations).

A visit to Bryce can occupy a few hours or a few days. Because the end and beginning of day are so spectacular, when the pink-orange sandstone goes through its dramatic transformation of light, shadow, and color, an overnight stay is highly recommended. A view of Bryce by full moon is an experience you will never forget. But at some point you will have to tear yourself away and continue the drive east. More of Utah awaits you.

Continuing east on UT 12, it is 7 miles to the village of Tropic. Though Ebenezer Bryce had a homestead here in the early 1870s, the town did not really come into being until ten years later. Today it is a pleasant place with a surprising abundance of flowers and fruit orchards. Ebenezer Bryce's cabin can still be seen alongside the highway at the south end of town.

From Cannonville, Kodachrome Basin State Park, with its fascinating multi-colored formations, is a highly-recommended 7-mile diversion to the south. Kodachrome Basin was named by a National Geographic author doing a story on the Escalante region in 1949. The 2,200-acre park has a campground nicely equipped with showers and plenty of picnic tables. The park also has six excellent trail hikes. Most recommended is the Panorama Trail: 3 miles of gentle terrain, interesting rock formations, and fine vistas.

The striking formations you see at Kodachrome Basin are variations of a sort of petrified geyser, sometimes called a "sandpipe." The theory is that Kodachrome Basin once was something like Yellowstone. Millions of years

Cannonville is one of just a handful of quiet little hamlets along Utah Highway 12.

Trail rides provide a unique way of exploring the wonders of Kodachrome Basin.

ago the geysers and mineral springs filled with debris and hardened into a cement-like substance of calcite and sandstone. When softer materials eroded, these structures were exposed.

Either return to Cannonville and UT 12 or continue southeast from Kodachrome Basin on the Cottonwood Canyon Scenic Backway (unpaved but passable in most vehicles when dry; inquire first about conditions). Along this backway, it is about 10 miles to Grosvenor Arch, a natural arch of delicate pastel-colored stone, named for founder and past president of the National Geographic Society, Gilbert Grosvenor. The 46-mile Cottonwood Canyon Road continues south to the Paria River and intersection with US 89 just west of Glen Canyon National Recreation Area.

Continuing east on UT 12, you pass through the pretty little town of Henrieville, after which the road climbs past colored clay cliffs called "The Blues" and then enters the rugged sandstone and shale country of Escalante. There is nothing for the next 30 miles except for some of the finest, most unspoiled high desert scenery you will ever see from a paved road.

One mile west of the old pioneer town of Escalante is Escalante Petrified Forest State Park. To appreciate the many interesting sights here, you will have to get out of the car and hike the excellent interpretive trail describing the park's many examples of petrified wood and dinosaur bones. The park has two main trails: 1-mile Wide Hollow Trail and a 0.75-mile branch called the Rainbow Loop. To see the really good stuff, do the Rainbow Loop. The park has a small but well-appointed campground (with showers).

Escalante is a classic Mormon village that retains the aura of the pioneer West. Not settled until 1875-76, Escalante was most prosperous right around the turn of the century, as confirmed by the number of larger brick buildings from this period. Limited farmland made this primarily a ranching community. You may still see livestock grazing on town lots.

Escalante is famous for the number of "backhouses" that remain on residential lots. Not to be confused with "outhouses," backhouses were common in the nineteenth century as summer kitchens, wash houses, guest cottages, studios, and workshops. Many of these began as the original house and were retained when the larger house was built. The DUP Museum is located in the old LDS Bishop's Tithing Storehouse at 40 South Center Street. This rock building was constructed in 1894 to store the eggs, bushels of wheat, woolens, and other goods contributed to the church by every good Mormon. These were then distributed to the needy and helped contribute to the common weal of church and community. It is common for the DUP museums of older Mormon towns to be housed in the old tithing offices, and this is one of the state's best. As always with the DUP museums, a call to one of the numbers posted on the door will bring a volunteer to let you in.

One odd item about Escalante is its name. If there is one place in southern Utah the Dominguez-Escalante expedition of 1776 did *not* get to, it was Escalante. In fact, the closest the fathers came to the town named for Silvestre Escalante was somewhere north of Panguitch, on the other side of the Paunsaugunt Plateau.

A sidetrip drive from Escalante, for those with vehicles suitable for rough terrain, is the Smokey Mountain Scenic Backway, highlighted by tremendous views of the rugged Kaiparowits Plateau. This 78-mile drive is passable in good conditions by passenger cars, but high clearance is helpful in the inevitable rough spots. Check in Escalante for more detail on the route.

Now that you have gotten yourself out here to the back of the beyond and the rather arbitrary end of this drive, the quickest way out of this fantasy land and back to the real world is to retrace the route back to US 89. This may not be such a bad prospect, as scenic as the drive was; but what the heck, now that you have come this far, why not just continue with the next drive? You will not be sorry if you do.

7

Utah Highway 12 Scenic Byway
Section 2: Escalante to Torrey

General description: Fifty-seven miles of the most spectacular desert and mountain wilderness in the entire state.

Special attractions: Slickrock country of the Escalante River, Calf Creek Falls, Anasazi Indian Village State Park, Boulder Mountain, Capitol Reef and Henry Mountain views.

Location: Southern Utah.

Drive route number and name: UT 12, UT 12 Scenic Byway.

Travel season: Year-round, though the road north from Boulder can be difficult in winter conditions and has been known to close after a heavy snow.

Camping: State Park campground at Escalante, BLM campground at Calf Creek, four national forest campgrounds on Boulder Mountain, commercial campgrounds at Escalante and Torrey.

Services: Most services in Escalante and Torrey; limited services in Boulder.

Nearby attractions: Escalante backcountry hikes and drives, Hole-in-the-Rock Scenic Backway, Hell's Backbone Ridge, Burr Trail Scenic Backway.

The drive

This is the second installment of the 120-mile drive on perhaps the most scenic highway in the nation, UT 12. We are now deep in the heart of slickrock country, in a part of Garfield County that still looks like a wilderness. Until just twenty years ago, the drive on UT 12 from Escalante to Boulder and the alpine drive across Boulder Mountain was a journey into one of the most remote places in the entire country. Begun as an ambitious Civilian Conservation Corps building project of the late 1930s, this stretch of UT 12 was opened in 1940 and was not entirely paved until 1971 (the stretch north of Boulder to Torrey was finally fully paved in the late 1980s).

The pioneer settlement of Escalante was described briefly at the end of the previous drive. Five miles east of Escalante is the turnoff on the right for the Hole-in-the-Rock Scenic Backway. This very scenic, somewhat rough dirt/gravel road traces the original route of the Mormon pioneers sent from Escalante in 1879 to colonize the remote and unsettled southeast corner of Utah. The party made their way to a crossing of the Colorado River below

Hole-in-the-Rock, a steep, narrow defile through which they amazingly blasted, cut, and fabricated a rough road, then lowered their wagons and teams in one of the truly great travel epics in the pioneer West. The story was memorialized in film in the 1949 John Ford classic, *Wagon Master*.

The 57-mile trip to Hole-in-the-Rock is rather easier today than it was for those pioneers. The drive can be done in about 2 hours, but the round-trip is best considered an all-day adventure. Though highly recommended (some of the very finest views of Lake Powell are from Hole-in-the-Rock), this is definitely *not* for RVs, trailers, or low-slung vehicles. The last 5 miles, over slickrock, will be difficult for conventional passenger cars. Inquire first in Escalante about current road conditions.

East of the Hole-in-the-Rock Road, UT 12 trends north through vast expanses of slickrock country. The road skirts south of a huge fold of white sandstone, then drops into the Escalante River Canyon. Ten miles east of Escalante, just on the downside of a low pass, is a spectacular overlook where (as the sign matter-of-factly states) you really *can* see forever on a clear day. As you look north toward the Aquarius Plateau, you get a good sense of what Wallace Stegner meant when he described this high plateau country as "remarkable mountains that are not mountains at all but greatly elevated rolling plains." The descent from this pass is a terrific driving and scenic experience. While the road is certainly driveable in any vehicle (with good brakes!), it is narrow and quite steep. If you are in a large RV or pulling a trailer, it will tax your driving skills a bit.

At about mile 14 is yet another outstanding viewpoint, Boynton Overlook, on the left. And here the thought may occur: if a person were to stop at every single scenic overlook along UT 12, it might take a week to drive from Red Canyon to Torrey. And it would probably be worth the time.

At the bottom of this long descent are the trailheads for some of the renowned Escalante Canyon backpacking and river trips. When you cross the Escalante River and start the climb up the other side, the first mile or so passes through a very narrow canyon of typical Utah redrock. At just under a mile of ascent from the river is the turnoff for Calf Creek Campground. It is a 3-mile hike from the campground to Lower Calf Creek Falls, a 126-foot cascade of ice-cold water.

The Calf Creek trail is a fine example of the great diversity of attractions to hiking in southern Utah. En route to the falls you will walk through groves of Utah junipers (locally called "cedars") and pass between steep, pastel-colored cliffs of Navajo Sandstone. Interpretive signs along the way point out ancient rock art left by members of the Fremont Culture and a thousand-year-old Indian granary. Though the hike can be hot and somewhat strenuous, its numerous attractions and the shady, cool reward of the falls area make it well worth the effort. Pick up a guide to the numbered interpretive trail at the trailhead.

Drive 7: Utah Highway 12 Scenic Byway

Section 2: Escalante to Torrey

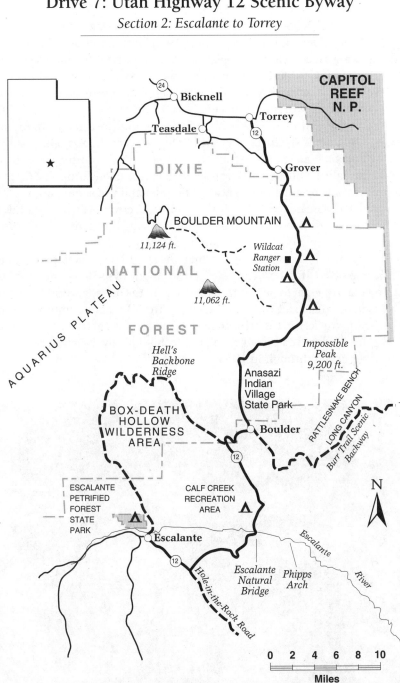

CAPITOL
REEF
N. P.

Bicknell

Torrey

Teasdale

DIXIE

Grover

BOULDER MOUNTAIN

11,124 ft.

Wildcat
Ranger
Station

NATIONAL

11,062 ft.

Impossible
Peak
9,200 ft.

FOREST

Hell's
Backbone
Ridge

Anasazi
Indian
Village
State Park

RATTLESNAKE BENCH

LONG CANYON

Burr Trail Scenic
Backway

BOX-DEATH
HOLLOW
WILDERNESS
AREA

Boulder

ESCALANTE
PETRIFIED
FOREST
STATE
PARK

CALF CREEK
RECREATION
AREA

N

Escalante

Escalante

Escalante
Natural
Bridge

Phipps
Arch

River

Hole-in-the-Rock Road

0   2   4   6   8   10

Miles

If UT 12 to this point has been impressive, beyond Calf Creek the road is *extraordinary*. The road appears to have been blasted through solid rock, climbing to a perfectly straight hogback ridge so narrow that in places you can enjoy views of 1000-foot drops on either side. From the end of this high-level drive you catch your first glimpse of the green Boulder Valley below. This is scenic driving at its very best.

Just at the end of the long hogback ridge and just before the final descent to Boulder is the turnoff on the left for Hell's Backbone. This road is rather rough but makes an extremely dramatic backcountry adventure drive—especially if you are into steep switchbacks and long dropoffs. Amazingly, this was the original route between Boulder and Escalante until UT 12 was completed. Local legend has it that milk and cream, carried by mules from Boulder to Escalante over Hell's Backbone, sometimes turned to butter from the rough trip. (Well, sour cream most likely. . . .)

Boulder was first used by cattlemen in the late 1870s, but no permanent settlement evolved until ten years later. This was one of the last communities in the lower forty-eight to be connected by road to the outside world. Boulder was so isolated that mail came by *packhorse* from Escalante until the mid 1930s. Pickup trucks carried in by mule were reassembled and run on packed-in fuel. The original road from Escalante to Boulder over Hell's Backbone was finally pushed through in 1933.

The views from Utah Highway 12 east of Escalante are some of the most expansive and dramatic in all of Utah.

Snow lingers into June on remote Boulder Mountain. (This photo was taken on June 12.)

Today, despite well-traveled UT 12, Boulder still appears absolutely and stunningly remote. The wooded wilderness of the Aquarius Plateau dominates the northern and western horizons, the canyons and roughlands of the Escalante River lie to the south, while the valley is defined in the east by forbidding desert cliffs.

At the north end of Boulder, Anasazi Indian Village State Park, with some excellent ruins and a museum, offers a good glimpse into Utah's very interesting early Indian culture. This was the site of a 1958–1959 University of Utah archaeological dig that uncovered a total of eighty-seven rooms in an eight-hundred-year-old dwelling.

Boulder is where the Burr Trail Scenic Backway begins. The paving of this route through the Waterpocket Fold area of Capitol Reef was a huge controversy and the source of spirited debate between environmentalists who did not wish to see a traffic increase through the desert wilderness and state and local officials who viewed the paving as a solution to critical road travel difficulties in the area.

You can follow this route all the way to Bullfrog Marina on Lake Powell or use it to connect with the Notom Road drive (see Drive #8). The Burr Trail remains unpaved in a 17-mile section where it crosses Capitol Reef National Park. Switchbacks on these unpaved sections may cause problems for larger rigs; otherwise, the route is passable for most vehicles. You should drive at least the first 18 miles of Burr Trail, to the end of Long Canyon. This stretch is one of the most interesting and most dramatic, and makes an easy sidetrip from UT 12.

As UT 12 leaves Boulder you enter Dixie National Forest and begin to climb steeply onto the Aquarius Plateau. Within 4 miles of Boulder, this is a true mountain drive (really *terrific* in autumn). A few miles farther and you come into beautiful groves of aspen. Watch for deer on the road, especially in the evening.

The names Boulder Mountain and Aquarius Plateau both apply to the same landform; both names appear on current maps. Aquarius, the "waterbearer" of the zodiac, seems most appropriate for this vast alpine upland. Source of the Escalante River and major tributaries of the Fremont and Sevier, the Aquarius Plateau spills its waters down upon the desert.

Though by now you have probably realized the impracticality of stopping at every single scenic overlook, do not fail to stop at the truly incredible Homestead Overlook about 11 miles past Boulder and close to the 9,400-foot apex of this drive. It was a view like this that prompted Clarence Dutton, author of perhaps the finest book on early exploration in Utah's canyon country, to remark: "It is a sublime panorama. The heart of the inner Plateau Country is spread out before us in a bird's-eye-view. It is a maze of cliffs and terraces lined off with stratification, of crumbling buttes, red and white domes, rock platforms gashed with profound canyons, burning plains barren even of sage—all glowing with bright color and flooded with blazing sunlight. Everything visible tells of ruin and decay. It is the extreme of desolation, the blankest solitude, a superlative desert."

Dutton recorded these sentiments in approximately this same location, high up on the southeastern flank of the Aquarius Plateau. The view still lives up to his description.

The road stays high for several miles, with especially spectacular views off to the right across the Waterpocket Fold and Capitol Reef and toward the Henry Mountains. At about mile 8.5 past Homestead is another not-to-be-missed overlook, called Larb Hollow, with even better views of the Henrys. Just past this overlook begins a serious (steep) 5-mile descent. You leave Dixie National Forest just north of Grover in some of the most beautiful high ranch country you will ever see, covered with sage and juniper. Grover is not an actual town, but a handful of ranches nestled in the valley.

UT 12 ends at the intersection with Utah Highway 24 just east of Torrey. Here you have the option of turning left/west to Loa and the quickest return to Interstate 15. If you wish to continue with Drive #8 through Capitol Reef and on to points east, turn right. In either case, you really ought to take a few minutes to visit the small residential community of Teasdale (about 4 miles west of Torrey and 1.5 miles south of UT 24 at a well-marked intersection). This quiet little town with its lovely LDS church is a perfect example of why the Mormon pioneers, kicked out of town after town across America and just looking for some unwanted place to call their own, didn't get such a bad deal after all. Wouldn't you rather live in Teasdale?

Torrey is a pretty little town with tree-lined UT 24 as its main street. Just west of the modern LDS church, note on the right the small, original church building, usually open for visitors. Across the street there is a cute little community picnic area with a bandstand. You will find most basic services here.

8

Utah Highway 24 Scenic Byway
Loa to Hanksville

General description: Starting in one of the state's prettiest farming/ranching valleys, this drive quickly enters classic Utah canyon country, highlighted by the many scenic attractions of the Waterpocket Fold.

Special attractions: Attractive agricultural communities along the Fremont River, Capitol Reef National Park, views of the Henry Mountains, outstanding geological formations.

Location: South-central Utah.

Drive route number and name: UT 24, UT 24 Scenic Byway.

Travel season: Year-round.

Camping: One national park campground at Capitol Reef; commercial campgrounds at Bicknell, Torrey (3), Caineville, and Hanksville (3).

Services: Most services in Loa, Torrey, and Hanksville; gas and food at Caineville.

Nearby attractions: Fishlake Scenic Byway, Escalante-Torrey (UT 12) Scenic Byway, Notom Scenic Backway, Cathedral Valley Scenic Backway, Goblin Valley State Park.

The drive

It is approximately 75 miles along UT 24 from Loa to Hanksville. Make that 75 *extraordinary* miles. This drive is non-stop, knock-out scenery, from the green valley of the Fremont River through the dramatic geologic upheaval of the Waterpocket Fold to the wild shale and sandstone high desert mesas and buttes that spread out to the north of the rugged Henry Mountains.

This entire scenic drive, including the 25-mile Capitol Reef National Park Scenic Drive, can be done in four hours. Plan on a full day, allowing at least half a day to poke around Capitol Reef, and longer if the park grabs your interest. Several excellent sidetrips might extend this drive even longer.

Start this journey in the pretty farm community of Loa, which is briefly described at the end of Drive #14. Loa is easily reached from Richfield in the Sevier Valley. UT 24 from Loa to Torrey is scenic in a peaceful, bucolic way, following a pretty river in a verdant valley. The land along the Fremont River is all private and mostly farm and ranchland. It is easy to understand why early settlers found this valley so attractive. There is a small national

Drive 8: Utah Highway 24 Scenic Byway
Loa to Hanksville

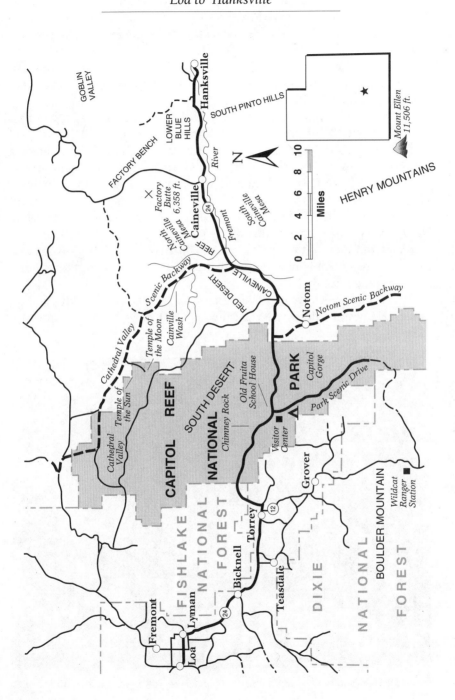

forest campground, called Sunglow, just east of Bicknell on the left. Five miles east of Bicknell a paved road on the right leads a mile or so to the lovely little hamlet of Teasdale, a worthwhile diversion to see a fine example of a classic Mormon farming community.

Torrey is described at the end of Drive #7. This is the gateway to Capitol Reef National Park as well as to the mountain wilderness of the eastern flank of the Aquarius Plateau.

Driving east, past the intersection with UT 12 on the right, you pass through classic Utah redrock for the 4 miles to the boundary of Capitol Reef National Park. Established as a national monument in 1937 and made a national park in 1971, Capitol Reef is one of America's greatest natural treasures. The park preserves the 100-mile Waterpocket Fold, a mammoth buckling of the earth's surface. The name combines the popular term for an uplifted landmass, "reef," with a visual resemblance of the park's many white Navajo Sandstone domes to that of the nation's Capitol. Capitol Reef is an incredible mixture of the finest elements of Bryce and Zion Canyons in a park that many feel is more enjoyable to visit than either of those more-famous attractions.

This is an evocative world of spectacular colored cliffs, hidden arches, massive domes, and deep, twisting canyons. Of all of Utah's many impressive

LDS church at Teasdale, a picturesque old settlement in the Fremont River Valley.

national parks and monuments, only Canyonlands National Park and the endless wildlands of Glen Canyon rival Capitol Reef's sense of expansiveness; of broad, sweeping vistas; of a tortured, twisted, seemingly endless landscape; of limitless sky and desert rock. While Bryce and Zion are like encapsulated little fantasy lands of colored stone and soaring cliffs, Capitol Reef is almost like a planet unto itself. Here you get a real feel for what the earth might have been like millions of years before life appeared, when nothing existed but earth and sky.

Actually, the Waterpocket Fold was created relatively recently, at about the same time and by the same forces as the entire Colorado Plateau. A mere 65 million years ago (give or take a few millennia), when the uplift of the Colorado Plateau began, rock strata here were bent into a huge broken fold. Wind and water gradually eroded the ancient fold into the landforms and canyon systems we see today.

Due to the low humidity year-round, there is really no "wrong" season for visiting this park; while the frequent thunderstorms of late summer sometimes cause flash floods, they also provide extremely dramatic skies and some of the best lighting of the year. And while this may seem a lifeless, barren place, a surprising wealth of flora and fauna makes its home here. You just have to look hard sometimes to see it.

There is no fee for travel directly through the park on UT 24. If pressed for time, you can see plenty of Capitol Reef from the highway; but it would be a real tragedy to miss the park's attractions just to the south. It is easily possible to spend three days or more exploring this park. A basic introduction (including the park scenic drive, drives to the ends of Grand Valley Wash and Capitol Gorge, and perhaps one short hike) should occupy at least three hours.

About 7 miles after entering the park boundary on UT 24 is the well-marked turnoff on the right for the park visitor center and Capitol Reef Scenic Drive. The visitor center is open daily (except certain federal holidays) year-round. The National Park Service suggests about 90 minutes for the 25-mile scenic drive, but plan on more time if you want to stretch your legs a bit (which you should). Be sure to pick up the literature on the park and on the old Mormon community of Fruita. At the fee station ($4.00 for the drive), pick up the very handy park driving brochure (free), which contains detailed descriptions of the numbered interpretive stops as well as useful geological information.

Views in Capitol Reef are considerably more "open" than those in Zion, which is rather confined by the narrow canyons. Even more so than Zion, much of Capitol Reef can be seen right from the car. There are several nice, short side-drives on well-maintained dirt/gravel roads that can be negotiated in virtually any vehicle. The first of these, Grand Valley Wash, is extremely attractive—sort of like taking a Disneyland ride in your own car.

You should definitely drive out to the end of Capitol Gorge. This 2.2-mile road is a little narrow for RVs, and nothing you would want to pull a trailer through, but other vehicles will make it without difficulty. It is hard to imagine a more unusual driving experience for a conventional vehicle.

There are also excellent walks in the park and very good rock climbing in vertical cracks of hard Wingate sandstone. Inquire at the visitor center for information on specific hikes and climbing routes. The rangers at the visitor center will also issue free backcountry (overnight) hiking permits along with recommendations for backcountry campsites.

The hike through The Narrows, from the trailhead at the end of the Grand Valley Wash drive, is highly recommended. About 0.25 mile into this hike there is a cutback trail (somewhat steep) on the left to visit Cassidy Arch, where the ubiquitous Butch is said to have hung out. There is an easy and interesting 1-mile hike from the trailhead at the end of the Capitol Gorge drive. On a rock wall called Pioneer Register you can see the names of miners, settlers, and other adventurers who passed through here starting in 1871. In fact, the labyrinthine Capitol Gorge road was the main transport route through this region from 1884 until UT 24 was opened in 1962.

After a visit to Capitol Reef's rocky wilderness, the green groves and fruit orchards around the intersection of UT 24 and the park scenic drive will seem a cool and welcome sight. Just after the turn of the century, the Mormon community of Fruita, nestled in the shaded canyon formed by the Fremont River, was a lively, vibrant town of nearly fifty. Though most of Fruita's residents gradually moved away after Capitol Reef's establishment as a national monument, the fields and orchards (and an abundance of wildlife) remain for your enjoyment. Visitors may even pick small quantities of fruit: cherries in June, apricots in July, pears in August, and apples in September.

The park campground, with seventy-one sites, water, and toilets (but no showers) is located in the shady area of old Fruita. Apart from water and the orchard fruit, the park provides no other services or amenities. Nearby Torrey is the best bet for accommodations and food.

So tear yourself away from the wonders of Capitol Reef and continue east along UT 24; there is much more to enthuse over on this drive.

Just after returning to UT 24, note on the left the old Fruita schoolhouse, nicely restored and in a beautiful setting beneath towering sandstone cliffs. The one-room schoolhouse, built in 1896, remained in use until 1941. It also served the community as church and town meeting place, with the desks pushed aside for Saturday dances. Just after the old schoolhouse, also on the left, is a petroglyph trail; beyond the petroglyph trail is the trailhead for the easy (2 miles round-trip) hike to Hickman Natural Bridge. This is perhaps one of the best park walks in all of Utah, with terrific scenic views and glimpses of Fremont Culture ruins. Hickman Bridge itself is a must-see.

*The sheer sandstone cliffs of the Waterpocket Fold
define the scenery of Capitol Reef National Park.*

The drive into Capitol Gorge is one of the more unusual driving experiences you can have in a family sedan.

From this trail you can also see one of the large white sandstone domes that inspired the park's name.

About 5 miles east of the turnoff for the park visitors center is the well-marked Grand Valley Wash trailhead on the right. From here, you can do the aforementioned hike through the Grand Valley Wash Narrows but in reverse.

The landscape along UT 24 outside the fee area is exceptional, even for this most scenic state. As might be expected, as soon as you leave the park boundary the landscape diminishes in interest—from incredible to just terrific. It is still extremely beautiful, and because this is still *public* land there is absolutely no commercial development outside either park entrance. The only obvious transition is that the most dramatic landscape features are enclosed within the park boundaries; otherwise, it is just as pristine and wild out of the park as within.

Just east of the park boundary, on the right, is the turnoff for the Notom Scenic Backway. This 29-mile scenic drive parallels the Waterpocket Fold and gives one of the better perspectives on its magnitude. To the east of the backway, the Henry Mountains loom above the high-desert badlands. The road is rough in places and high-clearance vehicles are recommended. Inquire at Capitol Reef as to current conditions.

About 4.5 miles east of the Capitol Reef boundary the road enters an interesting valley with odd, soft-looking, tannish-yellow sandstone cliffs.

Next comes an area of blue-gray Mancos shale, much younger in geological time than the more colorful rock of Capitol Reef. Just after you cross the Fremont River at the little gas station/cafe/campground (with showers) called "Sleepy Hollow," look quickly to the right through a gap in the sandstone cliffs at the curious area of gray sand dunes. More of this gray stuff follows soon after.

The landscape has really changed by this point. The views are more expansive, the rock formations look much softer, sort of halfway between sand dunes and sandstone cliffs. The landscape here is not so grand as what lies to the west but in some respects is more visually interesting.

About 5 miles east of Sleepy Hollow, watch for the turnoff on the left for Cathedral Valley Scenic Backway. This 56-mile dirt track heads back to the northwest through the northern tip of Capitol Reef and into Cathedral Valley, ending at Fremont Junction on Interstate 70. The main attractions along this desert and canyon drive are the views of such dramatic formations as Temple of the Sun and Temple of the Moon. High-clearance vehicles are advised for this rather rough drive, which includes a ford of the (very shallow) Fremont River.

There are some pretty little hamlets in the Fremont River Valley, along with a whimsical cluster of teepees at the Luna Mesa Cafe at Caineville (the Luna Mesa appears to be about all there is to Caineville).

Just past Caineville, look to the right where the large sandstone cliffs end and the Henry Mountains appear off to the south. East of Caineville the landscape flattens and the scenery seems remarkably undramatic compared with what you passed through earlier. Reminiscent of the Dakota badlands, this is a rough, empty land. On the good, fast road, this is also a fine place to make up time after all the dawdling you probably did earlier.

Hanksville is a crossroads town in the desert wilderness of eastern Wayne County. It makes a good refueling spot and is one of the few places within 50 miles where you can find a soft bed. The town has two attractions of note: a gas station and convenience store burrowed into a sandstone wall, Anasazi-style, and a relic of an old mill. The gas station you cannot miss; it is just south of the intersection with Utah Highway 95 (the route to Glen Canyon, Natural Bridges National Monument, and Blanding—Drive #9 in this guide).

The Wolverton Mill was built in 1921 by Edwin Thatcher Wolverton, a New England mining engineer who was absolutely sure he would find gold on Mount Pennell in the Henry Mountains. The mill was unique in its dual function of ore mill and sawmill, designed to both crush ore and saw timber. Wolverton never found his gold, and he abandoned his search in 1929. Today his mill stands as a monument to perseverance and blind optimism. In 1974, the BLM moved the mill from the Henrys to the BLM office in Hanksville and completed its restoration in 1988.

From Hanksville, it is a very scenic 55-mile drive north on UT 24 to Green River on I-70. Along the way you will pass Goblin Valley State Park and the really fantastic San Rafael Reef. As with so many drives in this part of Utah, this stretch of UT 24 deserves to be designated a scenic drive. But this is Utah, and there is only so much space on the map.

So here you are in Hanksville. You *could* head north for the interstate . . . but now that you are down here, why not just continue with the next scenic drive? You could do far worse than let yourself be a captive to the southeastern Utah tourist trail. More natural wonders lie just ahead.

9

Bicentennial Scenic Byway

Hanksville to Blanding

General description: A 133-mile high-desert drive across some of the state's most rugged canyon country.

Special attractions: Views of the Henry Mountains, Glen Canyon crossing, Natural Bridges National Monument, Anasazi dwellings.

Location: Southeastern Utah.

Drive route number and name: Utah Highway 95, Bicentennial Highway.

Travel season: Year-round.

Camping: National recreation area campground at Glen Canyon, national monument campground at Natural Bridges, BLM campground at Hog Springs, commercial campgrounds at Hanksville and Blanding.

Services: Most services at Hanksville and Blanding; limited services at Hite Marina.

Nearby attractions: Goblin Valley, Henry Mountains, Bullfrog Basin Marina, Trail of the Ancients, Moki Dugway Scenic Drive, Hovenweep National Monument, Abajo Loop Scenic Backway.

The drive

Completed in 1976, Utah's Bicentennial Highway runs 133 miles from Hanksville to Blanding. South of Hanksville the highway offers fine views of the Henry Mountains to the west, then winds through rugged canyon country before crossing Lake Powell at Hite Crossing. The road surface is excellent the entire route, and traffic is generally light in this sparsely populated part of the state. This drive can be done in half a day, with few stops and just a quick breeze through Natural Bridges. Plan on a full day if you wish to do a hike in Natural Bridges and poke around some of the Anasazi ruins between there and Blanding.

This drive begins at Hanksville, which was described briefly at the end of the previous drive. Hanksville is the last stop for reasonably priced gas and supplies until you reach Blanding (gas at Hite Marina is $.10 to $.15 per gallon more expensive), so you will probably want to fill up here. Besides, you should definitely check out the gas station and convenience store dug into the rock wall: a desert architectural classic. At the eastern edge of town is the intersection of Utah Highway 24 and UT 95, where UT 24 hooks north (left) and UT 95 (signed for Hite, Ticaboo, Glen Canyon) is the right/south turn.

As you drive south from Hanksville, you have really tremendous views off to the right of the Henry Mountains. Mount Ellen is the first high point, Mount Pennell the second. This was the last mountain range in the lower forty-eight to be explored and named. One of the nation's few free-roaming buffalo herds makes its home in the Henrys. A handful of the animals were transplanted from Yellowstone in the early 1940s, and today the herd numbers approximately three hundred head. Don't strain your eyes too hard looking for them; unless you are willing to penetrate their mountain preserve, it is doubtful you will see them.

On the other hand, if you *do* want to make the effort, the BLM has designated the Bull Creek Pass Road into the Henrys as a National Back Country Byway. Access for this drive is 20 miles south of Hanksville on the right. Anyone considering this rough and very remote drive should first check with the BLM office in Hanksville for detailed road information. Also called Bull Mountain Backway, it is *not* recommended in anything but a stout, high-clearance vehicle.

You will certainly have noticed, as you drive south on UT 95, the huge mesa on the right called "Little Egypt." The formation was named by early cowboys who were reminded of the Egyptian Sphinx. The drive will probably remind you less of Egypt than of the high desert prairie of, say, Wyoming: mostly flat with low mesas on the horizon, sagebrush-covered land, and snow-capped mountains in the background.

At the prominent fork for Lake Powell/Ticaboo, take the left-hand branch; right will take you to Ticaboo and Bullfrog (where you can continue your drive to Natural Bridges by taking the ferry to Hall's Crossing, if you have plenty of time). Here you may begin to notice you have returned to a more characteristically Southwestern landscape. Below the fork, the road winds through a gorgeous redrock canyon whose walls, though not particularly high, are magnificently carved and pock-marked. This really is one of the outstanding portions of this drive. About 6 miles south of the Bullfrog fork is the attractive Hog Springs rest area, which, according to the BLM map, also functions as a camping site. There are no facilities and no water, though there are toilets and a few shaded picnic areas. While it does not look particularly good for tenting, this could serve for an overnight stop.

Once south of Hog Springs the canyon opens up wider and the mesas on both sides (especially to the right) become much higher. About 3 miles south of Hog Springs you cross into Glen Canyon Recreation Area. Within a few miles you will start to notice a generally ugly brownish-green body of water on the right; at about 4 miles into the area you get your first really big vista. It is tempting to stop here for pictures, but you are better off waiting

Drive 9: Bicentennial Scenic Byway
Hanksville to Blanding

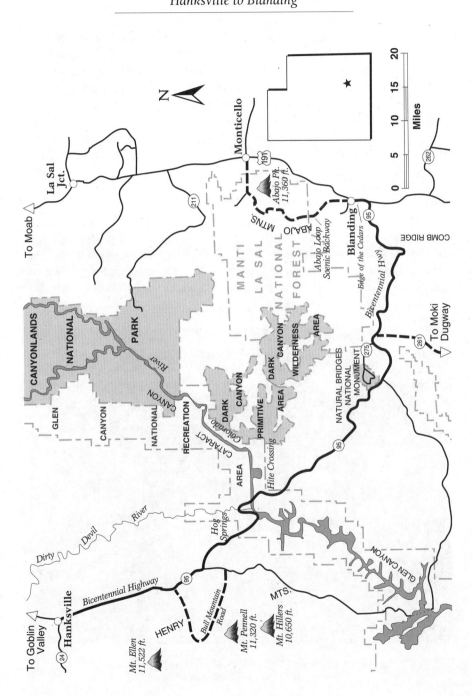

until Hite Overlook (4.5 miles past the recreation area entrance) to stop for snaps, as this is the best viewpoint you will have of Glen Canyon.

The enormous body of water you see below is part of the much-widened 200-mile stretch of the Colorado River now known as Lake Powell. In 1956 construction began on the Glen Canyon Dam some ninety (air) miles to the southwest. The dam was finished in 1964 (it took three years of round-the-clock work just to pour the concrete) and began generating power two years later. By 1980 Lake Powell had reached its current level. The lake was named for the indefatigable explorer of the Colorado River Basin, Major John Wesley Powell, who named this rough stretch of the Colorado "Glen Canyon."

This rugged combination of land and water had been home to early Desert Archaic people and later Anasazi Indians for many centuries before Powell made his epic 1869 descent of the Colorado. The river and its deep canyon had long been an obstacle to the few travelers who passed through the region since the coming of the first white explorers and settlers. Far downstream, the returning Dominguez-Escalante party spent nearly two weeks searching for a place to cross the Colorado before finally chopping

The rugged and remote Henry Mountains were the last peaks in the lower forty-eight to be mapped and named.

steps into the sandstone to descend to the river at what became known as the Crossing of the Fathers. In similar dramatic fashion, the Hole-in-the-Rock pioneers breached the canyon just above the junction with the San Juan River (see Drive #7).

A member of the Hole-in-the-Rock party, Charles Hall, found a more practical crossing point about 35 miles upstream from the Hole-in-the-Rock, where he started a ferry between what is now Hall's Crossing and Bullfrog Basin. This was the main Colorado crossing point until Cass Hite established a ferry and post office at approximately the spot below you. The ferry and the town of Hite were covered by current Lake Powell.

The dual purposes of the Glen Canyon Dam project were electrical energy and water management. The widening of the backed-up Colorado and its tributaries (notably the San Juan and Escalante) inundated thousands of acres of what had once been shoreline and branch canyons, drowning forever uncounted geological and archaeological treasures. But there are positive aspects of this massive transformation in the desert as well. Today more fast-food restaurants in Phoenix can sport neon lights, and the folks from nearby Mexican Hat have a great place to jet ski. And, of course, we tourists have a brand new landscape to enthuse over.

It really is a new landscape, with nearly 2,000 miles of shoreline. And the most positive aspect of the entire should-it-ever-have-been-built controversy is the simple fact that today's Glen Canyon National Recreation Area was established in 1972 to preserve the river and nearly one million acres of adjacent desert country for public recreational use.

Since Glen Canyon is designated a national *recreation area*, **not** a park, you can camp virtually anywhere. About 2.5 miles beyond the descent from Hite Overlook, there are all sorts of undeveloped campsites on the right, just above the water. About 10 miles from the overlook is the turnoff on the right (just after the second bridge) for Hite Marina. At Hite you will find a campground, gas station, basic convenience store, cafe, and boat rental; unless you are into boating or in desperate need of gas or a cold drink, there's no reason to go down to the marina. The camping is free but, like the rest of the lake, completely treeless with no shade, no drinking water, and no picnic tables.

As popular as Glen Canyon is with boaters, it is remarkably undeveloped, probably because this is all public land. The landscape may be rather bleak and cheerless, but at least it's *naturally* bleak and cheerless, unspoiled by development (hmmmmm . . . maybe what they really *need* is a waterslide here).

A little more than 6.5 miles beyond the Hite Marina turnoff you leave the recreation area. Twenty-four miles from Hite you will pass the cafe/gas station/motel at the non-town of Fry Canyon—don't blink! Past Fry Canyon the landscape gets a little greener with a sparse covering of juniper/

pinyon, but there is still not much chance for a shaded picnic site until you reach Natural Bridges. Twelve miles past Fry Canyon, at the turnoff on the right (Utah Highway 276) for Hall's Crossing, continue straight ahead for Blanding and Mexican Hat.

As you start to descend toward Natural Bridges National Monument, the groundcover becomes more luxuriant and the trees taller. You cannot see the chaotic landscape of Natural Bridges from the highway, tucked away as it is off to the north. The entrance to the monument, with visitor center and scenic drive, is approximately 44 miles from Hite Marina, on the left, then a 4-mile drive in.

There is ample evidence that Anasazi Indians, probable ancestors of the Hopi, occupied this complex system of canyons from about 500 B.C. until around 1270 A.D. The earliest inhabitants probably lived in pit houses on the mesa tops, while the later Pueblo Anasazi built cliff dwellings that can still be seen today. It is thought that the Pueblo Anasazi farmed up on the broad mesas, not in the narrow canyons. Cass Hite explored the region in 1883 while on a gold-prospecting sortie from his camp on the Colorado. Twenty-five years later, Theodore Roosevelt made this the first National Monument in Utah. A 1904 *National Geographic* expedition first brought the area to the public's attention.

There are few facilities at Natural Bridges and no services at all. At the visitor center you will find nice interpretive displays to introduce the area and describe the attractions of Bridge View Drive. There is a very attractive (but spartan) thirteen-site campground here. There is no water, but campers can fetch up to five gallons per day from the visitor center. This is the only drinking water within the monument, so fill your water bottles here. It is also requested that you leave trailers here, rather than pull them along the Bridge View Drive.

Arches and bridges, as geological formations, differ chiefly in the way they were formed. Natural bridges are the result of erosive action by running water, while arches are formed by gravitational collapse and erosion from wind and freeze/thaw action. These bridges are relatively new and will soon (in geological time) collapse. The largest natural bridges are believed to be only about five thousand years old.

The Bridge View Drive has been sensibly organized as a one-way loop, so you can rubberneck all you want and not worry about head-on collisions. The paved, 9-mile drive leads to overlooks and trailheads above the three bridges that are the drive's chief attractions. While all of the bridges can be viewed from the overlooks, short and relatively easy trails provide more intimate contact. The easiest hike is to the last bridge, Owachomo.

Natural Bridges makes a very nice one- to four-hour diversion, depending on how much you like to hike. The only real problem here is the lack of suitable picnic sites. The sole designated picnic area has but two tables.

So back to UT 95 continuing east. About a mile or so past the Natural Bridges turnoff is the intersection on the right with Utah Highway 261. This is the much-recommended Moki Dugway Scenic Backway, which presents something of a logistical dilemma for travelers (and for driving-guide writers). It is a recurring problem in Utah whenever you reach a crossroads: too many interesting things to see down too many roads running in too many different directions. So some choices need to be made.

At the lower end of the drive down UT 261 is the very dramatic (read: "steep, scary, unpaved, and with no guardrail") 1,000-foot switchback descent of the Moki Dugway. The views from the Dugway Overlook and nearby Muley Point are among the finest in southern Utah, and the view of the meandering San Juan River from Goosenecks State Park is extremely interesting. But once you have driven as far as Goosenecks, you probably will not want to retrace your route back up to finish the UT 95 drive to Blanding. This is especially true if you are driving an RV or pulling a trailer, since you will *not* want to re-ascend the gravel, 10% grade of the Moki Dugway. In fact, *descending* the Moki Dugway in a large vehicle will test your nerve and driving skills—perhaps more than your passengers will appreciate.

Goosenecks can be reached easily as a sidetrip from Drive #10, but reaching the Dugway/Muley Point overlooks from the south would require ascending the Dugway. That would be my recommendation for drivers willing to make the long ascent. Another alternative would be to terminate this drive here, do the Moki Dugway drive, and join Drive #10 at Mexican Hat. A final (longest) option would be to drive down to the overlooks, return north to UT 95, then visit Goosenecks from Drive #10. This would avoid the short, steep, unpaved descent entirely, though it would mean driving 24 miles mostly for the overlook views—they *are* worth it. This last option is probably the best for drivers of large vehicles.

If you do take this sidetrip, by all means stop in at the Kane Gulch Ranger Station for information on the fascinating wilderness through which you will drive. The Grand Gulch Primitive Area, accessed by a trail near the station, is one of the richest areas in Indian artifacts in all of southeastern Utah. The ranger station (open April–September) is on the left about 3 miles south of UT 95. The 5-mile drive out to Muley Point is on maintained gravel, departing UT 261 on the right, just where the pavement ends and the road begins to descend. Most vehicles, with the exception of larger RVs, should have no difficulties reaching Muley Point.

So, decisions, decisions. . . . If you are still with me to the eastern end of UT 95, from here to Blanding you will pass a succession of interesting archaeological sites, part of a large loop known as "The Trail of the Ancients." East of Natural Bridges you enter a more open landscape, where *way* off to the east you may notice the snow-capped peaks of the western ranges of the San Juan Mountains in neighboring Colorado.

*Today, Lake Powell spreads out over the desert where Mormon pioneer
Cass Hite established his important crossing on the Colorado River.*

At 10 miles from the Natural Bridges turnoff is a nice short stop at the
Anasazi ruins at Mule Canyon. Just 100 yards from the road, they can be
seen in ten minutes. The ruins include a kiva, a tower, and a small block of
rooms. Just beyond this site is Cave Towers viewpoint. Seven Anasazi stone
towers perch on the canyon rim, three of which are clearly visible here. Ten
miles east of Mule Canyon is Butler Wash Indian Ruins, another nice archaeological attraction, this time involving an easy 1-mile trail walk leading
to an overlook of several Indian dwellings.

A little more than 30 miles east of Natural Bridges is the intersection
with U.S. Highway 191. North goes to Blanding, Monticello, and escape
routes to the interstates; south leads to Drive #10 (although you may want
to drive up to Blanding first for fuel and provisions).

One more important archaeological site is worth a visit on the way
north to Blanding. About 2 miles north of the UT 95/US 191 intersection,
watch for Blue Mountain Trading Post. A few blocks past the trading post is
a paved road on the left, signed for Westwater Ruin. The overlook for the
fairly extensive ruins is just 2 miles down this road.

The town of Blanding has a distinct aura of "somewhere-elseness." It
is a fairly substantial community of nearly four thousand residents but a

long way from any urban center. Places like Blanding and nearby Monticello have to be extremely self-sufficient, commercially and culturally.

The chief attraction in Blanding is the very fine Edge of the Cedars State Park. Actually, this is more a museum than a park, with outstanding exhibits describing the various inhabitants of the region: from prehistoric Anasazi, through the later Navajo and Ute Indians, to the more recent Euro-American settlers. The museum houses one of the finest collections of Anasazi pottery in the entire Southwest. Behind the museum is an interpretive path leading through an actual Anasazi excavation, some of the buildings of which may be entered. Open daily, 8 A.M. to 5 P.M., Edge of the Cedars is located on the northwest edge of town; just follow the many signs.

Blanding also has a new dinosaur museum with life-sized models, fossils, skeletons, and a nice free exhibit called the "Nations of the Four Corners Cultural Center." This attraction features a self-guided walking tour that leads to a Navajo hogan, a Ute teepee, a Mexican hacienda, and a settler's log cabin.

If you are headed north from Blanding, the drive to Monticello is scenic though not spectacular. Just south of Monticello you begin to catch glimpses of the snow-capped La Sals to the northeast. If you have two hours to spare (and a high-clearance vehicle), a more interesting alternative to US 191 is the Abajo Loop Scenic Backway. This 22-mile mountain drive loops up through the Abajo Mountains north of Blanding, climbs to nearly 11,000 feet, then descends to Monticello. The road is single-lane dirt/gravel and is impassable when wet. The mountain scenery and the views of the southern part of Canyonlands National Park are superb. Inquire in Blanding about road conditions to determine whether your vehicle is up to the task.

10

Bluff Scenic Byway
Bluff to Monument Valley

General description: A 45-mile drive through the desert grandeur of southern San Juan County and the Navajo Indian Reservation, highlighted by views of desert spires and mesas.

Special attractions: Mexican Hat Rock, views of Monument Valley, Navajo crafts and culture, float trips on the San Juan River.

Location: The extreme southeast corner of Utah. The second half of the drive is on the huge Navajo Reservation.

Drive route number and name: U.S. Highway 163/Bluff Scenic Byway.

Travel season: Year-round.

Camping: Limited choices. One BLM campground at Sand Island; one state park campground at Goosenecks; commercial campgrounds at Bluff, Mexican Hat, and Monument Valley.

Services: Most services at Blanding; some services at Bluff and Mexican Hat; limited services at Monument Valley.

Nearby attractions: Hovenweep National Monument, Four Corners, Valley of the Gods, Muley Point, Goosenecks.

The drive

This is beauty on a grand scale. While the landscapes to the north and east are characterized by dramatic ancient bucklings of the earth and by intricate, maze-like canyons carved by the persistent action of rushing waters, the country encountered on this drive is more *spacious* and more serene in its magnificence. Rather than narrow, choatic canyons and steep, confining barrier reefs, US 163 traverses land that is broad, open, and windswept.

It is hot at the height of summer in this corner of the state. Otherwise, no real seasonal distinctions can be made, and driving poses no impediments for any sort of vehicle.

While this scenic drive is congruent with the state's US 163 Scenic Byway, the rugged country between Blanding and Bluff is not without interest. If you have just finished the Utah Highway 95 drive (Drive #9) and don't want to make the detour north on U.S. Highway 191 to Blanding, there is gas at White Mesa, just south of the UT 95/US 191 intersection, and at Bluff, 22 miles south.

Drive 10: Bluff Scenic Byway
Bluff to Monument Valley

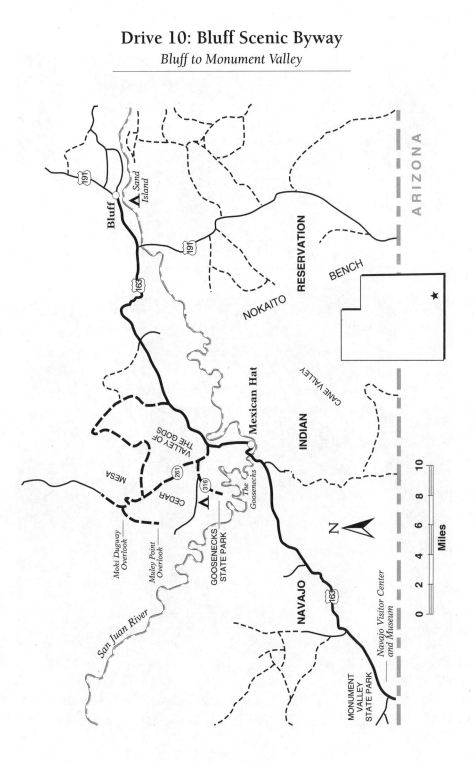

Graceful sandstone spires rise above the arid desert of the Valley of the Gods.

Just south of the UT 95/US 191 intersection, on the left, is a monument to Chief Posey. The Ute Indians of White Mesa and Allen Canyon were the last free-roaming Indian band in the country, and their frequent conflicts with white settlers culminated in the Posey Wars of 1915 and 1923, some of the last open gunfights between Whites and Indians in America.

Eleven miles south of the UT 95 intersection is the well-marked turnoff on the left for Hovenweep National Monument. Hovenweep is the site of the best Anasazi ruins in Utah. It is the least-visited national monument in the state and a highly recommended sidetrip for anyone interested in the cultural history of the Southwest. You will be disappointed if you expect to see cliff dwellings, as at Mesa Verde and Canyon de Chelly. These are stone structures organized into six villages built sometime around 1200 AD. The name is Ute for "deserted valley," which this definitely was by the time the Utes happened on it; it still seems an appropriate name today. The monument, with visitor center and campground, is 24 miles east on this paved road.

If you are wondering about the frequency of the word "recapture" on the map in this area (Recapture Pocket, Recapture Creek, Recapture Reservoir), it may relate to the use of the name "Montezuma" (for a creek, a town, and a trading post). According to a rather apocryphal local legend, the last Aztec ruler of Mexico escaped his Spanish captors and fled north to this region. He was supposedly "recaptured" and executed here. Extremely unlikely, it makes a good story nonetheless.

The scenery really starts to get good just north of the village of Bluff. This part of Utah was settled late, when hardy pioneers from Escalante came via the famous Hole-in-the-Rock Trail in 1880 and established homesteads at the present site of Bluff. From the start, ranching prevailed over farming in this land of unpredictable water. After eight years of increasingly difficult times at Bluff, several families saw the light of reason and moved north, establishing a more practical agricultural community at the present site of Monticello, which soon took the status of county seat from hardscrabble Bluff.

Today Bluff is a peaceful place whose biggest attraction seems to focus on San Juan River excursions. Bluff has a nice little historic loop of its own on the right just as you enter town. Note especially the Bluff library, a fine old stone building. The Bluff City Historical Preservation Association publishes an excellent tour brochure describing historical houses and other sites in Bluff with a guide to nearby rock art sites. Don't miss the Twin Rocks Cafe, incredibly situated just underneath a couple of rock spires. The tour brochure is usually available here.

At nearby Sand Island Recreation Area, 2 miles past Bluff, an excellent Anasazi petroglyph panel features five representations of Kokopelli, the hump-backed flute-player. Watch carefully for the Sand Island Road, on the left, just *before* the major turnoff for Mexican Water. There is a very small, basic (no drinking water) campground here that fills up quickly.

About 3 miles west of Bluff, US 191 makes a sharp left turn and heads south to Mexican Water, Arizona. Continue straight at this intersection on what is now US 163.

The highway crosses Comb Wash, revealing the dramatic cliffs of Comb Ridge, a huge redrock escarpment running north-south. This eroded monocline begins just south of the Abajo Mountains (west of Blanding) and runs eighty miles south to Kayenta, Arizona. After driving through the gap in this striking formation, it is definitely worth stopping to look back and study the impressive natural barrier more carefully. Just past Comb Ridge you climb out of the ravine and begin to see the outline of the dramatic formations of Monument Valley way off in the distance.

It's about 16 miles from Bluff to the eastern entrance, on the right, of the Valley of the Gods, a highly recommended sidetrip. Valley of the Gods is like a miniature version of Monument Valley without people. Its mesas and spires are formed of the same Cedar Mesa sandstone as the somewhat larger formations at Monument Valley. The 17-mile loop drive on (mostly good) dirt road is suitable for most passenger vehicles in good weather. Definitely

Approaching famous Monument Valley, the vistas become broader and more spectacular along U.S. Highway 163.

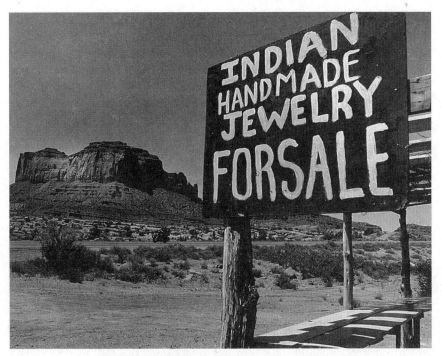

U.S. Highway 163 cuts across the huge Navajo Indian Reservation in Utah's remote southeast corner.

consider driving this beautiful, lonely loop—though not in a large RV and not dragging a trailer. The road surface is slightly rough at its northern limit; stay away after heavy rains.

Valley of the Gods is also a very good place to camp if you are entirely self-sufficient. There are no established campgrounds and no facilities, but there are plenty of secluded places to camp in the wild. It is incredibly quiet here.

The loop finishes on Utah Highway 261 (paved) just south of the descent from the Moki Dugway and north of the turnoff for Goosenecks State Park. Half a mile before reaching UT 261, you will pass one of the only manmade structures in the entire valley: a bed-and-breakfast ranch that might be an excellent base for exploring this wild region. To visit the impressive Muley Point overlook (see description under Drive #9), turn right and immediately climb the 1,000-foot graded gravel road up the Moki Dugway. Just at the crest and right before the pavement resumes, look for the turnoff to the left. Trailers and large RVs will find the long climb slow going.

Turn left on Utah Highway 291 to return to your scenic drive tour of US 163 about 8 miles south. The turnoff for Goosenecks State Park is about 7 miles south on the right. It would be a shame to miss this fascinating attraction. The overlook at the park will reward you with one of the most impressive views of entrenched river meanders in all of North America. The San Juan River snakes for more than 5 miles here in its deeply-cut canyon to cover just 1 mile as the crow flies. There is a nice picnic area with a few primitive campsites (free) here but no water.

The namesake monument for the town of Mexican Hat is actually about 1.5 miles north of town on the left, well-marked and with good dirt roads leading right to it. Local legend tells of the love of a young Mexican vaquero for an Indian maiden who, alas, was already married to an evil old medicine man. When the medicine man learned of the affair, he turned the vaquero to stone. If the rock doesn't seem to look much like a sombrero to you, it might help the illusion to consider it to be *upside down*, suggesting the medicine man first turned his rival on his head. Behind the sombrero is an interesting geologic formation called the Navajo Rug, a wavy pattern in the cliff strata.

The little town of Mexican Hat has depended largely on several minor oil and mining booms; today it benefits from the fair stream of tourists to this remote corner of Utah. This is home base for several land and river tour companies and makes a good base for exploring the surrounding wilderness areas.

From Mexican Hat, cross the San Juan River and, as the sign says, you are entering Navajo land. This is the Utah section of the 25,000-acre Navajo Indian Reservation, home to 250,000 Navajo. While the Navajo have long been considered one of the most peaceful of the Indian nations, during the middle part of the nineteenth century they were a fierce and powerful people who caused more trouble for the invading white Anglo-Americans than almost any other indigenous group. In the Southwest, only the Apache were more dangerous.

In 1864, after a long period of hostility between the Navajo and white settlers, the Navajo were forcibly evicted from their home in the Four-Corners region and made to march east across New Mexico. When these attempts at forced relocation ultimately failed, the Navajo were allowed to return to their traditional home.

Today the Navajo are a friendly, hospitable people, proud of their desert home, rich culture, and beautiful crafts. The Navajo Nation depends greatly on tourism, and they are happy to share their land and demonstrate their culture. Still, the perpetual wave of tourism must at times seem annoying; perhaps some feel somewhat uncomfortable with the idea that the homeland for which they struggled so hard remains subject to constant invasion, albeit of a more friendly sort. On no other reservation in America is there more of a sense that we are visitors on *their* land. It is important that we keep this fact in mind.

As soon as you climb out of the San Juan gorge, the views of Monument Valley spread out before you, turning your front window into an oversized, moving postcard. The next 25 miles are among the most attractive highway stretches in the entire country.

After 21 miles you reach the well-marked turnoff on the left for the tribal visitor center at Monument Valley. This intersection is like an open-air shopping mall for souvenirs and Indian art, full of quaint little stands. From here it is 4 miles to the Monument Valley Tribal Park.

The Monument Valley visitor center and scenic drive are actually on the Arizona side of a dividing line that is only nominal on the reservation. Good literature on the park and the drive is available at the visitor center. There is a small park entrance fee ($2.50 in 1995); it is definitely worth the visit. The visitor center parking lot teems with numerous local jeep tour companies, eager to whisk you off on guided tours of varying duration and difficulty. They are worth considering, especially if you want to get to the more out-of-the-way spots in the valley, which require a guide.

From Monument Valley, your options are to return (via US 163) to Bluff and US 191 northward or to continue south to the Arizona town of Kayenta at the intersection with U.S. Highway 160. The Arizona portion of this drive (along with a detailed description of the Monument Valley scenic drive) are outlined in Stewart Green's excellent guide to scenic drives in Arizona, also from Falcon Press.

11

Squaw Flats Scenic Byway
Monticello to Needles District, Canyonlands

General description: A 50-mile desert canyon drive with a variety of geologic, scenic, and historic attractions.

Special attractions: Newspaper Rock petroglyphs, Needles District of Canyonlands National Park, trail hikes, rock climbing.

Location: Southeastern Utah.

Drive route number and name: U.S. Highway 191/Utah Highway 211, Squaw Flats Scenic Byway.

Travel season: Year-round.

Camping: One state park campground, one national park campground, two Forest Service campgrounds west of Monticello, commercial campgrounds at Monticello and Needles Outpost.

Services: All services in Monticello; basic services at Needles Outpost; no services north on US 191 until La Sal Junction.

Nearby attractions: Abajo Mountains, Abajo Loop Scenic Backway, Needles and Anticline overlooks.

The drive

The official state byway is limited to UT 211 between US 191 and the Needles entrance to Canyonlands National Park. The entire corridor of US 191, however, along with the fantastic geological jumble to the west, are deserving of exploration. This drive begins in Monticello, focuses on the very attractive and interesting drive east along UT 211, and ends with a recommendation for continuing north to Moab.

Monticello (pronounced *Monti Sello*) seems somehow out of place here in remote southeastern Utah. It has an almost Midwestern look, like one of those marginally prosperous farm towns in downstate Illinois. The lawns are green and nicely trimmed, and the many nice old houses have an almost genteel look about them. In fact, Monticello was named for Thomas Jefferson's famous home after the citizenry tired of the town's more typically wild-west earlier names of Paiute Springs and North Montezuma Creek.

The San Juan County Travel Council, Canyonlands National Park, the USDA Forest Service, and the BLM operate a joint information office in the civic center at Main Street (US 191) and Second South. Open weekdays

Drive 11: Squaw Flats Scenic Byway
Monticello to Needles District, Canyonlands

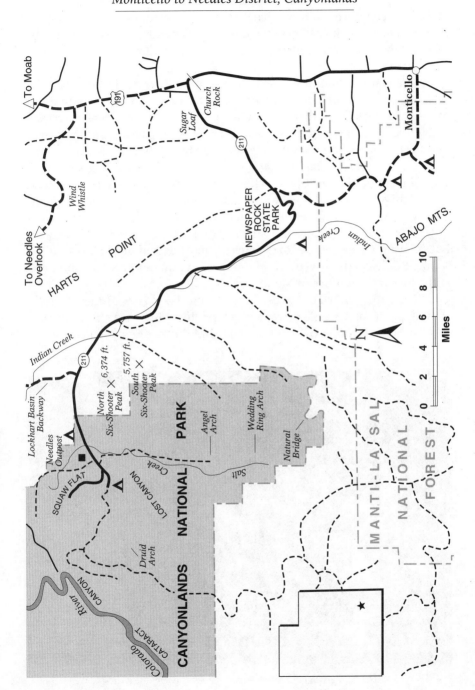

8 A.M. to 5 P.M., weekends and holidays 10 A.M. to 5 P.M., they provide the most detailed information on whatever you need to know about the region. While there is a park visitor center at the Needles entrance to Canyonlands, picking up your Canyonlands literature here will allow you to plan your visit in advance.

There are several nice scenic drives up into the Abajo Mountains to the west of town, including one that might serve as an alternate route to Newspaper Rock and Indian Creek Canyon. The Blue Mountain Loop/Hart's Draw Road is an attractive, 20-mile drive on good paved road that leaves Monticello to the west, loops 9 miles up past Blue Mountain Ski Area (currently defunct) to the Hart's Draw Road on the right, then descends to meet UT 211 just east of Newspaper Rock State Park. Five miles west of Monticello on this drive are two national forest campgrounds that might prove handy. This route might also be useful as a return to Monticello at the conclusion of this drive. Other Abajo drives from Monticello are the Blue Mountain Loop/Spring Creek Ranch Road (paved) and the Monticello to Blanding Alpine Route (partly paved, mostly rough). Inquire for current conditions at the information office in Monticello.

The entire stretch of US 191 from Monticello to La Sal Junction really should qualify as a scenic drive, with increasingly fine views to the northeast (ahead and to the right) of the La Sal Mountains. As you drive north

The petroglyph panel at Newspaper Rock is one of the richest displays of rock art in the state.

*Detail from Newspaper Rock. The horse-mounted hunter is from
the recent Ute period, centuries later than the Anasazi humanoid forms.*

through attractive ranch and farm country, there are also nice views of the distant snow-capped San Juan Mountains off to the east in western Colorado. The early Spanish Trail ran approximately parallel to US 191.

About 7 miles north of the Monticello town limit the road descends and you get your first glimpse ahead of the very prominent, tan, roundish rock called Church Rock, your landmark for the left turn on UT 211. Church Rock is an isolated chunk of harder Entrada sandstone material, around which softer mudstone layers have been eroded. The most remarkable aspect of this rock is that it is partially hollow. According to local lore, Church Rock was actually used for prayer services by area settlers. Today it sits on private land. A road leads up to the cave entrance, suggesting that perhaps the owners may one day turn this into one of the world's more interesting roadside hamburger stands.

The turn here on the left is signed for Canyonlands National Park and Newspaper Rock. This is the start of the Squaw Flats Scenic Byway. The byway travels southeast across beautiful high desert and ranch land for 12 miles before descending into the wooded canyon of Indian Creek.

A little more than 3 miles along UT 211, note on the right the simple sign stating "Marie's Place." This was the site of Marie Ogden's Theosophist colony, one of several religious cults of the 1930s calling themselves the Home of Truth. Marie and her followers arrived here in 1933 from Boise, where she had been lecturing on the occult. This precise spot was chosen for the site of the colony based upon a revelation she had received that this was the true axis of the world and the appointed place to establish "The Inner Portal," the only place on earth that would survive the rapidly approaching end of the world. Marie received her periodic divine communications during spirit-guided typing sessions. Her colony was essentially monastic and communal, renouncing all material wealth, contemplating the imminent end of the world as we know it, and waiting intently for the next divine message from Mrs. Ogden's theo-telegraphic typing machine. The local Mormon residents seemed not to give the Home of Truth folks much mind, even when Mrs. Ogden purchased the county newspaper and began to publish her divine wire service reports.

In 1935, a regional scandal erupted when a member of the colony died and Mrs. Ogden refused to give up the body for burial, claiming the deceased was, in fact, simply in suspended animation pending return in a higher, more sanctified state. She even reported in the paper various communications she had received from her dormant disciple. This went on for about two years, despite official attempts at claiming the corpse, which witnesses said had been mummified in the dry desert air. Somewhat disgraced by the affair, the colony dwindled to Marie and just a handful of the faithful who lived on here for several decades. Marie moved to a nursing home in the mid-1970s and died shortly thereafter.

There is nothing of real touristic interest at the old colony site, although the original cabins remain. The present owners plan to open a traditional cafe and basic campground, which will make this a good base for visiting the Needles entrance to Canyonlands.

Right where the road meets Indian Creek is Newspaper Rock State Park, one of the better roadside rock-art viewing sites in Utah. A fifty-foot-high sandstone face is covered with a variety of fine petroglyphs from several periods. Most of the several hundred figures appear to be Anasazi, but there are also later examples of Ute artwork, including one prominent figure of a hunter on horseback. There is also a small basic campground (no drinking water).

From here the byway follows Indian Creek through a gorge lined with white sandstone walls, which then opens up a bit wider on the left. At this point the character of the rock on the right changes to a towering red palisade of sheer Wingate sandstone. This is one of Utah's premier sandstone rock climbing areas, site of the famous *Supercrack of the Desert*. All along the buttresses on the right are long vertical cracks, and you may have the opportunity to watch climbers at play.

It is a little less than 20 miles from Newspaper Rock to the Needles entrance of Canyonlands National Park. Much of the land along Indian Creek is farmland and ranchland, perhaps the most striking agricultural setting in the world. About 1.5 miles beyond the park boundary is the well-marked

A climber works out on Supercrack of the Desert *above Indian Creek just east of the Needles District of Canyonlands.*

turn on the right for Needles Outpost. This is a private, commercial facility with a small store, cafe, gas, and an excellent campground with hot showers. The Outpost is closed from late October until late March.

Canyonlands National Park is a very large, very complex place. At 337,570 acres, this is Utah's largest national park, its newest (1964), and its wildest. Because of the remoteness of this corner of Utah, Canyonlands sees far fewer visitors than the parks located along the more popular tourist corridors to the west.

Around 300 million years ago a depression formed where this canyon system now lies. At about the same time, the highlands of the Uncompahgre Uplift were created to the north and east of here. Over millions of years, a thick layer of salt was deposited on the bed of an ancient sea that covered what is now Canyonlands, and sediment flowed down onto this bed from the wet highlands. The sea drained away and sand dunes covered the entire area for millions of years until the process was repeated, more than two dozen times. The many different layers of hardened strata rested on an unstable bed of salt that buckled and flowed, causing cracks in the surface that widened into chasms, which later became the course of least resistance for the streams and rivers that further etched the earth's surface.

All this abuse of *terra firma* resulted in the chaotic landscape presented so graphically in the Needles District of Canyonlands. The "needles" are actually rock pinnacles, often red-and-white striped as indication of the repeated layering of different strata. The Needles District differs from the other main section of the park, Island in the Sky (see Drive #12), in the same way that Capitol Reef differs from Bryce (or the Grand Canyon). In the Needles, as in Capitol Reef, you are down in the midst of intricate canyons and sheer formations; at Island in the Sky you are essentially up on the rim looking out across broad vistas below.

The Needles is probably a more interesting place to drive around than Island in the Sky, and definitely better suited to walking tours. Perhaps the *best* part of Canyonlands for both driving and walking is the rough and remote third section of the park, called the Maze District; but this area of limited access and difficult roads is strictly for hard-core canyon junkies. The Needles offers a good compromise of relatively navigable roads and trails and a real sense of wilderness.

Do not expect much in the way of visitor services or amenities. About 4 miles past Needles Outpost you reach the park visitor center (open 8 A.M. to 6 P.M.), where you can pick up any material you may have missed at the information office in Monticello. The center has a nice, small interpretive museum about the park. A few miles beyond the visitor center is Squaw Flat Campground, in a very nice setting but without hookups or showers. It is worth noting that the $3 park entrance fee is good for seven days unrestricted entry and is also honored at Island in the Sky; hang onto the receipt if you are continuing north to Moab.

The park has only 10 miles of paved roads, with 54 miles of dirt tracks of varying roughness. The paved road leads to Big Spring Canyon Overlook. The best thing to do in the Needles is get out of the car and walk. There are short interpretive walks and longer hikes of all degrees of difficulty to a total of 55 miles of trails. Consult with the rangers at the visitor center to determine the most appropriate trails for your fitness level and itinerary.

The two premier hikes in the Needles are the 11 mile round-trip outing to Confluence Overlook (with the confluence of the Colorado and Green rivers a thousand feet below) and the long-day/overnight excursion to Druid Arch and Chesler Park. At Chesler Park you will find nearly a thousand acres of grassy meadows surrounded by tremendous stone formations. It has some of the finest scenery in the park.

From the Needles it is possible, with a stout four-wheel-drive vehicle and plenty of time, to return to US 191 at Blanding (south of Monticello) via a series of very rough roads to the south. It is also possible to drive directly north to Moab on the Lockhart Basin Scenic Backway. This is a fairly rough 57-mile jaunt that requires high clearance and four-wheel-drive. It departs UT 211 to the north about 4 miles east of Needles Outpost. Check at the outpost for specific directions and current road conditions.

For the less adventurous, retrace the route back out to US 191. The drive north along US 191 to Moab is continuously scenic and deserves some mention.

Six miles north of UT 211 is the turnoff on the left to Canyon Rims Recreation Area and Anticline/Needles Overlook. This drive, called the Needles/Anticline Scenic Backway, is a *highly* recommended sidetrip. From Needles Overlook you have the best view of the Needles area and get perhaps the best idea of just how *big* Canyonlands is. These are by far the grandest views of the rugged canyon country to the east of the Colorado River. It is 21 miles on good paved road to Needles Overlook, another 17 on good gravel to Anticline Overlook. At Anticline Overlook you look directly across to Dead Horse Point about 6 miles to the west (and just over 100 miles by road!). You also get a unique view of Arches National Park from here. There are two BLM campgrounds in the Canyon Rims Recreation Area: Wind Whistle Campground (seasonal drinking water) is about 7 miles west of US 191, and Hatch Point Campground (drinking water here) is about 7.5 miles along the gravel road to Anticline Overlook.

Just south of La Sal Junction on US 191 you get a really good visual lesson on just how the wind works on these sandstone mesas to create the arches for which this part of Utah is so famous. Be sure to stop at the Wilson Arch Viewpoint for a look at an actual, for-real arch—without even having to leave the car. A very informative BLM sign gives a clear and succinct explanation of the formation of sandstone arches.

Hollowed out of a gigantic sandstone boulder, HOLE N" THE ROCK is a popular roadside attraction along U.S. Highway 95 south of Moab.

Don't miss Hole N" the Rock [sic], just past La Sal Junction. In general, it is unfortunate what so often happens to roadside landscape left in private hands; in this case the landowners were *so* over-the-edge in what they did with their own private chunk of redrock that it turned out to be an inspired masterpiece of roadside ultra-kitsch. Over a twelve-year period, Albert Christiansen excavated 50,000 cubic feet of sandstone to create a 5,000-square-foot cave dwelling and gift shop, consisting of 14 rooms with huge stone pillars. Hole N" the Rock is open daily from 9 A.M. to 5 P.M., with continuous guided tours.

It is about 15 miles from here to Moab.

12

Round About Moab

Shafer Canyon, Dead Horse Point, and Arches

General description: Indescribable scenic beauty and fascinating geology on a somewhat disjointed three-part drive.

Special attractions: Terrific sandstone formations, views of Canyonlands and the snow-capped La Sal Mountains, dinosaur tracks, petroglyphs, rock climbing, thrillingly steep driving.

Location: Southeastern Utah.

Drive route number and name: Utah Highway 279/313, U.S. Highway 191, Potash Scenic Byway (Shafer Trail Scenic Drive).

Travel season: Year-round.

Camping: National park campgrounds in Canyonlands and Arches, state park campground at Dead Horse Point, Moab Jaycee Campground, undeveloped camping along Colorado River/Utah Highway 128.

Services: All services in Moab; no services along route.

Nearby attractions: Colorado River; Canyonlands National Park; four-wheel-driving, hiking, and biking trails out of Moab.

The drive

The country around Moab presents distinct logistical problems for writers of driving guides—problems common to much of Utah but especially so in this corner. Basically, there is just too much to see in too many directions; except for the La Sal Mountain Loop (described as a sidetrip to Drive #13), there are no neat, concise loops that take in all of the attractions in any systematic fashion.

There are any number of ways to tackle the somewhat daunting, though visually apppealing, challenge of the Moab area. The town is a veritable campaign headquarters for half-day outings in every direction. Your driving strategies here will likely depend on the type of vehicle you are driving and where you plan to overnight. This drive, therefore, is less a continuous excursion than a series of three distinct drives that might easily be combined as a day-long (*quite* long) project or extended over several days. The bottom line is that the roadside scenery around Moab is as spectacular as it gets anywhere in Utah (which is to say, anywhere in the world) so just strap yourself in and hit the road.

The roads described here are appropriate for all vehicles, with the sole exception of the latter part of the Shafer Trail road, which is unpaved, a tad narrow, and a little rough for larger RVs. At the end of this road is the chief obstacle to what otherwise would be an *almost* concise loop drive. The climb from the canyon floor to the canyon rim at Island in the Sky is steep, thrilling, demanding, and not suitable for some vehicles. Drivers with the nerve and appropriate vehicle will be able to use this steep ascent route and complete a more-or-less continuous loop, with spur drives out to Dead Horse Point and into Arches. Unfortunately, the ascent to Island in the Sky is the only way up to the canyon rim; if you do *not* make this climb, you will have to retrace your route back to US 191, then use the more conventional approaches to Arches, Island in the Sky, and Dead Horse Point. This obstacle doesn't present itself until the end of the Shafer Trail segment of this drive, so you can do the drive into Canyonlands in anything but a large RV. It would be a shame to miss the scenery along the Shafer Trail just because you were worried about the shocks on your mini-van.

What Banff is to the Rocky Mountains, Moab is to canyon country. This is the capital city of Utah's sandstone wilderness, a focal point for desert and river adventure, a mecca for slickrock tourism. People come to Moab from all over the world to hike, bike, raft, and drive the rough roads that penetrate the fantastic desert landscape. They come for less strenuous pursuits as well, to visit nearby Arches and Canyonlands national parks and for the view from Dead Horse Point.

Grand County was named for the Grand River, the original name of the Colorado. The first Europeans to enter the area were Spanish explorers who discovered a Colorado River crossing at the approximate site of today's highway bridge at Moab. Until the early Mormons established crossings at Lee's Ferry, Hall's Crossing, and Hite's Crossing, this was the closest place for traffic from the old Spanish settlements of New Mexico to breach the barrier of the Colorado River and its imposing canyons.

Mormon pioneers arrived at Moab early (1855), where they established the Elk Mountain Mission but were quickly driven out by Indians. It wasn't until the end of the 1870s that the Mormons sunk permanent roots here. They named their new settlement for a remote desert land referred to in the Bible as "the land beyond Jordan." A ferry operated across the Colorado here from 1885 until 1912, when the first bridge was built. For most of this century Moab toddled along as a quiet ranching center, until a small uranium boom in the 1950s caused the population to soar—there were a few more residents in 1960 then the 4,100 who live here today.

As in other Western mining boom towns that ran dry, tourism came in to fill the economic void, and catering to visitors appears to be the primary source of livelihood for Moab today. Arches and Canyonlands are the headliners on the tourism bill, but outdoor recreation has become increasingly

Drive 12: Round About Moab
Shafer Canyon, Dead Horse Point, and Arches

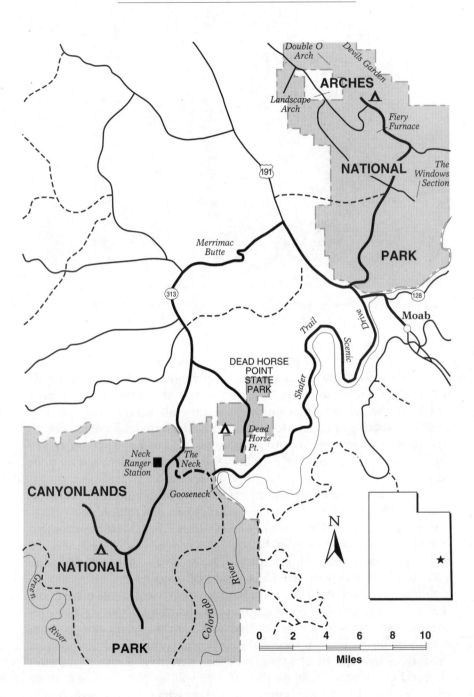

One thousand feet below Dead Horse Point, the Shafer Trail Road traverses a mesa ledge above the Colorado River.

more important. Over the past twenty years Moab has established itself as one of the most important centers for river-running and for the relatively new sport of mountain-biking. One interesting legacy of the region's mining activity is the number of rough roads "leading off to nowhere," which is precisely where cyclists and four-wheel-drive enthusiasts seem to want to go. Moab has an excellent information center, at Center and Main streets in the heart of town, where you can find all the literature you need for your stay.

Moab has been a film-making center since John Ford filmed his version of the Hole-in-the-Rock pioneer journey (see description under Drive #7), *Wagon Master*, in 1949. In more recent years, Moab locations appeared in such films as *Choke Canyon*, *Indiana Jones and the Last Crusade*, *Thelma and Louise*, *Geronimo*, and *City Slickers II*. An excellent "movie location auto tour" brochure is available from the Moab visitor center.

The first segment of this drive is a state-designated scenic drive called the Potash Scenic Byway. Head north out of Moab on US 191. At the north edge of town, cross the Colorado River and resist the temptation to shoot directly on up to Arches. Instead, take the first left turn (UT 279), signed for Potash. Immediately after turning, note the interesting (if rather unscenic) chemical evaporation pond on the left; you will see plenty more of these soon enough. *NOTE:* If you hope to camp this night at Arches, drive first to the park entrance (just a mile farther along US 191) and register for a campsite; do this at the visitor center from 7:30 to 8 A.M. or at the entrance station after 8 A.M. You will then have to drive 18 miles to Devil's Garden Campground to stake your site. Your chances of getting a campsite after mid morning are slim.

This road follows the contour of the Colorado River, directly across the river from Moab. At mile 3.2 is a sign for Indian ruins, referring to a somewhat difficult-to-discern granary in the cliffs. At exactly 4 miles is an attractive little campground (six sites) called Jaycee Park, maintained by the BLM.

It is doubtful you will find another drive with as much vertical redrock rising so abruptly from right beside the road. This is a very popular roadside rock climbing site; from just past the Jaycee campground you may see a mile or so of an odd combination of beginning rock climbing classes and Indian petroglyphs. With redrock rising immediately on the right and the more-green-than-red Colorado River on the left, this is a most picturesque drive. At mile 5.5 is a nice undeveloped camping area, then a sign for dinosaur tracks.

Potash (as you may have guessed) is a large chemical extraction operation and *not* a town. Utah is the nation's leading producer of phosphates, used primarily for fertilizer. South of Potash the canyon is not so hemmed in; the landscape opens a bit and there are fine, broad vistas of the La Sal

The Window Arches in Arches National Park are an easy walk from the park road.

Mountains to the east. A lot of things change here. The road just past Potash is still paved, but narrower and not as well maintained. The pavement ends 1.5 miles south of Potash, right where the road begins to climb out of the Colorado River Canyon. Look on your left to see where some of the commercial float companies put in for the popular trips through Cataract Canyon. Stated mileages will be from the end of the pavement.

This is the end of the officially designated Potash Scenic Byway, and the practical limit of travel for large RVs and trailers. Conventional vehicles, minivans, and truck-top campers can continue—with care—all the way into Canyonlands Park, but unless you have a robust, high-torque vehicle suitable for the climb to Island in the Sky, at some point you will have to turn around and retrace this drive to US 191. Do continue as far as you feel comfortable, since the scenery gets better and better the farther you go. In fact, this is the point at which this drive *begins* to get interesting.

Beyond Potash the road winds up through a tortured landscape, a rough and inhospitable place. You have the opportunity to drive right beside a couple of huge evaporation ponds. Some will react negatively to the imposition of industry on this wilderness, while others may find the ponds interesting and, certainly, visually striking. The Potash folks have done a good job of marking off the numerous side roads that they do not want you on, so it is easy enough to stay on route.

There are a couple of short, steep intervals, then at about 2.5 miles beyond the pavement's end you come upon a fascinating expanse of *level* redrock. You might want to get out of the vehicle and explore this on foot a bit. At mile 8.5 you come up on top of one of those great, broad, grass-covered mesas overlooking the Colorado River. The views here are absolutely breathtaking, and you will probably have them mostly to yourself. This is a fascinating and beautiful drive, especially in the evening. It makes a good overnight trip for self-sufficient campers; past the chemical operation at Potash you can camp anywhere short of the national park.

The road forks here at the first big river vista. Take the more prominent fork to the right. If you look up and to the right at the big, dark, blocky formation about 1,000 feet above, you can actually see the observation deck at Dead Horse Point. At mile 9.5 there is about 100 feet of slightly nerve-wracking road (with a *big* drop on the left—ooooooeeee, *scary!*). Just hold your breath and it'll be okay. . . .

Just past mile 11 you enter Canyonlands National Park (via a very back way, so there's no entry station). At just under mile 13 is a major "T." At this point, conventional vehicles are best advised to retrace the route. A left turn here will take you down an eternity of rough road and wild canyon country. If you are prepared for a real driving adventure, take the right turn, well marked for Island in the Sky and Visitors Center. You will need a low-geared vehicle and plenty of nerve for the next 3 miles or so of white-knuckle switchbacks, as the road (an engineering wonder) climbs out of the canyon. This road was pioneered by ranchers Frank and John Shafer—whose cattle must have been fearless critters—and later improved by uranium prospectors.

If you saw the road-adventure film *Thelma and Louise*, you may recognize this as the location of the final dramatic chase scene (although it is represented in the movie as the Grand Canyon). If you are into scary, steep, "thrill driving," you'll love this one. There are no guardrails, and it is definitely better driving *up* it than down. (Thinking, again, of that final dramatic scene from *Thelma and Louise*, the thought of "life imitating art" would make the descent rather nerve-wracking.) In ascent, however, this is highly recommended! If you do make the climb up to Island in the Sky, you can return to Moab via Dead Horse State Park and Arches National Park, making this a long, but very eventful, loop. With this option, your route is obvious from the canyon rim.

If you choose *not* to make the climb up to the Canyonlands Visitor Center, you must retrace your route to US 191 and do the conventional approaches to Island in the Sky and Dead Horse State Park or return to Moab. There are potentially serious consequences to misjudging your vehicle's ability to make this climb: this is one place where discretion really *should be* "the better part of valor" for those driving underpowered or overweight rigs.

For those returning to US 191, your only real decision is in which order to visit Arches, Island in the Sky, and Dead Horse Point, or whether you will even try to visit them all in one day. I would probably recommend the order stated, since the day's end from Dead Horse Point is especially nice.

Return to US 191 and turn left (north). The turnoff for Arches is on the right, just under a mile up the road.

Arches is a wonderland, and the sort of place that brings out the amateur geologist or landscape photographer in even the most citified of us. Arches was established as a national monument in 1929 and upgraded to national park status in 1971. The park contains more than 1,500 recognized natural arches, ranging in size from just a few feet to the 306-foot span of mammoth Landscape Arch. As always, stop first at the park visitor center, just inside the entrance, for an orientation and for information on drives and hikes within the park. There is a very nice self-guiding booklet for the park road drive. The park road was very well designed to bring visitors close to park attractions, so it is possible to have a very positive, memorable experience in just a few hours of touring Arches. On the other hand, you can spend days here. If you do intend to overnight in the one campground here, you'll have to reserve your space early at the entrance station; in the summer tourist season it is doubtful there will be sites available after mid morning.

Sagebrush and desert landscape of Arches National Park.

These fabulous geological oddities are thought to be the result of the movement of unstable strata deep beneath the earth's crust, then subsequent erosion by wind and water along with the weakening action of freezing and thawing on delicate sandstone formations. Beneath the earth's surface here lies a thick salt bed, the residue of a vast sea that covered the land hundreds of millions of years ago. Millions of years of later, geologic deposits as much as a mile deep further built up over this thick bed of salt, and the sea gradually disappeared. The unstable salt layers buckled and shifted beneath the weight of the hardened upper layers, creating faults and domes on the surface. As the surface was eroded by wind and water, delicate fins, spires, and balanced rocks of harder stone were exposed and sculpted. These formations were further acted upon by wind, water, and extremes of temperature, leaving us this incredible geological treasure.

(At least that's the *reasonable* theory. No one really knows for certain. So, if your kids think these formations were probably left by gigantic prehistoric space invaders playing in a big terrestial sandbox, they just might be right.)

The turnoff for Canyonlands and Dead Horse Point is at UT 313, 6 miles north of the Arches turnoff, well marked on the left. After the wonders of Arches, this landscape may seem perfectly *prosaic* until you stop and take a fresh look at it without the unfair comparison to the dramatic landscapes of the park. A few miles along UT 313, note on the right Monitor and Merrimac Buttes, looking very obviously like their Civil War nautical namesakes. At mile 15 is a prominent fork: left 4 miles to Dead Horse State Park, straight 4.5 miles to Canyonlands/Island in the Sky. Let's head first to Island in the Sky (though it really is "take your pick" on this choice).

Island in the Sky, the name given to the elevated northern section of Canyonlands National Park, is almost precisely that: an isolated piece of land far above the deep canyons of the Green and Colorado rivers. And it certainly does have the airy and Olympian aura of a floating island, detached from the earth below. This narrow "peninsula in the sky" was, in fact, carved by the two great rivers as they flow ever closer to their confluence at Cataract Canyon.

The views from this height are spectacular in all directions, with fine panoramas from the several strategically placed overlooks. From each of the turnouts are short, easy trails with interpretive signs describing the incredibly intricate maze of canyons below. It is highly recommended that you get out of the car and do some of these hikes—perhaps even more encouraged here than in other parks.

Canyonlands, which was created as a national park in 1964, is a wild and wonderfully undeveloped place. Even the nature of the visitor facilities at Island in the Sky reflect this minimalist approach to park development.

Unlike the elaborate facilities and amenities at Bryce and Zion, Canyonlands does not offer much here in the way of creature comforts. There is a water fountain at the visitor center (along with helpful rangers and plenty of useful literature on hiking and geology) but that is about it for frills. The small Willow Flat Campground has no water either, so come prepared.

The terrain between Island in the Sky and Dead Horse Point is BLM-administered public land. If all other camping options have been exhausted, those prepared for self-sufficient (and minimum-impact) camping might find decent primitive sites along dirt roads to the west of UT 313 between Island in the Sky and the Dead Horse Point turnoff. Keep in mind that camping on public land at undesignated sites requires special diligence to maintain the pristine nature of the land. Do not build new fire rings; either use existing rings or do without your evening campfire.

Dead Horse Point is administered as a state park; consequently, it has slightly more-elaborate facilities than its spartan neighbor, Canyonlands. The park maintains a visitor center, campground, and museum that are open year-round. The campground here has electrical hookups and water, and, unlike the first-come-first-served national park campgrounds, you can use your VISA/MC to reserve a site (1-800-322-3770).

The name supposedly comes from an unfortunate incident that occurred back when local cowboys used this point as a natural corral to round up and break the many wild horses inhabiting the region. According to the most popular story, a band of undesirable horses was left behind on the mesa, the assumption being they would find their way off the mesa to freedom. They didn't, and they died there of thirst.

Dead Horse Point is, like Island in the Sky, an isolated promontory of stone jutting out over the deep gorge of the Colorado River. The overlook provides some of the most famous views in the region, especially of the Colorado River two thousand feet below. Between the overlook and the river you can see clearly the Shafer Trail road, giving a nice sense of cohesion and closure to this admittedly disjointed drive.

13

Colorado River Scenic Byway

Moab to Interstate 70

General description: A 44-mile run through the redrock canyon carved by the Colorado River, then across the desert to the major east-west travel corridor of central Utah.
Special attractions: Colorado River, Professor Valley, Fisher Towers, views of the La Sal Mountains.
Location: Southeastern Utah.
Drive route number and name: Utah Highway 128, Colorado River Scenic Byway.
Travel season: Year-round.
Camping: Five BLM campgrounds and two BLM semi-developed camp clusters along the Scenic Byway; commercial campgrounds in Moab.
Services: All services in Moab; no services along the route.
Nearby attractions: Negro Bill Canyon hikes, La Sal Mountain Scenic Backway, Sego Canyon Rock Art Site.

The drive

What distinguishes this drive from other canyon drives in southern Utah is that while this drive does follow a narrow canyon with steep sandstone walls, it also follows the Colorado River—a fairly substantial body of water. This is one of the very few places in the state where you have the opportunity to actually drive beside one of the major rivers that cut the dramatic gorges for which this part of the country is famous. In fact, UT 128 is the *only* road that runs along either the Colorado or the Green River. This is a favorite area for both bicyclists and river floaters, and you are likely to see both on this drive. The rafters are fun to watch, the cyclists require your attention.

This is a relatively short drive; at 44 miles it makes a nice afternoon excursion from Moab. Though short, note that you will not find services along this drive until Crescent Junction or Grand Junction (depending on your direction) if you are not returning via this route to Moab. So be sure to gas up in Moab and bring as much food and drink as you will need for the drive. (Moab, the tourist center of Utah's eastern canyon country, was briefly described at the start of Drive #12.)

There are two options to make a longer outing of this drive: you might loop back to the west on the interstate, then return to Moab via U.S. Highway 191, 31 miles south of the Crescent Junction exit; or you might combine this drive with the La Sal Mountain Loop on your return to Moab. This drive also makes an attractive connecting route from the canyon country of southeastern Utah to the interstate and points beyond.

Leave Moab on US 191 north, as if headed to Arches. Just before the Colorado River (a mile or so out of Moab) is the turnoff on the right for UT 128. A little more than 3 miles from the start of UT 128 you will reach the pullout on the right for Negro Bill Canyon. Named for the early settler William Granstaff, who kept cattle in the canyon, this is the location of one of the most popular short trails in the Moab area. This moderate trail is just under 2 miles and ends at Morning Glory Natural Bridge. At 243 feet, this is the sixth longest natural bridge in the nation.

Starting about 3 miles beyond Negro Bill Canyon are three BLM campgrounds: Hal Canyon, Oak Grove and Big Bend Recreation sites. In addition, there are two camp clusters (Drinks Canyon and Upper Big Bend) on either side of the developed campgrounds. At about mile 15 from the start of UT 128 the canyon opens up at Professor Valley, where you pass some ranches and areas under cultivation. This area is famous in film history as the site of such films as: *Rio Grande, Ten Who Dared, Wagon Master, Rio Conchos, Cheyenne Autumn, The Commancheros, Against a Crooked Sky,* and *Choke Canyon.*

Approximately 16 miles from Moab is the turnoff on the right for Castle Valley and the La Sal Mountain Scenic Backway. This very attractive, 60-mile desert/alpine loop is mostly paved and comes out on US 191 6 miles south of Moab. This also makes a nice afternoon excursion from Moab, returning you to town for the night. The drive takes from two to four hours to complete and is driveable in most passenger vehicles. A couple of steep and narrow switchbacks make this drive impractical for larger RVs and trailers. The route is impassable when snow-covered.

Attractions along the drive include the beautiful woodlands of the Manti-La Sal National Forest and terrific views of the La Sals, the Abajo Mountains, Arches, and Canyonlands. One of the bloodiest confrontations between white settlers and Indians in Utah history took place at Pinhook Draw on the northwest edge of the La Sals. A band of Paiutes ambushed a posse that was after them for the murder of two ranchers. Nine members of the posse and an unknown number of Indians died in the ensuing fight. A monument to the battle has been erected alongside the road.

Once you enter Professor Valley, the view ahead is dominated by Fisher Towers, rising some 1,500 feet above the surrounding desert. To visit Fisher

Drive 13: Colorado River Scenic Byway
Moab to Interstate 70

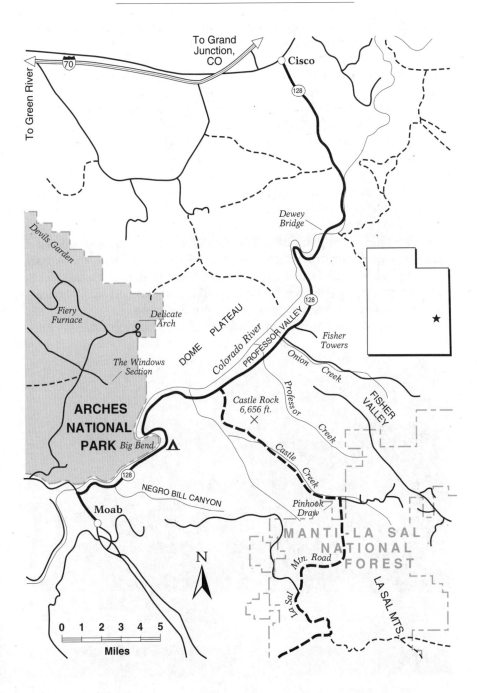

To Grand Junction, CO

To Green River

70

Cisco

128

Dewey Bridge

128

Devils Garden

Fiery Furnace

Delicate Arch

DOME PLATEAU

Colorado River

PROFESSOR VALLEY

Fisher Towers

Onion Creek

FISHER VALLEY

The Windows Section

Castle Rock 6,656 ft.

Professor Creek

ARCHES NATIONAL PARK

Big Bend

Castle Creek

128

NEGRO BILL CANYON

Pinhook Draw

Moab

MANTI-LA SAL NATIONAL FOREST

Mtn. Road

La Sal

LA SAL MTS.

N

0 1 2 3 4 5
Miles

Towers do *not* take the second dirt road on your right (well marked for Fisher Valley Ranch/Taylor Livestock). This is a really nice, fun drive on good dirt road (for any vehicle but RVs/trailers) along Onion Creek, with excellent scenery, but it is not the road to Fisher Towers.

The *proper* turnoff for Fisher Towers is well marked, about 0.75 mile past Fisher Valley Ranch Road. It is about a mile to the parking area/information board at the trailhead. From here, if you look straight back from where you've come (southwest), there is an excellent view of Castle Rock (also known as Castleton Spires/Castleton Rock), where a famous Chevy commercial was filmed in the 1960s. Castleton is the largest spire; to the right is a large blocky formation called The Rectory, then two smaller spires called the Nuns, and a final spire called the Priest. The Fisher Towers Trail is a somewhat-grueling 2.2 miles but definitely worth the hike if it is not too hot. There is no water and there are lots of ups and downs, but the views of the towers are interesting as you contour around their base from north to south.

Five miles or so past Fisher Towers, as the highway rises up toward a gap, look back for really terrific views of the Fisher Towers with a backdrop of the La Sal Mountains and the Colorado River in the foreground. This view encapsulates all that is best about Utah roadside scenery: desert spires, snow-capped peaks, and a rugged, river-worn desert gorge.

A few miles past this viewpoint is Hittle Bottom Recreation Site, the

The Colorado River above Moab is popular with commercial float companies.

Closed service station, now a roadside folk-art installation, along Utah Highway 128.

put-in for most of the commercial float trip companies out of Moab. Approximately 29 miles from Moab you cross the Colorado at Dewey Bridge. There is a seven site BLM campground located here. Just after the bridge, look on your right for an extremely interesting roadside folk-art site at an old Texaco station, covered with religious, patriotic, and moralistic slogans, photographs, American flags, the Ten Commandments, and other good stuff.

Beyond Dewey Bridge the scenery decreases in interest. At this point you may decide to return to Moab (or perhaps do the La Sal Mountain Loop), unless you intend to access the interstate. Past Dewey Bridge the road follows the river for a few miles, then strikes out across the desert. Once out of the confines of the river valley, you can see how much the land depends on the river: this is very much scrub desert for the next 5 miles. At about this point, the scenery stops being *picturesque*; while certainly interesting, the landscape is definitely not pretty.

Fortunately, this drive need not actually go to the townsite of Cisco, which is about 2.5 miles to the right at the end of UT 128. Poor, bedraggled Cisco could win prizes for unsightliness; there is nothing here but boarded-up, falling-apart houses—no store, no gas station, no permanent residents. It is pretty much a twentieth-century ghost town. Turn left at the end of UT 128 and it is just under 3 miles to the interstate entrance.

If you are heading west on the interstate, consider stopping off in Green River to see the very fine John Wesley Powell River History Museum, one of

*The Colorado River flows past Fisher Towers and the La Sal Mountains
on its way to meet the Green River in Canyonlands.*

the better places to learn the story of exploration and travel on the Green River and about one of Utah's most important explorers. The museum is open daily from 8 A.M. to 8 P.M.

Another worthwhile stop, just off the interstate, is the Sego Canyon Rock Art Site. This is no doubt the most accessible of Utah's major rock art panels. The panels had been on private land, which the Bureau of Land Management recently acquired through a land trade, and is now open for public viewing. The east-facing panels contain both painted pictographs and incised petroglyphs, some dating back as far as 500 B.C. There is also Fremont Culture art from around 1000 A.D. and Ute Indian art from the past century and a half. Exit the interstate at Thompson, drive through town, and where the road curves proceed straight ahead on the narrow but paved road for 3 miles until you arrive at two washes. This site is relatively new to public exposure. It is hoped that visitors will adhere to the strictest low-impact strategies: please do not touch the panels in any way.

14

Fishlake Scenic Drive
Fish Lake to Loa

General description: A 40-mile alpine and high-desert drive, commencing with the 13-mile Fishlake Scenic Byway.

Special attractions: Beautiful Fish Lake, with abundant opportunities for fishing and boating.

Location: Central Utah, in the Fishlake National Forest.

Drive route number and name: Utah Highways 25 and 72, Fishlake Scenic Byway.

Travel season: Year-round, though heavy snow may be a problem between Fish Lake and UT 72.

Camping: Numerous national forest campgrounds along Fish Lake, primitive campsites at Mill Meadows Reservoir.

Services: All services in Loa and Richfield; basic services at Fish Lake.

Nearby attractions: Grass Valley/Otter Creek, Cove Mountain Scenic Backway, Gooseberry-Fremont Scenic Backway, Thousand Lake Mountain Scenic Backway, Loa to Hanksville Scenic Byway.

 The drive

    This drive through lush mountain scenery and high sagebrush flats is highlighted by a visit to one of the prettiest large alpine lakes in the West. When the eminent geologist-soldier Clarence Dutton first saw Fish Lake he was prompted to write: "No resort more beautiful than this lake can be found in southern Utah. Its grassy banks clad with groves of spruce and aspen; the splendid vista down between its mountain walls with the massive fronts of mounts Marvine and Hilgard in the distance; the crystal-clear expanse of the lake itself, combine to form a scene of beauty rarely equalled in the West."

    It was like that in 1875 and remains so to this day. There are a few more folks visiting the lake resorts now than in Dutton's day, but the beauty of the lake and surrounding mountains, and the clear air, have been preserved for the public's pleasure.

    The 13-mile stretch from the start of UT 25 to the northeast corner of Fish Lake has been designated a state scenic byway, though the drive is equally attractive beyond this arbitrary limit. Therefore, this drive is described

Drive 14: Fishlake Scenic Drive
Fish Lake to Loa

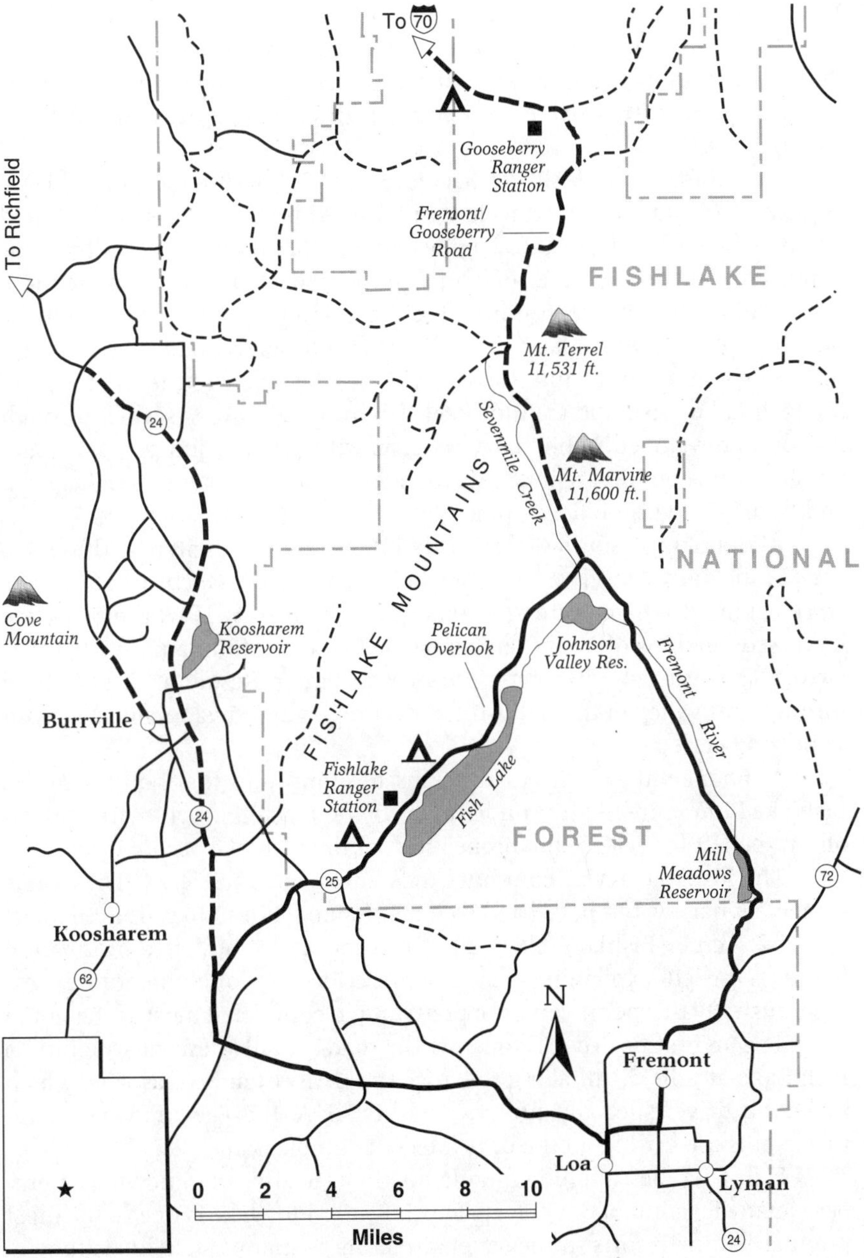

To 70

Gooseberry
Ranger
Station

Fremont/
Gooseberry
Road

FISHLAKE

To Richfield

Mt. Terrel
11,531 ft.

Sevenmile Creek

Mt. Marvine
11,600 ft.

NATIONAL

24

Cove
Mountain

Koosharem
Reservoir

FISHLAKE MOUNTAINS

Pelican
Overlook

Johnson
Valley Res.

Fremont River

Burrville

Fishlake
Ranger
Station

Fish Lake

FOREST

Mill
Meadows
Reservoir

72

24

25

Koosharem

62

N

Fremont

0 2 4 6 8 10
Miles

Loa

Lyman

24

as a 40-mile loop continuing to Loa. The road is paved and well maintained along its entire course and suitable for all vehicles. Traffic is generally moderate except for weekends in the immediate area of the lake resorts. Winter driving may be slowed by icy conditions, especially beyond the Fishlake basin, but the inconvenience is compensated by the extreme beauty of the area in snow. There are several designated scenic backways (unpaved) branching from this drive, providing a fine variety of alpine driving experiences.

The start of the Fishlake Scenic Byway is the intersection of Utah Highways 24 and 25. Most travelers will reach this intersection via Richfield on Interstate 70 or from U.S. Highway 89 in the Sevier River Valley. This approach from the north is an extremely pleasant drive and deserves mention.

Utah Highway 119, east from Richfield, is a very scenic route, starting out through pretty farmland then climbing into wild, undeveloped desert hills. It is 9 miles to the intersection with UT 24. Angle to the right, signed for Fish Lake, Loa, and Capitol Reef. Highway 24 is *very* scenic, through mostly undeveloped public land covered with pinyon, juniper, and sagebrush. This is high-desert prairie surrounded by low mountains: rough, green, and beautiful, with no development at all.

About 8 miles south of the UT 24 intersection you will pass through a zone of the most densely packed sagebrush. If you like sagebrush, *this is the place* (didn't Brigham Young say that?). At about mile 10 you may notice increased ranching off to the left below the Fishlake Mountains. A few miles farther you reach the northern end of Koosharem Reservoir. If you drive through this valley in the right sort of evening light, it just might strike you as bucolic perfection.

At about mile 17 the road begins to climb into the foothills of the Fishlake Mountains. At just under mile 23 you reach the well-marked turnoff on the left for UT 25, the proper start of the Fishlake Scenic Byway.

The Fishlake byway continues the climb begun on UT 24. The road is somewhat narrow but paved and well maintained. Four miles from the start of UT 25, enter Fishlake National Forest and note the large information board on the left, explaining the use of prescribed fire for eliminating excess sagebrush. By this point you have pretty much completed most of the initial altitude gain on this drive. From here the road actually descends slightly to Fish Lake at mile 5. All along this road are dense stands of aspens, which make this drive especially attractive in the fall. At this elevation even summer nights are brisk, and the days are cool and pleasant.

Fish Lake lies in a down-faulted valley (technically known as a *graben*) at an elevation of 8,843 feet. The 5.5-mile-long lake is one of the most popular fishing resorts in the state, attracting as many as 7,000 visitors on summer weekends. Fish Lake is well known for its trophy lake trout (mackinaw) that often exceed twenty pounds. Across the lake, the long ridge of the

*Johnson Reservoir is the source of the Fremont River and
a popular trout lake in Fishlake National Forest.*

Mytoge Mountain forms the eastern limit of the Fish Lake basin. To the north, mounts Marvine and Hilgard, both well over 11,000 feet, remain snow-capped for most of the summer.

The lake shore is dotted with three commercial resorts, two RV facilities, three campgrounds, and numerous picnic areas and boat launches. At just under mile 7, note the large board locating the several campgrounds within the Fishlake Recreation Area. Though camping is abundant, count on the campgrounds filling up quickly on summer weekends. There's a full-on

National Forest Service brown-log-cabin resort development here, but it is on a low key and fairly unobtrusive scale. Here you will find a gas station, general store, marina, RV park, cabin rentals, and even a laundromat.

At about mile 7.5 is the truly outstanding Fish Lake Lodge. The present lodge (the third on this site) was built between 1928 and 1932 and still retains a distinct rustic charm. In many ways the lodge is reminiscent of some of the classic Adirondack or White Mountain resorts built around the same period—like something right out of a 1930s movie. The dining room is rustic perfection and is open to the public for all meals. There are also twenty-five wooden cabins for rent here. The lodge is also the best place to pick up national forest information, including detailed maps outlining the numerous area hikes and biking trails. There is a useful self-guided auto tour brochure that will help explain the geology of the Fish Lake basin.

About 2.5 miles beyond the lodge, past Bowery Campground, you leave most of the hubbub of the Fish Lake resort development behind. Even as laid back as the development is, it's nice to be past the cabins, marinas, and paved bicycle paths. Here you can see the unspoiled northern end of the lake as you drive through gorgeous meadowland and sagebrush flats. The marsh and meadowland is perhaps the most beautiful aspect of this entire basin and a real delight for bird watchers. Keep your eyes open for moose.

Utah Highway 25 crosses the Fremont River just below
its source in the lush Fishlake National Forest.

Loa, a picturesque farming and ranching community on the upper Fremont River, was named for Hawaii's Mauna Loa volcano.

In another few miles you reach the lake's northern limit and you leave the recreation area. Two miles farther is Frying Pan Campground, and 1 mile beyond you descend to 1-square-mile Johnson Reservoir. A look in any direction makes you wonder why the scenic byway designation was limited to just the first 13 miles of this drive. (What, this isn't scenic?!)

Just at the northern edge of Johnson Reservoir, on the left, is the northern extension of the Gooseberry-Fremont Scenic Backway. This backway runs approximately 37 miles between Salina Canyon on I-70 to the north and the intersection of UT 25 with UT 72 just north of Fremont. You will follow the paved southern section of the backway from here to Fremont. To the north, the Gooseberry Road is good graded dirt for about 15 miles to Gooseberry Campground, then paved to the interstate. (This road will probably be fully paved in the near future; for now the road seems fine for most passenger vehicles, but it is best to check on current conditions at Fish Lake.) This backway accesses some of the region's finest forest and meadow scenery and is locally renowned as a spectacular fall drive. This road closes in winter.

A mile or so beyond the high point above Johnson Reservoir, UT 25 crosses the Fremont River at Zedds Meadow. The road rises quickly and steeply for about 1 mile, then begins a long descent into the valley on the other side. The landscape is drier on the far side, with fewer trees and more open views. The views to the south are especially fine. The more you descend, the more this begins to look like desert. There are no pine trees here. A few aspen are up high, but trees at the lower elevations are mostly pinyon and juniper.

The river bottom is lush and dense with cottonwood and boxelder. The road crosses the Fremont River again, where the now greatly expanded stream announces the small earthwork dam, Mill Meadow Dam, just downstream. There are lovely spots to camp along the little reservoir here. It is 3 miles farther to the intersection with UT 72, where you will turn right to reach Loa. From this intersection you may also choose to drive 27 very scenic miles north on UT 72 to join I-70 at Fremont Junction.

About 4 miles north (left) on UT 72 is the start of another attractive sidetrip: Thousand Lake Mountain Scenic Backway. This 35-mile backway loop runs over the northern flank of Thousand Lakes Mountain, then descends to loop through the northern tip of Capitol Reel National Park. The scenery along this backway is an impressive combination of high alpine and high desert. The road is somewhat rough, can be very dusty in dry periods, and is impassable when wet. High-clearance vehicles are definitely recommended.

Headed south toward Loa, Utah 72 is as scenic as Utah 25 began. From here you can see south into Canyonlands. The land here is a mix of BLM and private, though it is hard to distinguish one from the other: mostly undeveloped pasturage and rugged desert hills. About 2 miles from the UT 25/UT 72 intersection you come into the irrigated valley at the community of Fremont, an eclectic mixture of new ranch homes and old ranches, trailer homes, and log cabins spread out for about three miles along the valley. There are no services. From Fremont to Loa it is 9 miles of ranchland and farmland.

Loa is one of the prettiest farm towns in central Utah. Settled in the 1870s, it was named for Mauna Loa volcano by a fellow who had served a Mormon mission in Hawaii during the 1850s. The Wayne Stake Tabernacle is a classic LDS community church.

In order to complete this drive as a circle, head west on UT 24, 12 miles, back to the Fish Lake turnoff. The last leg of your drive traverses undeveloped BLM land, mostly sagebrush-covered desert hills: nothing spectacular, but completely unspoiled. A possible option for a scenic return to Richfield might include a sidetrip along Cove Mountain Scenic Backway, a popular drive during fall colors. The backway runs from Koosharem north to Glenwood, 10 miles east of Richfield, offering beautiful views of the Koosharem and Sevier valleys. Reach Koosharem from the well-marked intersection of UT 24 and Utah Highway 62, 7 miles north of the start of the Fishlake Byway. The Cove Mountain backway, though unpaved, is generally suitable for passenger vehicles when dry.

Other options from Loa include striking east on UT 24, which is described as Drive #8. Since Loa is the start of this very interesting drive, well, why not just go for it?

15

Beaver Canyon Scenic Byway/Sevier River Valley

Beaver to the Sevier Valley

General description: The Beaver Canyon Scenic Byway is a 17-mile mountain canyon drive between the town of Beaver and Elk Meadows Ski Resort. An unpaved mountain road continues the drive over the Tushar Mountains and down to Junction in the Sevier River Valley. The Sevier Valley is a well-watered corridor filled with diverse historic and geological attractions.

Special attractions: Historic Beaver, high mountain scenery, Fishlake National Forest, Puffer Lake, scenic/historic Sevier River Valley, hiking, fishing, camping.

Location: Central Utah, in the western section of Fishlake National Forest.

Drive route number and name: Utah Highway 153/Beaver Canyon Scenic Byway, Kimberly/Big John Scenic Backway, Utah Highway 89.

Travel season: Year-round as far as Elk Meadows. UT 153 beyond Elk Meadows is closed in winter and impassable to most vehicles when wet. This is an especially fine autumn-colors drive.

Camping: Four national forest campgrounds, with unlimited opportunities for primitive, undeveloped camping.

Services: All services in Beaver; limited services in Junction.

Nearby attractions: Kimberly/Big John Scenic Backway, Butch Cassidy's boyhood home, Historic Marysvale, Big Rock Candy Mountain, Fremont Indian State Park.

 ## The drive

Beaver Canyon Scenic Byway (UT 153) climbs from the town of Beaver into the Tushar Mountains and Fishlake National Forest. The scenic byway ends after about 17 miles of forest and mountain driving to a high point at Elk Meadows Ski Area. This drive continues the route east across the spine of the Tushars (Utah's designated Kimberly/Big John Scenic Backway) descending to Junction in the Sevier River Valley. From Junction, the drive turns north on US 89 along the scenic Sevier River to the junction with Interstate 70.

Drive 15: Beaver Canyon Scenic Byway/Sevier River Valley

Beaver to the Sevier Valley

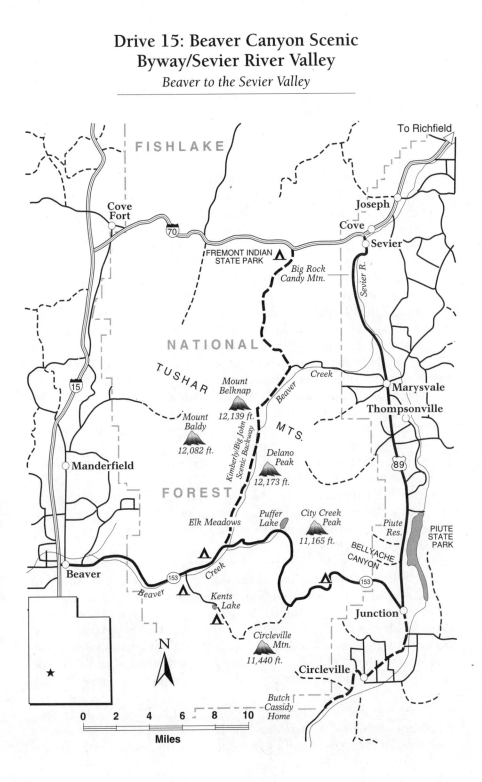

To Richfield

FISHLAKE

Cove Fort

70

Joseph

Cove

Sevier

FREMONT INDIAN STATE PARK

Big Rock Candy Mtn.

Sevier R.

NATIONAL

TUSHAR

Mount Belknap
12,139 ft.

Beaver

Creek

Marysvale

Thompsonville

Mount Baldy
12,082 ft.

M T S.

15

89

Delano Peak
12,173 ft.

FOREST

Manderfield

Elk Meadows

Puffer Lake

City Creek Peak
11,165 ft.

Piute Res.

PIUTE STATE PARK

Kimberly/Big John Scenic Backway

BELLYACHE CANYON

Beaver

153

Creek

Beaver

Kents Lake

153

Junction

Circleville Mtn.
11,440 ft.

Circleville

N

Butch Cassidy Home

0   2   4   6   8   10

Miles

This 62-mile drive provides a nice diversity of scenery and roadside attractions, from the beautiful and seldom-visited Tushar Mountains to the gentler landscapes and rustic communities of the Sevier River Valley.

The initial scenic byway section of this drive is paved and suitable for all vehicles. Traffic in the canyon is nearly always light, though the road is rather narrow near the mouth of Beaver Canyon. Because of heavy snow in the canyon, snow tires or chains are required from November 1 through March 31; the road may be inconvenient for larger vehicles during that period. Because UT 153 east of Puffer Lake is unpaved (and technically closed during winter), it is a good idea to check in Beaver about the current status of this road. In dry conditions, travel east of Puffer Lake, across the ridge of the Tushars and down into the Sevier Valley, will be no problem for passenger cars and smaller campers. The first stretch of the unpaved road beyond Puffer Lake is narrow and uphill (briefly), which will make travel impractical for RVs and trailers.

Unlike the Wasatch Plateau, to which the Tushar Range bears a resemblance, this isn't a true plateau, but the remains of a series of stratovolcanoes that were in a period of massive eruption about 24 million years ago. The region is extremely rich in minerals and was the site of a small mining rush around the turn of the century. These are some of the highest summits in Utah, with mounts Baldy, Belknap, and Delano all higher than 12,000 feet. The entire range is seldom visited, making this a good place for high-level hiking, bicycling, and backpacking trips "far from the madding crowd."

The drive begins in Beaver at the foot of the west slope of the Tushars. Beaver is a fascinating old town that seems to be living in the past. It is full of inexpensive motels and attractive old buildings and boasts at least one of those small-town variety stores that some of us remember from the 1950s and 1960s—the sort of place that appears to have just a little bit of everything and about anything a person would really need to get along . . . back in the 1950s and 1960s.

In the 1870s and 1880s Beaver was the most important community in southern Utah. Today it is one of the best examples of a larger southern Utah town, with many stone and brick buildings (dozens of Beaver homes are listed on the National Historic Register). Most of the town's current residents are descendants of the original settlers sent here by Brigham Young from Parowan in 1866. The Beaver Co-Op (1872) was once one of the largest stores south of Salt Lake City, profiting from mining and transportation activity. The beautiful old courthouse, now a community museum well worth a visit, dates from 1877.

One hundred years earlier, the Dominguez-Escalante expedition took advantage of this well-watered and verdant site to refresh themselves on their long journey in search of a short route from New Mexico to California.

Historic Beaver County Courthouse, built in 1877.

During Utah's pioneer era, Beaver was the birthplace of Utah's favorite outlaw, Butch Cassidy, and the boyhood home of one Philo Farnsworth, credited as "the father of television." Allow at least an hour to poke around this very interesting old town.

From downtown Beaver, 200 North (next to the old high school) is UT 153, clearly marked for Elk Meadows and Puffer Lake. A large LDS church and the adjacent Beaver Canyon Campground/RV Park mark the eastern limit of town. Half a mile farther, note the famous old racetrack on the left. After another mile you've left all residential and commercial development behind and you are in a very pretty mountain canyon with Beaver Creek flowing alongside the road. A little under 5 miles from downtown Beaver you enter Fishlake National Forest. The road surface is fine, but the road is narrow and down here in the forest the views are closed in, so take it slow if you are in a big rig.

The byway quickly climbs 4,000 feet through groves of mountain mahogany, passing four hydroelectric plants on its way. Two miles from the entrance to the national forest is Little Cottonwood Campground; it's 2.5 miles farther to Ponderosa picnic site. Just past Ponderosa is the turnoff on the right for Forest Road 137. This good dirt road provides access to some attractive high mountain lakes and nice camping sites at Little Reservoir, Kent's Lake, and Anderson Meadow Reservoir. The byway climbs steeply from here, and about a mile past this turnoff (mile 11.4 from town) is Mahogany Cove Campground. Above here the views really open up in spectacular fashion.

Three miles beyond Mahogany Cove you will reach Merchant Valley Dam, which supplies the water for the power plants below. Above the dam is a flat meadowland area. This is extremely beautiful, pristine alpine terrain, and the Forest Service is so serious about keeping it that way that they prohibit parking in many places.

The road levels off through the meadowland. About 2 miles above Merchant Valley Dam is a turnoff on the left, well marked for Big John Flat, a designated scenic backway. This 22-mile section of the Kimberly/Big John Scenic Backway climbs over the Tushar Mountains and leads up to the old Kimberly mining district. Kimberly developed rather late as a mining camp, when the Annie Laurie Mine was established in 1899. Between 1901 and 1908 the town residents numbered 500 here, and the mill was processing 250 tons of ore per day. Today all that remains are a handful of log ruins and the remains of the Annie Laurie mill.

The Kimberly/Big John Scenic Backway ends at I-70 near Fremont Indian State Park. Here you can see more than five hundred examples of rock art, both the incised *petroglyphs* and the painted *pictographs*, messages in stone from the people who inhabited this canyon from the times of the earliest hunter-gatherers until recent pioneer days.

The unpaved Kimberly/Big John Scenic Backway is generally suited for passenger cars (not for large RVs or trailers), though high-clearance vehicles are strongly recommended. The road is closed in winter.

About a mile farther along the Beaver Canyon drive is a turnoff on the right, signed for Beaver High Adventure Base (apparently a Boy Scout camp). This road descends a little less than a mile to extremely beautiful Three Creeks Reservoir in an absolutely splendid alpine setting. It's a good fishing spot and a great place for a picnic.

Just past the turnoff for Three Creeks you will leave the national forest, and you begin to encounter private homes as you approach Elk Meadows Ski Area. After another mile you reach the very low-key development that's grown around the base of the ski area. Just past the end of this development you reach the Puffer Lake Resort (cabins, camping, convenience store) and the end of the paved road.

From the pavement's end, UT 153 is actually the southern and eastern section of The Kimberly/Big John Scenic Backway. The dirt road beyond Puffer Lake is fine (when dry) for conventional vehicles and truck-top campers. This road is technically closed in winter, which can last from November until mid-June. After the first couple of miles, this route descends, presenting no real obstacles for most vehicles. If you are still concerned about the suitability of your vehicle for the road ahead, check with the folks at Puffer

Roadside grave of a Sevier Valley pioneer, north of Junction.

Lake Resort. If for no other reason than the near total absence of people on the east-side descent (either as development or traffic), continuing on to Junction is highly recommended.

Climb steadily and steeply for just under 2 miles to a very beautiful high-meadow area where the views broaden out. You will see the trailhead here for Trail 129, one of several fine trails that depart the road from this high point. This meadowland is designated as a wildlife feeding area, where you will likely see both deer and elk. Exactly 3 miles from the end of the paved road you intersect a road on your left signed for the Skyline Recreation Trail. The Skyline trail is the showcase trail for this section of Fishlake National Forest. It runs approximately 8 miles north and west from UT 153 to intersect the Big John Road. Along the way, it climbs high to skirt the highest peaks of the Tushar Range.

At this point UT 153 is somewhat higher than 10,000 feet. There are excellent primitive campsites up here. Just be sure to camp where there is an existing fire ring, so as not to add to the already over-abundant selection.

Two miles farther and the road begins its serious descent. After about 2.5 miles of descent you will reach a major dirt-road intersection with FR 137 on the right, signed for Kent's Lake (12 miles to the lake or 25 miles back to Beaver via this route). It is 11 miles straight ahead on UT 153 to Junction. After a couple of miles of descent you will come out of the forest and meadows to an absolutely spectacular overlook of the Sevier River Valley, just before the long descent to Junction (which can be seen down in the valley).

The descent on this side of the Tushars is visually striking for the nearly complete absence of trees. There are a few aspens but not much else up high and not much more below. This gives unrestricted views into the valley as you descend. With the steepest part of the descent behind you, you pass the road doubling back on the left for City Creek Campground, with a handful of nice undeveloped sites tucked away in a shady grove. It is 5 more miles to the farming and ranching community of Junction, on US 89.

Junction and nearby Circleville were settled in 1864. Livestock was important from the start and remains so today. The county seat of Piute County, Junction has one of the most attractive red brick courthouses in the state. Take some time to poke around here. It won't take long since there's not much to see, but this is as fine an example of idyllic, small-town ranching America as you'll see anywhere. Junction has a gas station, cafe, small motel, and another one of those great small-town general stores that has a little of everything.

Now that you've made it this far, you might as well make the 6-mile sidetrip south to Circleville, where that outlaw Butch grew up.

Folks in Circleville are no doubt a lot prouder of their favorite infamous son than of a particularly nasty incident that took place over the mountains in Beaver at just about the same time Cassidy was born. During the 1866 Black Hawk War, Circleville was the site of the massacre of an entire Paiute village. Following the outbreak of hostilities, all of the male members of a neighboring village were placed under armed guard, while the women and children were locked in a cellar. Some of the braves attempted to escape, and all of them were shot and killed by their guards. After some discussion on how to handle the women and children, they were led up singly from the cellar and their throats cut.

An old settler's cabin, 2.5 miles south of Circleville and clearly visible on the right from the highway, is Butch Cassidy's boyhood home. Cassidy, born Robert Leroy Parker, lived here on his father's ranch from age thirteen. It was here that the boy met Mike Cassidy, who had run with a group of horse thieves before taking a ranch-hand job with the Parkers. Cassidy taught the youngster all he needed to know about growing up tough and independent, and the boy must have idolized him, for he later took his old friend's name as an alias.

Mike Cassidy left for Mexico one step ahead of the law. Shortly after, young Parker stole some horses and lit out for Colorado. Sometime later he teamed up with two other adventurers and robbed a train in Grand Junction and a bank at Telluride. It was about this time that he emerged as a full-fledged outlaw, the soon-to-be-famous bandit Butch Cassidy.

Cassidy and his notorious band, "The Wild Bunch," robbed banks and stagecoaches, held up mining payrolls, and rustled cattle throughout the region around the turn of the century. He was said to have been a likeable fellow, a Robin Hood-like character who was known to have been helped out many times by ordinary citizens in his evasion of the law. There is even a story of the Piute County Judge in nearby Junction buying Butch beers when he came to town.

Cassidy, along with his partner, the Sundance Kid, was allegedly killed in a shootout with a company of cavalry in Bolivia. Yet stories of his reappearance in the region, and subsequently in the Pacific Northwest, persisited for years. According to the research of at least one historian, he lived out a quiet life in Spokane before dying of pneumonia in the 1930s.

North of Junction, US 89 follows the Sevier River Valley. This is mostly BLM land on both sides of the road, scrub sagebrush desert used for grazing, so there is no development at all. Off to the left are the high peaks of the Tushar Range. On the right you occasionally catch a glimpse of the Sevier River and where it widens into Piute Reservoir a few miles north of Junction. At the northern end of the reservoir (5 miles north of Junction) is Piute Lake State Park, with primitive camping and not much else.

It is 19 pristine, scenic, wide-open miles to the very pretty old town of Marysvale. Marysvale's several substantial commercial buildings—mostly boarded shut and in varying states of decay—along with the names of several of the streets branching off from US 89, are evidence that this was once a mining town of some importance. Marysvale began in the 1860s as a Mormon farm town. In 1868 ore strikes in the Tushars, west of town, brought hordes of miners. Always alternating between mini-booms and hard times, nearby uranium mining in the mid-1900s resulted in one of the highest rates of cancer in the world. Marysvale has a small selection of motels, gas stations, and convenience stores.

Just north of Marysvale, US 89 follows the Sevier River as it winds through a very picturesque sort of desert canyon called Clear Creek Canyon. Here you will start to notice some really fantastic coloration and eroded shapes in the hills. The colors are the result of hydrothermal activity (much like the soft, yellow rock at Yellowstone), evidence that the volcanic activity of the Tushars is quite recent.

At about mile 4.5 north of Marysvale, watch on your left just above the road for the interesting yellow-brown formation that inspired the popular folk song "The Big Rock Candy Mountain," made famous by the late Burl Ives (but written by a railroad man before the turn of the century). About a

"The Big Rock Candy Mountain," alongside U.S. Highway 89 in the Sevier Valley.

half-mile farther is a pullout with a sign for Lemonade Spring. Oddly enough, the trickle that issues from this bizarre heap of soft yellow rock *does* look and even taste slightly lemony. The coloration comes from oxidized iron in the clay-rich earth (limonite), but the taste indicates clearly there must still be some sort of low-grade acid concentration up in these hills (the volcanic Tushars have long been known as a source of sulfur). In all likelihood, the acidity is probably more closely related to battery acid than to citric acid, but "Lemonade Springs" is certainly more romantic sounding than, say, "Battery Acid Springs."

About half a mile farther is a scenic pullout that gives the best view back toward The Big Rock Candy Mountain. From this vantage point, you may decide for yourself (and argue with your kids, no doubt) whether this does, in fact, look like a huge chunk of marbled candy. (Actually, they might have called it "The Big Chocolate and Caramel Syrup-Covered Ice Cream Sundae Mountain," but that's not very melodic.)

Once north of the small cluster of low-key development around Big Rock Candy Mountain, the valley increases in beauty. The Sevier River flows immediately to the right of the road. At just under mile 12 from Marysvale, you reach the important intersection with I-70. To return to Interstate 15, take I-70 west; to continue along US 89, north to Richfield, get on I-70 **east**. Fortunately, since this is Utah, even the interstate drives are scenic, the only difference being the speed at which the scenery rolls by.

Richfield is a full-on mini city, with fast-food restaurants, supermarkets, large discount houses, and all the other manifestations of civilization as we know it.

16

Tintic Scenic Drive
Eureka to Delta

General description: A basin and range drive across broad, dry valleys and rough desert hills.

Special attractions: Tintic District mining towns, Great Basin desert views, Little Sahara Recreation Area, site of Topaz internment camp, Fort Deseret.

Location: Central Utah, on the edge of the Great Basin.

Drive route number and name: U.S. Highway 6.

Travel season: Year-round. Can be very warm in summer.

Camping: Limited primarily to two large campgrounds at little Sahara, commercial RV park at Delta.

Services: All services in Delta; most services in Eureka; limited services in Lynndyl.

Nearby attractions: Nebo Loop Scenic Byway, Pony Express Trail Scenic Backway, Notch Peak Loop Scenic Backway.

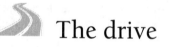 The drive

This is one of but a handful of drives in this guide that touch on the rough, desolate region of the Great Basin, the desert land that lies to the west of Utah's famed mountain and high plateau country. This is not an easy region to appreciate on first sight; it resists the modern tourist almost as staunchly as it did the early settlers who quickly learned simply to avoid it. This place is the dry, cracked alkali flat, the volcanic plain devoid of vegetation, home to rattlesnake and tumbleweed. But in its remoteness and its sheer resistance to Man's attempts to domesticate it, it has a raw, imposing, and eternal power.

In some ways, this drive describes various attempts at coming to terms with the Great Basin; or, at least, of Man's tenuous and sometimes failed efforts to put this rough land to some practical use. The drive runs from the old Tintic Mining District south along US 6 to Delta, the last urban outpost on the edge of the Great Basin and site of a Japanese-American internment camp during World War II. Along the way, the route offers glimpses of the vast desert wasteland to the west, of the fascinating accumulation of shifting sand dunes at Little Sahara, and of a river that just gives up and dies here in the desert. The 50-mile drive is on excellent, flat, paved road.

Views along the Paria River Valley Scenic Backway. (Drive 4)

Brilliant red sandstone at the west end of Red Canyon. (Drive 20)

Flaming Gorge Reservoir (Drive 20)

Petroglyphs from several distinct historic periods, at Newspaper Rock State Park. (Drive 11)

Views into the amphitheater from Sunset Point.

June is the time for vibrant cactus blossoms like these near St. George.

Johnson Canyon movie set, the location for many western movies and television shows (including Gunsmoke).

Replicas of the Central Pacific's JUPITER and the Union Pacific's OLD 119 make daily appearances at Golden Spike National Historic Site. (Drive 28)

Kodachrome Basin State Park (Drive 6)

Little Cottonwood Creek, 20 minutes from downtown Salt Lake City.

Alpine meadows on the fringe of the High Uinta Wilderness Area, beside the Mirror Lake Scenic Byway. (Drive 21)

The marsh grasses provide a rich feeding environment for a wide variety of both waterfowl and common songbirds, like this yellow-headed blackbird.

Arches landscape, with La Sal Mountains in the background.

Coral Pink Sand Dunes State Park, a Utah treasure. (Drive 4)

Drive 16: Tintic Scenic Drive
Eureka to Delta

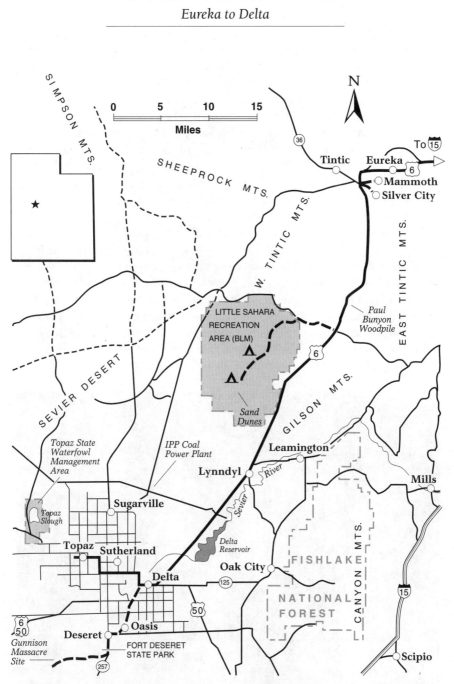

To reach the drive's starting point at Eureka, exit Interstate 15 at Santaquin and take US 6 west. The drive from Santaquin to Eureka is itself rather scenic and interesting. West of Elberta the landscape becomes more dramatic, as we leave agriculture behind and enter the rough desert hills called the Tintic Mountains, named for a Ute Indian chief.

In 1869, ore strikes in these hills resulted in the establishment of the Tintic Mining District. Within thirty years this had become one of America's most important mining districts, with most activity centered around the towns of Eureka, Mammoth, Diamond, and Silver City. The population here soared to an estimated 8,000 just before the turn of the century. Mining slowed in this century but continued through the 1950s. Altogether, the district produced an estimated $570 million in silver, gold, copper, lead, and zinc. Some small-scale operations have recently resumed here.

Present-day Eureka sort of toddles along, supported by the few regional mining jobs left and a slow but steady trickle of tourist business. Eureka has a very natural "mining town that's seen more prosperous days" appearance to it. This rough-edged, somewhat down-at-the-heels look is an indication that the tourist trade has not been substantial enough to warrant fixing the place up—or that the town's eight hundred residents just plain do not want to make it slick. This is a quiet, funky, very pleasant place, and your last opportunity for fuel and food for a long way. For a good overview

Eureka, principal town of the Tintic Mining District.

of the mining history in the Tintic area, stop at the excellent Tintic Mining Museum, upstairs in the old city hall on Main Street. As with the many DUP museums in small towns across Utah, call one of the numbers listed on the front door and someone will come down to open up for you.

As you leave Eureka at its southern end, note the old gallows frames used for lowering miners into the tunnels and for extracting ore. The most prominent of these, just on the right as you leave town, has a nice interpretive plaque that explains how the underground mining operations were carried out. Also note the humorous sign, proclaiming Eureka "Not just a hole in the ground."

A mile or so past Eureka, US 6 trends slightly to the left—ignore the fork to the right, signed for Tooele. Ahead of you stretches out the grim, dry expanse of the Great Basin. At this point the highway travels due south through a broad valley ringed with rough, arid, desert hills. A little more than 2 miles past Eureka is the well-marked turnoff on the left for Mammoth. Though there is not much to see here, it is worth the short (less than a mile) sidetrip up this paved road to the attractive cluster of houses, in a truly spectacular setting. Mammoth was the site of the Tintic District hospital just after the turn of the century.

It is just under a mile to a similar turnoff on the left, this one to the defunct town of Silver City. Depending on the status of the current small-scale mining operation up this road, you may or may not be able to reach the townsite, which sits on private property. In 1995 you could drive just under 2 miles up this semi-paved road, past extensive (and quite interesting) old mine dumps to a gate that appears to mark the limit of allowable traffic. The short drives up these two canyons are worthwhile to give a sense of how the mining in this district was spread out among many small canyons, each with its own little community, all centered around the larger town of Eureka.

Back down in the desert, driving south along US 6, it may seem surprising that this is *not* a state-designated scenic byway. This drive is really attractive: pristine, wild, high prairie dotted with rough hills covered with sagebrush, pinyon, and juniper. The views are terrific and, except for the interesting relics of old mining operations, there is no sign of development. The road is excellent, flat, and fast.

Just under 20 miles south of Eureka is the turnoff, on the left, signed for Paul Bunyon's Woodpile. The "woodpile" is a cluster of fluted lava formed about three million years ago, resembling a gigantic stack of petrified wood. You will have to get out of the car to see it, but the short walk along easy, wooded trail can be a nice break. Drive 3.3 miles on decent dirt road to a gate. Park conventional vehicles below the gate; a 4x4 will get you a whopping 0.1 mile closer. Pass through the gate (please close it behind you) and follow this rough road to the trailhead. The moderate trail is about 1 mile long, with a well-marked option for either the woodpile itself (left) or the overlook (right). I recommend the slightly easier trail to the overlook unless you have kids who insist on dragging you up to the woodpile.

A few miles to the south is Utah's largest dry beach. Most of the sand at Little Sahara Recreation Area was left by the Sevier River, which flowed into Lake Bonneville, the prehistoric sea that filled this part of the Great Basin until about fifteen thousand years ago. Southwest winds, after picking up particles of sand, were deflected upward by Sand Mountain until they lost impetus and dumped the sand here, forming this isolated, 124-square-mile system of free-moving dunes. The dunes are still moving to the north and east between five and nine feet per year.

From the well-marked Little Sahara turnoff it is 4.4 miles to a left turn, then 1.5 miles to the visitor center, the hours of which vary greatly. It appears to be open most often during the popular spring and fall seasons. If closed, there will usually be someone around to answer your questions, and there is plenty of self-service information on using the recreation area facilities.

There are very nice campgrounds here, with water and toilets, though the constant roar of dune-buggy and motorcycle engines can be annoying to those in search of peace and quiet in the desert. If the noise gets on your nerves, you can escape to the Rockwell Outstanding Natural Area, a 9,000-acre, vehicle-free zone set aside to preserve a sense of the natural ecosystem. Stay away from Little Sahara on weekends if you are sensitive about noise.

If you decide to skip the visit to Little Sahara, you will get an idea of what it is like as you continue south on US 6, when Sand Mountain comes into view on the right. This fascinating geological oddity (it is an isolated, gigantic dune) appears either black or sandy gray, depending on the light.

Just as you pass Sand Mountain, look off to the right, farther south and west, and you will see one of the world's largest coal-fired electric plants. Intermountain Power Project's immense power plant supplies electricity for communities as far away as Southern California. About 12 miles past Little Sahara the road passes the first cultivated fields, as you approach the small community of Lynndyl, tucked away in the cluster of trees seen far ahead. Lynndyl is an attractive, quiet farm town with a gas station and convenience store.

South of the oasis of Lynndyl, you return to the desert. In about 3 miles you will pass under the very impressive network of power lines that issue from the power plant. Note that the Sevier River now flows to the left of the road on the final leg of its long journey from the high snows of the Markagunt Plateau to its eventual dissipation in the dry wasteland to the southwest of Delta. Strange to see a river that, rather than flowing into some other body of water, just runs out of energy and dies.

Shortly after crossing the Sevier, you pass the small Delta airport and then the golf course, announcing you are in Delta's northern suburbs. Note on the right the cheese factory and restaurant, Delta Valley Farms, a good place for a simple lunch.

The modern town of Delta is neither very scenic nor especially interesting. It is, however, a convenient service center and the last community of any size before striking out across the Great Basin. There is a choice of supermarkets and several motels.

In the nearby Sevier Desert, remnants of Folsom Early Man culture have been found, dating back nearly eight thousand years. Yet it was a long

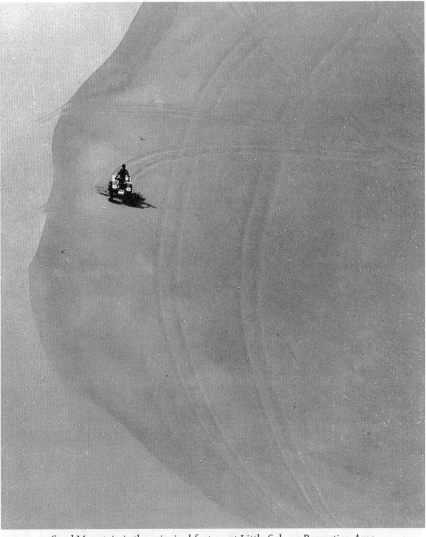

Sand Mountain is the principal feature at Little Sahara Recreation Area, and a mecca for dune buggies and ATVs.

time before the area was permanently settled. Delta was not a pioneer Mormon community. The town came into being in 1907 after construction of the Yuba Dam on the Sevier River made it practical to irrigate new fields here.

In 1853, Captain John Gunnison and six of his men were killed by an Indian war party while surveying a possible transcontinental rail line. There is a monument to the massacre but little else a few miles west of Hinkley on U.S. Highway 50/US 6 and then south at the well-marked dirt road to the monument. Fort Deseret is about 4 miles south of Hinkley. If you are expecting an elaborate pioneer stockade, this simple adobe structure will be a disappointment. The 10-foot mud walls were put up in a big hurry at the start of the Black Hawk War in 1866, when Brigham Young advised all of the Mormon settlements in Central Utah to prepare for hostilities. The Indians never came, so the fort was never tested. (Probably a good thing, from the looks of the place.)

Beyond Hinkley there is nothing but rough, dry, barren, inhospitable, and thoroughly *glorious* Great Basin desert for more than 80 miles, until you reach the Nevada line. The 50-mile desert/mountain Notch Peak Loop Scenic Backway is 43 miles to the west, just to the north of US 50/US 6. This backway is usually driveable in passenger vehicles, and it offers good opportunities for rock-hounding and trilobite hunting. Check on road conditions in Delta.

Memorial at the site of Topaz, a World War II relocation camp for Japanese-Americans, in the desolate Great Basin.

In spite of the town's rather prosaic birth and general lack of historical interest, there are things to see in the Delta area apart from the imposing desert scenery to the west. Delta's Great Basin Museum, at 328 West 100 North (right in the middle of town), is a good source of information on regional history and geology. Delta is one of the greatest rock-hounding centers in the West. Trilobites at Antelope Springs and topaz crystals at Topaz Mountain are among the more popular finds. Check in at the Great Basin Museum for tips on other likely spots, and pick up their useful little guide.

Delta's one significant historical claim to fame was a regrettable affair that took place here half a century ago. During World War II, 8,700 Japanese (many of them American citizens) were uprooted from their California homes and relocated to an internment camp named Topaz Relocation Center, set in a marshy area on the edge of the Sevier Desert.

All that remains of the old relocation center is a lingering mood of desolation and rough times, but the site is worth a visit as a reminder of how innocent people are sometimes made to suffer during difficult and stress-filled times. To reach the site, continue west on US 6 from downtown Delta; just after the railroad overpass, where US 6 curves to the left, go **straight** (signed for Sutherland). Turn right at the stop sign (1000 West) and drive north to Sutherland (the power plant will be visible straight ahead). The road takes a hard angle to the left at mile 1.2, but just follow this obvious main road (now called 1500 North) for 2 miles until you see a prominent sign indicating Sutherland to the right, Abraham and Topaz straight. (You are essentially working your way northwest on the most obvious main roads of an area criss-crossed with many roads at right angles.) Just under 6 miles due west of the big curve you reach 7000 West and a clearly marked right turn for Topaz. Go north on 7000 West for 2.5 miles to a stop sign and the end of the pavement. Continue north on good, graded gravel to the intersection with 4500 North. As the sign indicates, turn left on this off-and-on paved road.

At this point you are in the general vicinity of the relocation center, and you should begin to get a sense of just how unpleasant this must have been for the thousands of Japanese-Americans banished to this alkali wasteland. At mile 3.7 watch for the unmistakable memorial on the left.

The quickest way to reach the I-15 corridor from the Delta area is to drive 27 miles east on US 50. Salt Lake City is a little under three hours of direct driving from Delta.

17

Nebo Loop Scenic Byway
Payson to Nephi

General description: A high-alpine drive along the eastern flank of 11,877-foot Mount Nebo.

Special attractions: Payson Lakes Recreation Area, Mount Nebo Wilderness Area, Devil's Kitchen Geologic Interest Site, hiking, fishing, backpacking.

Location: Central Utah, in the Wasatch Range.

Drive route number and name: Forest Road 015, Nebo Loop Scenic Byway.

Travel season: Memorial Day to Thanksgiving, depending on snowfall. This is a spectacular autumn colors drive (late September until early October).

Camping: Five national forest campgrounds, two commercial campgrounds at Nephi.

Services: All services in Payson and Nephi. No services on route.

Nearby attractions: Tintic Mining District, Little Sahara Recreation Area, Provo/Utah Lake, attractive communities of the Sanpete Valley.

The drive

This really isn't a loop at all, despite its official name. The 38-mile Nebo Loop Scenic Byway is a north-south mountain drive that runs between the regional centers of Payson and Nephi. This extremely popular excursion provides spectacular close-up views of imposing Mount Nebo, impressive vistas of Utah Valley and the Wasatch Mountains, and abundant opportunities for high-level alpine hikes. It is a relatively short drive that makes a nice half-day outing.

The Nebo Loop byway is fully paved and fine for all vehicles. A bit of climbing to its 9,000-foot high-point may cause larger rigs to pant a bit, but there are no real problems with the road. Traffic on this popular byway can be slow on weekends, especially during the autumn colors season. The road closes during winter. In general, and for photographers in particular, this drive might best be done in morning, since it is predominantly to the east of Mount Nebo.

While the byway can be driven in either direction, it seems to be most popular as a north-south drive, setting out from Payson. Payson is a quiet

Drive 17: Nebo Loop Scenic Byway
Payson to Nephi

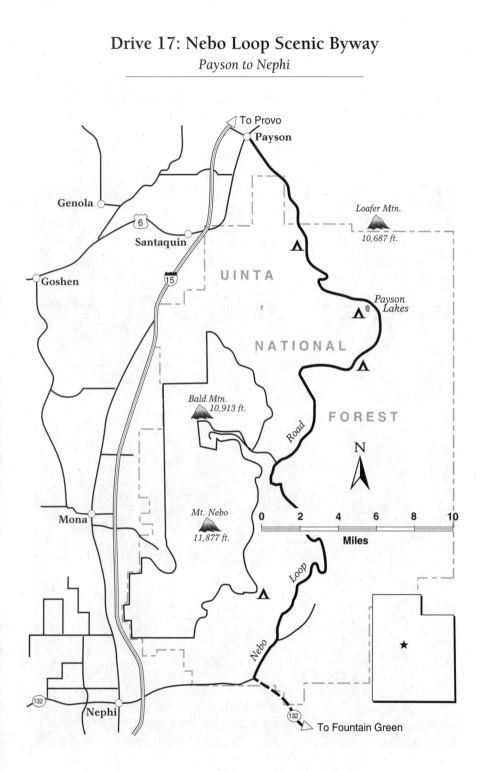

At 11,877 feet, Mount Nebo is the highest peak of the Wasatch Range and the featured attraction of the Nebo Loop Scenic Byway.

community of nearly ten thousand with a fine collection of attractive old brick homes on Main Street north of the business center. Main Street is one-way, running south. The downtown itself is somewhat devitalized, with many closed businesses. At the south end of this business district is a nice, well-shaded town park with a wading pool: ideal for a picnic.

U.S. Highway 6 is Payson's 100 North. Follow it east through town until you see (on the right) the large, ornate old Peteetneet Academy. You really cannot miss this outstanding architectural gem, one of the most elaborate old schoolhouses in the state. The red and beige brick building houses a traditional private academy, named for an Indian chief who had befriended the earliest Mormon settlers here. Peteetneet Avenue, on the right (also called 600 East), is well marked for the Nebo Loop Scenic Byway.

Head south through a fairly nondescript residential area. Two large LDS churches within four blocks should give you an idea of the sort of place Payson is. Within a mile you will be on a narrow but paved country lane, winding southward and upward away from Payson. Be careful of weekend traffic, especially if you are in a large vehicle. At about mile 3.5 the road comes up and out of the canyon into really gorgeous mountain meadowlands. This lovely, open interlude lasts but briefly before the road enters another narrow, steep canyon that is heavily wooded with a stream cascading on the right. A mile farther you enter Uinta National Forest. Just inside the national forest boundary, on the right, is the small (twelve sites) and secluded Maple Bench Campground.

By about 10 miles from Payson, you have gained enough elevation that the trees have thinned out and the views have become more expansive. At mile 12.7 is the turnoff on the right for Payson Lakes, with nearly one hundred tent and RV sites (0.5 mile to lakes). A mile and a half past Payson Lakes is the turnoff on the left for Black Hawk Campground, which is 2 miles from the byway. Just past this turnoff you should begin to notice that you are very high up on the northeast flank of Mount Nebo. At mile 15 there is a nice overlook on the left called Beaver Dam Creek Overlook. A plaque here describes the confrontation in 1865-67 between Ute chief Black Hawk and the Mormon settlers, famous throughout central Utah as the *Black Hawk War*.

Past this overlook, the views of Nebo's summit are extremely impressive. Mormon settlers named Mount Nebo ("Sentinel of God") for the biblical peak where Moses died, the highest mountain east of the Jordan River. It seemed appropriate, since this Nebo lies to the east of Utah's Jordan River (well, okay, it's a bit to the south as well). At 11,877 feet, Mount Nebo is the highest peak in the Wasatch Range and one of the highest in the state. The Mount Nebo Wilderness Area protects 28,500 acres of rugged alpine terrain surrounding the peak.

The road continues to climb. At just past mile 17, Utah Lake Viewpoint provides a very nice view off to the northwest. From here you can see clearly most of the Provo Valley, with Utah Lake (only eighteen feet deep at its deepest) and Mount Timpanagos, the massive snowy peak to the northeast of Provo.

There are numerous scenic overlooks along this route. The Bald Mountain Overlook is particularly impressive, with several excellent trailheads. Now that you have used your vehicle to gain all this elevation, this is a good place to embark on a mountain hike and gain views for which you would normally have to work a lot harder.

At about mile 25 the road begins to descend, and it really is remarkable just how close to the east face of Nebo the road brings you. There is an especially fine overlook just past mile 25. At mile 29, do not fail to stop at the very interesting Devil's Kitchen Geologic Interest Site. A short interpretive trail leads to a surprising sight. Here, in the heart of this most Alp-like mountain landscape, is a little scene lifted from the brightly-hued sandstone canyons to the south. A geological oddity, Price River conglomerate is an easily eroded, brightly colored material that stands out in sharp contrast to the surrounding alpine forest. The hoodoos, spires, and columns look like they belong in Bryce Canyon.

Mount Nebo, from the east. The name Nebo comes from the
Book of Mormon, and means "Sentinel of God."

The byway descends along Salt Creek and, at just under mile 38, reaches the intersection with Utah Highway 132. Here you leave the national forest and the scenic drive is essentially finished.

Turn right at this intersection to go to Nephi, 3 miles to the west, and Interstate 15. A left here takes you into the Sanpete Valley, where several very pretty old Mormon towns merit a sidetrip. The first of these is Fountain Green, 8 miles from the intersection with UT 132, a classic Mormon village of the Sanpete region. Fountain Green, traditionally tied to sheep raising, holds a sheep festival every July, and it is common to see the animals grazing in backyards throughout the town. Other Sanpete communities are described as a sidetrip from Fairview on Drive #18.

Nephi is an orderly little city of 3,500 that is starting to look a little down-at-the-heels these days. It doesn't look so much run-down as *well used*, as if it has passed its economic prime. The town occupies an interesting position geographically. The base of the towering Nebo massif is lovely spruce/pine forests and dramatic alpine terrain, but Nephi also sits at the eastern edge of the rough desert plains and dry, rocky hills of the Great Basin. It is the ideal place for someone who cannot decide between desert and mountain activity and scenery.

Settled in 1851, Nephi was named for the first of the prophets of the Book of Mormon. The place had seen plenty of traffic before the Mormon pioneers moved in. First Fremont Indians then Utes lived in this valley. The Dominguez-Escalante Expedition came through here in 1776, Jedediah Smith visited in 1826 and 1827, and John C. Fremont passed by in 1843-44.

The town prospered as a farm and ranching community, then received a major economic boost when the new rail line came down from Salt Lake City during the 1870s, making Nephi an important agriculture and livestock shipping point. One of Utah's premier rodeos, the Ute Stampede, celebrates Nephi's cowtown heritage.

18

Huntington Canyon/Eccles Canyon Scenic Byways

Huntington to Fairview and Scofield

General description: A traverse of the alpine terrain of the Wasatch Plateau.

Special attractions: Beautiful alpine driving, access to backcountry drives and hiking, quaint Fairview, historic Scofield mining town.

Location: Central Utah, in the Manti-La Sal National Forest. The drive includes Utah Highway 31 from Huntington to Fairview, and Utah Highways 264 and 96 from the intersection with Utah Highway 31 to the old mining town of Scofield.

Drive route number and name: UT 31/264/96, Huntington Canyon Scenic Byway/Eccles Canyon Scenic Byway.

Travel season: While roads are officially open year-round, snow closures are common from November until May.

Camping: Four national forest campgrounds, state park campground at Scofield Reservoir.

Services: All services in Huntington and Fairview; limited services in Scofield.

Nearby attractions: Cleveland-Lloyd Dinosaur Quarry and Scenic Backway, Skyline Drive Scenic Backway, attractive old Sanpete towns along U.S. Highway 89, Manti Temple.

The drive

The Wasatch Plateau is one of the most important geographical features of central Utah, marking the division between the vast Colorado Plateau and the Great Basin. This drive combines the Huntington Canyon and Eccles Canyon scenic byways and provides an excellent introduction to the spectacular high country of the Wasatch Plateau. The length of your drive will vary from 55-75 miles, depending on which options you choose. The route is paved, two-lane highway, suitable for all vehicles, with generally light traffic on both branches of the drive except during hunting season. Expect icy roads and even temporary snow closures in winter; snow tires or chains are required October 1-April 30.

Drive 18: Huntington Canyon/Eccles Canyon Scenic Byways

Huntington to Fairview and Scofield

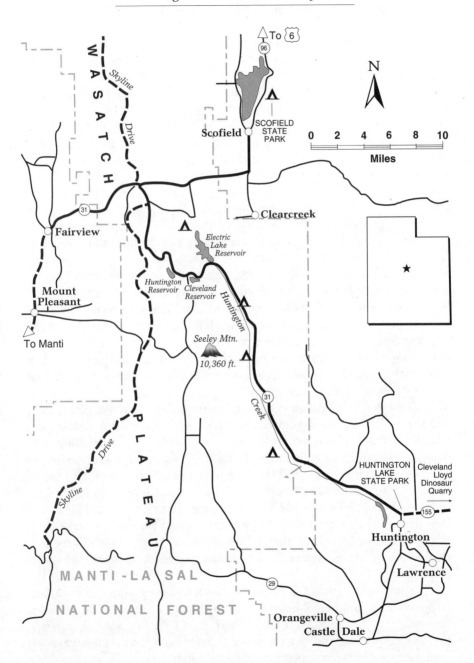

Huntington Canyon is the longest canyon on the Wasatch Plateau, and UT 31 is the only paved road *across* the plateau. The Eccles Canyon drive, which branches from the high point of the Huntington Canyon drive (approximately 10,000 feet elevation) down to Scofield Reservoir, is extremely impressive: lonely and desolate in all the best ways, it is perhaps the best part of this drive and not to be missed. The only real decision you will have to make is whether to finish the standard route of the Huntington Canyon drive down to Fairview (which I strongly recommend). In a conventional vehicle, I suggest doing both right and left forks of this drive, ending in either Fairview or Scofield, depending on which side of the mountain range you wish to finish this drive on. In a large RV, or pulling a trailer, you may not want to drive down one fork then reascend to do the other. If you must choose one over the other, I recommend the Scofield branch.

In either case, the drive begins in Huntington. Close to Huntington is an attraction that all area visitors should to take in, especially if you have children with you: The Cleveland-Lloyd Dinosaur Quarry, source of more than thirty complete skeletons and more than twelve thousand individual bones from seventy different prehistoric animals.

About 147 million years ago the plain to the east of present Huntington was a shallow, muddy-bottomed lake. Dinosaurs were trapped in the boggy areas and many bones accumulated here. The lake eventually dried up, and later geological activity deposited layer upon layer of strata over the site. Wind and water eroded these upper levels, bringing the fossilized bones close enough to the surface to be discovered by local ranchers. Word of these finds reached scientists at the University of Utah, who staged the first of many official digs in 1929.

There is a small visitor center and museum, an attractive picnic area, and a very interesting self-guided nature trail. Among the many dino-exhibits at the visitor center is a complete allosaurus skeletal reconstruction. Perhaps the most interesting feature is the quarry itself. A major excavation site contained within a large metal shed provides a good glimpse of the process of recovering the fossilized bones from the earth. Cleveland-Lloyd Dinosaur Quarry is open weekends, 10 A.M. to 5 P.M., from Easter until Memorial Day, then daily through Labor Day weekend. From Huntington, take Utah Highway 155 to Cleveland, then follow the many signs to the quarry. The road to the quarry is unpaved but well maintained and suitable for all vehicles.

From Huntington, UT 31 heads north and west through luxuriant farmland and ranchland before trending upward into the mouth of a narrowing sandstone canyon with Huntington Creek flowing on the left. Just at the mouth of the canyon, about 8 miles from town, is a large, coal-fired, electrical generating plant. Immediately after the power plant this drive takes on a mountain/canyon aspect as it enters Manti-La Sal National Forest.

This is an absolutely pristine mountain canyon. Three very basic National Forest Service campgrounds (none with drinking water)—Bear Canyon, The Forks, and Old Folks Flat—are located beside the canyon road at 7, 18, and 21 miles from Huntington, respectively. Old Folks Flat was the site of an annual LDS gathering. There are many nice picnic spots and places to fly fish, and the upper reaches of Huntington Creek for the final 4 miles to Electric Lake are designated "fly fishing only." At mile 23 you reach Electric Lake, named for its function as the storage reservoir that supplies the steam turbines at the Huntington generating plant.

This is an air-conditioned place. Most summers the snows here last into July (a good place for a summertime snowball fight), but when summer does come to these high meadows, it comes full bloom. Few places in the American West rival the Wasatch Plateau for abundance and variety of wildflowers.

The road stays high between Electric Lake and past Huntington Reservoir, winding level for 5 miles or so at elevations around 9,500 feet. Early in the summer expect snow here. There are impressive views to the west of the San Pitch Valley, San Pitch Mountains, and Mount Nebo to the northwest.

In 1988, the skeleton of an 11,000-year-old woolly mammoth was found just below the dam at the head of Huntington Reservoir. This important find is on display at the College of Eastern Utah Prehistoric Museum in Price (a replica is on display at the Fairview Museum).

The road finally tops out above 9,700 feet after winding along up high for about 7 or 8 miles from the southern tip of Electric Lake. Just before this high point, you will encounter what looks like a major turnoff on the right, signed prominently for Scofield. This is a branch road, *not* the main Eccles Canyon road to Scofield, which is farther along. Shortly after that right, there is a left for the southern part of the Skyline Drive.

The Skyline Drive is one of the Wasatch Plateau's featured scenic attractions. This partly paved road, a designated scenic backway, winds along the steep spine of the Wasatch Plateau for more than 87 miles, much of it above 10,000 feet. The most spectacular stretch of this drive is the 30 miles running from UT 31 south to the Joe's Valley-Ephraim Road, fairly consistently between 10,500-10,800 feet elevation. Some parts of this drive run along hogback ridges barely wider than the road itself, with outstanding views of Sanpete Valley farms and towns below. Far to the east are the plateaus of the Tavaputs; 50 miles to the north are the summits of the Wasatch Front. Portions of the Skyline Drive are passable in conventional vehicles year-round. If you intend to explore this very beautiful high-level road, check first in Huntington or Fairview (or any Manti-La Sal Forest ranger station) for current conditions.

Three-quarters of a mile in descent from the Huntington Canyon high point on the Fairview (northwest) side is a viewpoint that looks out to the

Utah Highway 264 winds across pristine alpine meadows above Electric Lake on the Wasatch Plateau.

west and north toward Mount Nebo. Just past this point is the well-marked turnoff on the right to Scofield, which is the right-hand branch of this driving route. You can take this right and skip ahead to do that leg or continue the descent to Fairview. Also here is the turnoff on the right for the northern part of the Skyline Drive.

The descent on UT 31 to Fairview runs through extremely beautiful forest of aspen and fir. After 7 miles of descent, you reach the not-terribly-scenic, rather ramshackle outskirts of the greater Fairview metropolitan area.

Do not be misled by the suburbs: Fairview is both attractive and interesting. With lots of old brick homes, this is a classic little Mormon country town. Take a few minutes to drive around the side streets, where you are liable to see sheep grazing in yards, kids riding horses, and other such bucolic sights. Toward the south of town is a well-used rodeo arena.

The Fairview Museum is huge, with everything from a mastodon replica to lots of interesting old Mormon pioneer artifacts. It really is a must-see for anyone interested in the history of the Sanpete Valley, or in small-town Utah life in general. There are excellent exhibits of nineteenth-century furniture, pioneer spinning wheels, agricultural machines and tools, and a nice collection of Native American basketry and pottery. Outside the museum are displays of cook wagons, farm implements, and coaches. If you like the eclectic jumble of neat old stuff you find in small-town museums across the West, you will *really* like this place. The museum is located at 100 North and 100 East. Admission is free, open Memorial Day through September, 10 A.M. to 5 P.M. (1 P.M. to 8 P.M. on Sundays), and by appointment the rest of the year.

Fairview is a classic Mormon village of the Sanpete Valley.

The Sanpete Valley is considered the best area in the state to see the cultural remnants of nineteenth-century Mormon settlement. An interesting sidetrip from Fairview is the drive south on US 89 through the picturesque old Mormon communities of Mt. Pleasant, Spring City, and Ephraim to the regional center of Manti. Spring City was first settled in 1852, abandoned during the Walker Indian War (1853-54), resettled in 1858, abandoned again during the Blackhawk War (1866), then resettled for good the following year. Its many nineteenth-century buildings have earned Spring City the nickname "the Williamsburg of the West." Ephraim and Manti are both attractive and substantial communities, settled early in Utah's pioneer era, and preserving the architecture of the period. Manti is the site of perhaps the most beautiful of the state's eight Mormon Temples, and the third oldest, after St. George and Logan.

From Fairview, 400 North (UT 31) heads back up and over the Wasatch Plateau. As you will have gathered from the earlier descent, the ascent of UT 31 up Fairview Canyon is much steeper (to eight percent grade) and narrower than Huntington Canyon. It is 8 miles to the Scofield/Skyline north intersection.

Just after this turnoff, make sure you angle to the right with the main road (100 yards past the turnoff); if you go straight here you will head north on the Skyline Drive. Once past the Skyline Drive turnoff, the well-marked road to Scofield is straight ahead. You are now on the Eccles Canyon Scenic Byway.

The road descends through lovely meadows and high summer pastures, well watered with creeks and ponds. Land up here alternates between national forest and tracts of private property, so there are high ranch pastures and the private homes of a few *very* fortunate individuals. Flat Canyon Campground is about 3.5 miles from the start of the Eccles Canyon drive. Just past the campground the road begins to descend steeply for a couple of miles to the northern end of Electric Lake before making a short final ascent and descent in earnest at about 11 miles from the start of the drive.

The terrain up here has a real alpine look, or perhaps more like somewhere in Norway. It is absolutely pristine. Beyond Electric Lake there is no mark of Man up here, except this road—completely desolate, in the best way. Because this is just about at timberline, the tree cover is very thin, so views are quite open. In late July and early August, these meadows are alive with California corn lily, wild geranium, green gentian, scarlet gilia, purple lupine, wild delphinium, wild sweet pea, alpine sunflower, woodland star, forget-me-not, bluebell, charlock, hyssop, blue penstemon, and columbine. There is perhaps no prettier alpine drive in all of America than this short stretch.

At this point you descend into Eccles Canyon. At mile 13 you reach the first of several large coal mines in the Scofield region. Note on the left the interesting coal tramway along the hillside, stretching for 2 miles down the valley. Just at the lower terminus of this very impressive transport system is the Skyline Mine, which produces between 3.5 and 5 million tons of coal each year. On the right is the turnoff for the old mining town of Clear Creek, a nice diversion 3 miles up this branch canyon on good road. The town is rather run down and forlorn, though there are a few well-maintained homes amidst many ruined miners shacks, and some evidence that this was once a robust little community.

About 3.5 miles beyond the Clear Creek turnoff is the hamlet of Scofield, nicely situated at the southern end of Scofield Reservoir. While Clear Creek is in the sort of narrow valley we generally associate with mining towns, Scofield occupies a wider, more open setting. The pretty pasturelands at the town's south end somewhat mask its mining-town look. The town is somewhat run down in a very picturesque way: large old stone and brick buildings, characteristic miners' cabins, and the usual trailer homes. It's a very nice hodge-podge that does include a gas station and grocery store.

Utah's officially designated Eccles Canyon Scenic Byway technically ends at the Clear Creek turnoff. It seems the official designators feel that as soon as you run into mining operations a drive can't be scenic anymore. In fact, while this may not be as picturesque as the high meadows and alpine terrain above, these mining operations and mining towns can be highly visual and certainly very interesting. This drive is definitely worthwhile all the way to the town of Scofield.

Scofield is famous in mining history annals as the site of one of the worst mine disasters of all time. On May 1, 1900, an explosion at the Winter Quarters Mine ignited clouds of coal dust, sweeping flames through the shafts and setting off two dozen kegs of blasting powder. Nearly two hundred bodies were recovered, some of them children as young as thirteen. One Scofield family lost six sons and three grandsons that day. It was common practice at the time for boys to be employed at menial tasks in the mines. The tragedy at Scofield was often cited as an example in continuing efforts, early in this century, to enact and enforce child labor laws.

The Scofield Cemetery sits on a bench to the west of town. Note the number of gravestones bearing the date May 1, 1900. In all, nearly 150 victims of the great tragedy are buried here.

Below the town of Scofield, this drive declines in interest and beauty. Scofield Reservoir is pretty uninspiring—just a big hole full of water—although it is said to be full of fish. Scofield State Park, with a full-service campground, is 5.5 miles farther along.

The rest of the way to U.S. Highway 6 is scenic enough, though unspectacular. Once past the minor residential development at Scofield Reservoir, the road leaves the canyon and heads across sagebrush flats. This land is mostly fenced off as private ranchland, so there's no telling what the

The small cemetery at Scofield is the resting place of nearly 150 of the almost 200 miners who died in the Scofield Mine Disaster of May 1, 1900.

future holds in the way of development. It is 10 miles to the highway, where a left turn takes you quickly to Interstate 15. A right on US 6 will take you to Helper, where you can pick up Drive #19 in progress from Duchesne.

19

Indian Canyon/Nine-Mile Canyon Loop

Duchesne to Price and north to Myton

General description: A highly diverse drive combining lovely forested canyons, the traverse of old Indian and settler trails, and many cultural and historical attractions.

Special attractions: Ashley National Forest, Indian Canyon, historic attractions and museums in Helper and Price, Nine-Mile Canyon, rock art sites.

Location: Central Utah.

Drive route number and name: U.S. Highway 191/Indian Canyon Scenic Byway, Nine-Mile Canyon Scenic Backway.

Travel season: Generally year-round. The unpaved Nine-Mile Canyon road may be a problem when wet. Snow can cause difficult winter driving on any part of this drive and can close Nine-Mile Canyon. The foliage in Indian Canyon is especially brilliant in fall.

Camping: Limited. State park campground at Duchesne, one national forest campground on US 191, commercial RV parks at Price and Wellington, free RV overnights at Duchesne.

Services: All services in Price and Helper, most services in Duchesne, basic services in Wellington and Myton.

Nearby attractions: Reservation Ridge Scenic Backway.

The drive

The two travel corridors described by this drive were the two early ways in and out of the remote Uinta Basin region. Until the mid 1880s the only way into the basin was on horseback. The old stage road, which followed an ancient Indian trail through Nine-Mile Canyon and over the ridge into the Duchesne River Valley, was instrumental in the development of the basin by connecting the established railroad community of Price with the frontier military post at Fort Duchesne. In 1886 the canyon road was widened and improved by troopers of the all-black Ninth U.S. Cavalry, and it served as the only real route into the Uinta region for more than twenty-five years.

This region remained true "Wild West" frontier longer than almost anywhere else in the American West. Butch Cassidy, who was known to have used the Nine-Mile Canyon road for eluding posses, made perhaps the most daring robbery of his career, in 1897, at the paymaster's office of the Pleasant Valley Coal Company just north of Helper.

In 1905, when the Uintah and Ouray Indian Reservation was opened to white settlement, thousands of settlers traveled this route to new homes in the wilderness. Even after the Indian Canyon Road (present US 191) was established in 1915, mail still came along the older road during the winter months until the late 1920s, as it is 1,700 feet lower than the high road over Indian Creek Pass and was less prone to snow closure.

This drive combines Utah's designated Indian Canyon Scenic Byway with nearby Nine-Mile Canyon Scenic Backway, creating a convenient (if somewhat time-consuming) 145-mile loop. The initial segment of this route is an alpine drive up beautiful Indian Canyon, 45 miles of wilderness scenery with a handful of picturesque farms and ranches at the Duchesne end. This part of the drive should take one to two hours, depending on how often you stop for pictures. The Nine-Mile Canyon Backway is approximately 78 miles and requires at least three hours to complete. Plan on spending at least an hour in Helper and Price—much more if you intend to visit the highly recommended College of Eastern Utah Prehistoric Museum at Price. It is possible to do the entire loop as a very long all-day excursion from Salt Lake City, but a more practical strategy would involve an overnight stay in Helper, Price, or Duchesne, or a night of camping en route. This would allow ample time to poke around historic Helper and Price.

This is one of only a few drives in this guide that involve substantial driving on unpaved roads. The mostly unpaved Nine-Mile Canyon Backway is, however, wide and well maintained. In dry conditions it presents no problems for any vehicle, though it is not recommended for vehicles longer than 22 feet. Check in Price about road conditions, especially if it has been wet.

The route starts at Duchesne, a town that seems remote and off the beaten track even today. According to one account, Duchesne was named for a nun, making this one of the few places in Utah named for a non-Spanish Catholic. There is a campground at nearby Starvation Reservoir State Park.

From Duchesne turn south on US 191, signed for Castle Gate (44 miles). The road climbs gradually up the canyon for 25 extremely beautiful miles past picture-perfect ranches along Indian Creek. The final 3 or 4 miles of ascent to 9,100-foot Indian Creek Pass climb steeply.

Just after leaving Ashley National Forest, watch for a dirt road on the right, signed as Reservation Ridge Scenic Backway. This mountain backway winds for about 45 miles along Reservation Ridge, with broad views out over Strawberry Reservoir and Ashley National Forest, before meeting U.S. Highway 6 near Soldier Summit. The single-lane dirt road is closed from November 15 to May 15, and four-wheel drive is recommended.

Drive 19: Indian Canyon/Nine-Mile Canyon Loop
Duchesne to Price and north to Myton

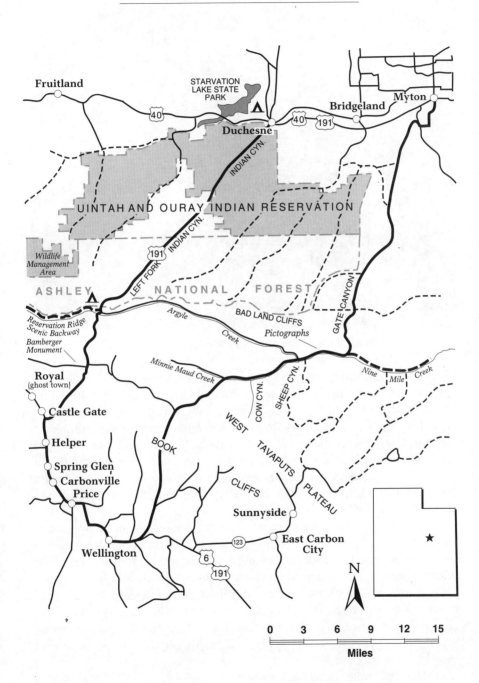

Fruitland

STARVATION LAKE STATE PARK

40

Duchesne

Bridgeland

Myton

40 191

INDIAN CYN.

UINTAH AND OURAY INDIAN RESERVATION

191 INDIAN CYN.

LEFT FORK

Wildlife Management Area

ASHLEY NATIONAL FOREST

GATE CANYON

Reservation Ridge Scenic Backway

Bamberger Monument

Argyle Creek

BAD LAND CLIFFS

Pictographs

Royal (ghost town)

Minnie Maud Creek

Nine Mile Creek

SHEEP CYN.

Castle Gate

Helper

BOOK

WEST

COW CYN.

Spring Glen
Carbonville
Price

CLIFFS

TAVAPUTS

PLATEAU

Sunnyside

123

East Carbon City

Wellington

6

191

N

0   3   6   9   12   15
Miles

Abandoned homestead in Indian Canyon, south of Duchesne.

The descent to the west of Indian Creek Pass is steeper than the east side. About 7 miles in descent, note the small but attractive monument on the right, dedicated to Governor Simon Bamberger. It is unclear precisely why this monument to Utah's first non-Mormon governor (an immigrant German Jew) was erected here, except that he was in office when most of the work on the Indian Canyon Road was completed. One story is that it was put up in gratitude for Bamberger's sending convicts from the Gunnison penitentiary to help build the road. (I can't imagine the *convicts* felt too grateful about that.)

The scenic aspect of this part of the drive comes to an abrupt end at the coal processing plant at the intersection of US 6 and US 191, just north of Helper. Turn left here for Helper and Price and a short touristic interlude based on some very interesting social and industrial history.

During the 1880s the Denver and Rio Grande Western Railroad discovered and developed the vast coal deposits of Carbon County. Since then, the ups and downs of the coal mining industry have determined the character of life in Carbon County, a place distinctly different from the rest of mostly Mormon Utah.

Helper, 2 miles from the intersection of US 191 and US 6, was named for the "helper" engines attached to heavily loaded trains for the long haul up to Soldier Summit. Helper was also known as "the town of 57 varieties," due to its ethnic diversity. About one-third of all Carbon County coal miners at the turn of the century were Italian. There were also large numbers of Southern Slavs and Finns. Shortly after the turn of the century, large numbers of Greeks added to the ethnic potpourri. All of this gives the Helper-Price area a distinct quality, more like other Western mining districts (places that shared this sort of ethnic diversity) than the agriculture-based valleys settled by the LDS pioneers.

Helper has an attractive and interesting main street and historic district, worth spending some time poking around. The town is a tad rundown and has that gritty mining-town character to it, but there are clear indications of the wealth that was floating around here at a time when people knew how to build on a grand scale. Helper's chief tourist attraction, and the best place for a quick overview of the recent regional history, is the Western Mining and Railroad Museum, at 296 South Main Street.

The best place for an overview of the *prehistory* of the region is down the road in Price. Like Helper, Price has a large non-Mormon population. Price's Hellenic Orthodox Church is reputedly one of the oldest continuously occupied Greek churches in America. But the big attraction here, and a must-see for anyone interested in things prehistoric, is the excellent College of Eastern Utah Prehistoric Museum. This museum has one of the country's best collections of dino-stuff. In the Hall of Dinosaurs stand four complete dinosaur skeletons; the museum also exhibits a complete woolly mammoth skeleton, unearthed in Huntington Canyon in 1988. Kids can measure their feet against dinosaur tracks preserved in coal. There are also excellent displays of Fremont Culture artifacts, including a very impressive collection of rock art photographs and reproductions. The museum, at 155 East Main Street, also houses a regional travel council office.

There is enough to see in the Helper-Price environs to warrant staying over and continuing with the Nine-Mile Canyon drive in the morning. When it is time to tear yourself away, drive south from Price 7.5 miles on US 6 through the town of Wellington. About 2 miles past Wellington turn left at the well-marked road for Nine-Mile Canyon Backway. After about 1.5 miles of non-descript suburbs, double-wide trailers, etc., you will have passed the build-up and pretty much be in the wilderness. WARNING: As the sign indicates, 75 miles with no services on this route.

Of the several explanations for why a canyon longer than forty miles should be named *Nine-Mile Canyon*, the most reasonable centers on the nine-mile triangulation survey of the area made by John Wesley Powell's mapmaker during the landmark 1869 Powell expedition. Maps presented to Congress clearly indicate Nine-Mile Creek.

Long known to Ute and earlier Fremont Culture Indians, this historic trail still has the feel of the past, an aura partly preserved by the dust of

Main Street in the old coal-mining town of Helper.

driving on (mostly) unpaved road. The drive will take three to four hours, depending on your pace (and how much time you spend searching for the fascinating rock art that abounds here). There are many attractions along this drive: I will try to give accurate mileages, all measured from the start of the scenic backway.

NOTE: Please keep in mind that there is a real mix of public/private land along this drive. There are many attractive old cabins (some ruined), some on BLM-administered land, but mostly on private ranches. It is especially important to honor the private property signs here, where the distinction between public and private is sometimes indistinct.

Ten miles from the Scenic Backway sign you will pass a ruined cabin in the vicinity of Soldier Creek. At the mouth of Soldier Creek Canyon the road begins to climb. At mile 12.5 you will pass a coal company, and the pavement ends. At about mile 16 you come into the wide valley called Whitmore Park. There was a stage station at the west end of this valley (probably near one of the several corrals).

Cross the bridge over Minnie Maude Creek at mile 21.3. Half a mile farther is a BLM sign describing the canyon. At about mile 26 you should begin to notice the first major petroglyph panels on a rocky point to the left of the road. In fact, you can see carvings all along the road from here if you look carefully at the dark, varnished areas of the rock.

The old townsite of Harper is a little past mile 30. About 1.5 miles past the remains of Harper is a balanced rock to the left of the road. When viewed from the west, this rock is said to resemble Porky Pig. (To those of us lacking imagination, it looks pretty much like . . . a big chunk of rock.) Just past this rock, on the left, is an excellent panel of rock art.

The cavalry troopers who improved the road in 1886 also raised the telegraph line through the canyon on surplus metal poles left over from the Civil War. Many of these poles can still be seen today. At mile 33 is the attractive stone house built by canyon resident and long-time telegraph operator Ed Harmon.

A BLM sign indicates the road up Harmon Canyon to the right. Just after the sign, on the left and about 30 feet above the road, are some of the canyon's best petroglyphs. After another 1.5 miles, stop at the prominent tall cottonwood that spreads its boughs across the road. Look up to the left, about 200 feet from the road, and note the very distinct snake design. For the next few miles the walls to the left will be full of ancient art.

At about mile 38 is the site of the Brock Ranch, a substantial cluster of log houses and newer concrete block buildings, all marked as private. This ranch served for some time as the headquarters for Preston Nutter's Utah cattle empire. Nutter had more than 25,000 head of cattle ranged on land from here south to the North Rim of the Grand Canyon. As the midway point between Price and the garrison at Fort Duchesne, this was also the

The sandstone walls above the road in Nine-Mile Canyon are a treasury of ancient rock art.

telegraph relay station—the stone building and log cabin next to the cliff were used for this purpose.

At 0.25 mile past Brock's is a bit of route confusion at a major split in the road. The sign reads straight ahead for Prickly Pear Canyon, Dry Canyon, and Cottonwood Canyon; left for Myton. If you go straight (continuing in Nine-Mile Canyon) there are lots of interesting Indian petroglyphs as well as some old granaries, but the road gets progressively rougher and eventually ends. Take the left turn for Myton or return to this point after exploring Nine-Mile Canyon further.

At this point you actually depart Nine-Mile Canyon, climbing up and out of the drainage to cross into the Duchesne River Valley. From the intersection, the road winds and bounces up a dry canyon for 6.5 miles (this is the roughest stretch of the entire route, but passable in any vehicle when dry) until it reaches a high point above the canyon, with great views off to the north. The road then descends back into the sage-covered scrubland below.

Outlaw Ambush Point (site of an aborted stage robbery attempt by some Butch Cassidy pals) is 1 mile from the intersection; the site of Gate

Arch is 0.5 mile farther. The natural arch that once stood here was dynamited in 1905 out of fear that it might collapse on a passing wagon. At just under 15 miles from the intersection are the extensive ruins of the important watering stop called, simply, Wells. After another 5 miles the Duchesne Valley and the Uintas come into view to the north. Then begins a gentle descent through scrub hills dotted with oil wells.

The pavement resumes at about mile 27 from the intersection in Nine-Mile Canyon. Two and a half miles past the start of the pavement, turn left at the yield sign to reach U.S. Highway 40 after another 1.5 miles. Turn left to reach Duchesne (8 miles) and the fastest return to the Salt Lake Valley.

20

Flaming Gorge - Uintas
Scenic Byway
Vernal to Manila and Dutch John

General description: A 150-mile drive along the eastern edge of the Uinta Mountains and along the southern rim of Flaming Gorge Reservoir, providing outstanding views of the river gorge and the High Uintas and a variety of roadside geology lessons.

Special attractions: Utah Field House of Natural History/Dinosaur Garden, Ashley National Forest and Uinta Mountains, Flaming Gorge Reservoir and Dam, Sheep Creek Canyon, Swett Ranch.

Location: Northeast Utah. The drive begins in Vernal, runs north to Flaming Gorge Reservoir, then explores branches to Manila and Dutch John.

Drive route number and name: U.S. Highway 191/Utah Highway 44, Flaming Gorge-Uintas Scenic Byway.

Travel season: Year-round. Ice and snow may create hazards during winter.

Camping: Eleven campgrounds in Flaming Gorge Recreation Area, numerous national forest campgrounds along US 191 and Sheep Creek Loop.

Services: All services in Vernal and Manila; limited services at Red Canyon, Flaming Gorge Lodge, and Dutch John.

Nearby attractions: Diamond Mountain/Jones Hole Hatchery, Dinosaur National Monument and Quarry, High Uintas Wilderness Area, Red Cloud/Dry Fork Scenic Backway, Brown's Park Scenic Backway.

The drive

Like so many of the places described in this book, Flaming Gorge presents an especially vivid lesson in geology at its most dramatic and most varied. This drive presents terrific contrasts in scenery: the rugged Uinta Mountains; beautiful alpine forests; a brilliantly colored, 91-mile reservoir at the bottom of a dramatic river gorge; and high desert country to the north.

Because of difficult terrain, poor access to the Uinta Basin, and extremes in weather, this was never a popular region for agriculturally minded settlers, either Native American or white pioneer. In terms of permanent settlement, the place is, simply . . . defiant. Throughout history, however, it has been a favorite hunting ground for Indians and mountain men and a

Drive 20: Flaming Gorge - Uintas Scenic Byway
Vernal to Manila and Dutch John

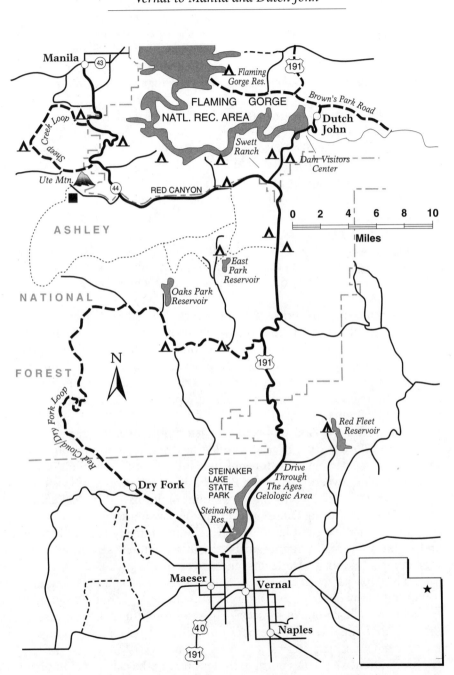

popular hideout for outlaws. Early explorers John C. Fremont and John Wesley Powell marvelled over the rugged beauty of the gorge.

Today the area is a favorite for tourists and recreationists, and a relatively undisturbed home for a tremendous variety of wildlife. Flaming Gorge National Recreation Area offers visitors two information centers, more than six hundred camping and picnic sites, and more than one hundred miles of trails.

The official state-designated Flaming Gorge Scenic Byway runs from Vernal north on US 191 to Greendale Junction, then takes the left (west) branch (UT 44) to Manila. I've added a recommended sidetrip of the eastern branch, continuing north on US 191 to Dutch John, and an especially recommended drive along the Sheep Creek Geological Loop.

This is a long drive, at least 150 miles as a round-trip from Vernal, with options for interesting sidetrips. With stops to enjoy the scenery, count on at least five hours to complete the drive. There are optional finishes, depending on whether you wish to return to Vernal. All roads along this drive are paved, in excellent condition, and appropriate for all vehicles; traffic is generally light. Snow can be a problem in the winter, though the road is kept clear year-round.

Begin this drive in Vernal, the dinosaur capital of the world and a town with a very distinct "on the edge of civilization as we know it" atmosphere. Few cities in America developed as late in our social history as Vernal did, or remained so isolated. This was still a pioneer outpost until well into the current century, partly because there was very little early LDS interest in settling the region, due to an unfavorable report by an exploration party sent forth by Brigham Young in 1861.

The Utah Field House of Natural History interprets the region's historical, prehistorical, ecological, and geological diversity. A large mural showing the various geological features of the Uinta region, from the Precambrian (2.7 billion years old) to the Pleistocene (11,000 years old) is especially useful in understanding the foundations of the drive through Flaming Gorge. The neighboring Dinosaur Gardens display fourteen life-sized statues of the region's ancient inhabitants (including a ninety-foot diplodocus and eighteen-foot-tall tyrannosaurus), all in an outdoor setting of native rock and period foliage. Don't miss these two attractions.

Now that you're in the mood for dinosaurs, it would be a shame to drive all the way out to Vernal and *not* visit Dinosaur National Monument. In addition to being one of the world's greatest prehistoric boneyards, the drives along the Green River here are extremely scenic. This highly recommended sidetrip begins in Jensen, 12 miles east of Vernal on U.S. Highway 40, then 4.5 miles north to the entrance to the national monument and visitor center. At the visitor center you can pick up a handy self-guided-tour brochure.

Utah Highway 44 traverses the east side of Flaming Gorge National Recreation Area.

Another recommended sidetrip from Vernal is the Jones Hole Scenic Backway. The drive traverses a variety of local ecosystems, from desert sagebrush to alpine aspen grove, before dropping into a narrow canyon at Jones Hole, where an important national fish hatchery supplies trout for Utah, Colorado, and Wyoming. This is one of the few fully paved scenic backways in the state. The road is narrow, however, and may be difficult in winter conditions. The backway starts 4 miles east of Vernal, departing from Utah Highway 149. The 80-mile drive takes at least two hours, plus time for sightseeing. The regional travel office in Vernal can give you a brochure describing the drive.

Flaming Gorge Recreation Area is approximately 41 miles north of Vernal. Head north on Vernal Avenue (US 191), and just beyond the outskirts of town (about 3.5 miles from the town center) you will see on the right a small information board for "Drive Through the Ages Geological Tour." Stop to read the short route description and pick up the brochure about the signed geological attractions that line the route. There is also a nice cross-section picture showing the eighteen layers of the earth revealed along the drive.

Just past this board you will pass four blue/white geological information signs in rapid succession, the first of many. Soon on the left is the very

Red Canyon Overlook provides perhaps the most spectacular views of Flaming Gorge Reservoir.

attractive Steinaker Reservoir. The landscape is still sage-covered here, but toward the north end of the lake it becomes wooded. Near this end of the lake, another sign indicates a Jurrasic Morrison formation—the graveyard of dinosaurs. No doubt these are the dinosaurs for which Vernal is famous. Steinaker State Recreation Area (camping) lies at the north end of the reservoir. About 4 miles past the reservoir is a sign on the right for Red Fleet State Park, where there is an especially nice campground and hiking trails. The road is remarkably well marked with geological info signs nearly every hundred yards.

Fourteen miles north of Vernal, on the left, is the turnoff on Forest Road 018 for the Red Cloud/Dry Fork Scenic Backway, also signed for East Park Reservoir. Four miles along FR 018, the route forks: the right fork goes north to East Park Reservoir (nice secluded camping), the left fork is the backway drive to Dry Fork. This is a lovely forest and mountain drive on one of the few roads that provide access to the lower part of the Uinta Mountains. Driving conditions on this backway vary greatly, from paved to quite rough. Check for current conditions in Vernal, especially if you are not in a high-clearance vehicle. Driving time for the 45-mile loop is about two hours.

At around mile 17 the sagebrush flats turn to pinyon and juniper. A few miles farther and this has become an alpine drive, with aspen the predominant roadside tree. The Uintah/Daggett county line is the high point of this drive at 8,428 feet.

The road passes two nice national forest campgrounds, Red Springs and Lodgepole, then enters Flaming Gorge National Recreation Area at about 33 miles north of Vernal. A mile and a half farther is the intersection at Greendale Junction; right is the continuation of US 191 to Flaming Gorge Dam and the town of Dutch John. We'll go straight here, designated UT 44 and signed for Manila.

About 3 miles past this intersection is the turnoff on the right for Red Canyon Overlook. One mile up the overlook road is Red Canyon Lodge, where you will find a restaurant, cabins, groceries, gas, fishing, horseback rides, a gift shop, and a kids fishing pond. Also up this road are two campgrounds, a visitor center, and picnic area. It is 3 miles to the overlook.

Red Canyon Overlook presents probably the most spectacular view of Flaming Gorge Reservoir. From this elevation, 1,700 feet above the reservoir, the water appears in deepest hues of blues and greens. And that 1,700 feet is *straight down*, with the cliffs below the overlook almost perfectly vertical.

It is about 12 miles of forest driving to reach the south access to the Sheep Creek Canyon loop, just past Deep Creek Campground, on the left. This interesting sidetrip is described on the return from Manila, but if you intend *not* to return via UT 44, you might want to do the Sheep Creek option from here, reversing the direction of the description. One reason for *not* doing the Sheep Creek Canyon loop on your way north is that it means missing the truly spectacular view from the turnout and overlook about 2 miles farther north on UT 44, just at the start of the long descent to Manila.

Tiny Manila is the county seat and largest community of Daggett County; Dutch John is the only other "town" in a county that probably has a larger population of bears than people. The official state census for the county is 690 (but that probably *includes* the bears.) Yet even with only 207 residents in the Greater Manila Metropolitan Area, it isn't the smallest county seat in Utah; Junction, in Piute County, enjoys that honor. Small as it is, Manila still provides most basic traveler services.

From Manila you can do the big loop north through Wyoming to Green River (Utah Highway 43 becomes Wyoming 530), then back down US 191 along the east side of Flaming Gorge. Or you can double back from here to take in the Sheep Creek Canyon Geological Drive and back to Greendale Junction. Another important option to consider is to head west on UT 43 (this soon becomes Wyoming 414) on good roads across the northeast flank of the Uintas to reach Interstate 80 at Fort Bridger, Wyoming. This is the quickest route back to Salt Lake City (a little more than three hours from here) and a nice drive in its own right. This option also presents a good opportunity to visit the interesting historical site of Fort Bridger.

In retracing UT 44 south from Manila, it is just under 6 miles to the northern entrance, on the right, to the Sheep Creek Canyon Geological Drive. This 15-mile sidetrip (one half to one hour) is highly recommended. The road is paved, though not in great condition. There are several campgrounds and picnic areas along way, including a very attractive campground immediately on entering the loop road. Two miles up Sheep Creek Road, on the hill to the right, is the burial site for Cleophas Dowd (1857-1897), who homesteaded here from 1885 until 1897, when he was killed by his partner. Two of his children are also buried here.

At mile 3, just past Sheep Creek Ranch (where you may see llamas grazing), you enter the Sheep Creek Geological Area. Sheep Creek Canyon was split by the Uinta Crest Fault, which exposed eighteen distinct layers of strata. All along this drive are nice markers (brown here) describing the geological formations.

This is a really stunning canyon, with outstanding formations. Just past mile 6 the road climbs out of the canyon (nothing radical) and leaves the official geological area. The road is still paved here, although a little rough, and has turned into a very nice alpine drive. At just under mile 10 is the turnoff for Ute Tower Fire Lookout (signed Forest Road 221 for Spirit Lake and Brown Lake). To get to the lookout, turn right, then a quick right again at the signposts. Follow FR 221 a little more than 1 mile to Forest

Road 5 on the left. It is about 1.5 mile up FR 5 to the tower. This road is unpaved and rather rough but no problem for most vehicles (you wouldn't want to drive it in an RV, and you might leave your trailer at the signposts).

Definitely try to get to the tower. Staffed by a Forest Service volunteer, its primary function today is as a tourist attraction, though it does still serve as a fire lookout. The tower was built as a Civilian Conservation Corps project and was in service from 1937 until 1968, when fire-spotting planes largely replaced towers. There are no public facilities and no water. From the tower you have some of the best views of the generally roadless High Uintas, and you can even see more clearly that the Uintas are really a massive, bumpy dome or bulge in the earth.

At mile 13 you finish the Sheep Creek loop and return to UT 44, turning right/south. It is about 14 miles from the south entrance of the loop to the intersection with US 191, where you will turn left/north for Flaming Gorge Dam and Dutch John. This road is sometimes closed in winter.

Whether you are interested in visiting the dam or not, you should at least drive up to see the Swett Ranch. Oscar Swett homesteaded this land in 1909 and developed the ranch over the next fifty-eight years. Swett sold the ranch in 1968, and the Forest Service bought it in 1972, preserving it as an example of a traditional Utah family ranch. Half a mile north on US 191 is the turnoff on the left for Swett Ranch. The ranch is 1.25 mile up this reasonable dirt road, which may not be suitable for large RVs and trailers. Swett Ranch is open 9 A.M. until 5 P.M. Thursday-Monday only, between Memorial Day and Labor Day.

It's a little more than 5 miles farther along US 191 to the visitor center at Flaming Gorge Dam. There is a very nice self-guided tour of the dam and power plant, beginning with an elevator descent to the riverbed.

If you have the time and energy, it is worth the effort to continue this drive out to the viewpoint beyond Antelope Flat, where you will get a sense of how John Wesley Powell must have felt in describing his first impression of the gorge: "The river enters the range by a flaring, brilliant red gorge that may be seen from the north a score of miles away." The gorge really *can* appear to glow red from down here, due largely to its composition of red quartzites and red shale.

The town of Dutch John, about 3 miles beyond the dam, was built in 1957 to accommodate workers at the dam. Today it is a strictly practical commercial center of fair usefulness but little touristic interest. About 2.5 miles past Dutch John, watch for the turnoff on the left for Antelope Flat. From the top of this eastern branch of the Flaming Gorge drive, it is possible to continue on US 191 north to Green River, Wyoming, and quick I-80 returns (approximately three hours on interstate) to Salt Lake City.

The old Oscar Swett Ranch is maintained by the
National Park Service as a historic attraction.

For a more adventuresome return to Vernal, Brown's Park Backway (described earlier), which runs east and south to join the paved Jones Hole Road, is highly recommended. This route passes through some of the finest scenery in northeastern Utah and gives a glimpse of the region's pioneer era at such historic sites as the Jarvie Ranch. The 55-mile unpaved backway, suitable for most passenger vehicles in dry conditions, requires approximately two hours to complete. Inquire first at the Forest Service office in Dutch John.

21

Mirror Lake Scenic Byway
Kamas to the Wyoming line

General description: Sixty-five miles of the most pristine alpine country to be seen from any paved highway in the country.

Special attractions: Mountain lakes and meadows, superb views, wildlife, camping, hiking, fishing.

Location: Northern Utah. The byway runs between Kamas and the national forest boundary, just south of the Wyoming state line.

Drive route number and name: Utah Highway 150, Mirror Lake Scenic Byway.

Travel season: Varies, depending on early snowfall and late snowpack. The highest part of the road can remain closed until early July. By early October it is likely to close with any good storm.

Camping: Twenty-four national forest campgrounds and ample opportunity for primitive camping.

Services: All services in Heber City and Evanston, Wyoming; basic services in Kamas; no services along the route.

Nearby attractions: Broadhead Meadow Scenic Backway, North Slope Scenic Backway.

The drive

This is one of the most spectacular mountain wilderness drives in America. The Mirror Lake Scenic Byway is one of only two places along the entire Uinta Mountain range where a paved road penetrates this wilderness enough to give an idea of just how grandly deserted this region is (the other is the west branch of the Flaming Gorge Byway, Drive #20).

Without their year-long snow mantle, the Uintas would not be particularly attractive peaks. They are hardly "Alp-like," being much broader, and they lack the elegant, steep summits and sharp ridgelines of, say, the Tetons to the north. But the Uintas form a proper wilderness, barely penetrated by roads of any sort, retaining a true sense of what the land was like before it became domesticated. On the Mirror Lake Scenic Byway you will come face to face with Nature, and you may feel rather in awe of the power of untamed places.

Trailheads along the Mirror Lake road lead to some of the best alpine hikes and backpacking trails in America. There are also more than two dozen designated campgrounds on or just off the byway. For really detailed information on trails, campgrounds, and other recreational opportunities, stop at the Forest Service information office in Kamas.

The Mirror Lake Scenic Byway is entirely paved, with numerous turnouts, and driveable in any size vehicle. Traffic is usually moderate mid week, heavy on weekends. It has been known to snow (hard) in the middle of summer at 10,687-foot Bald Mountain Pass, and the weather in the Uintas can be extremely unpredictable at *any* time; be prepared for emergencies, and be sure to bring along warm clothing. September can be a beautiful time for this drive, with generally clear, cool days and cold nights. This byway is generally closed from mid-October until May, though exact dates depend entirely on snowfall.

The drive begins in the pleasant mountain village of Kamas. To reach Kamas from Salt Lake City, take Interstate 80 east to the U.S. Highway 40 (Heber City) exit, then watch for Utah Highway 248 on the left, 5 miles south of the interstate. Kamas is about 8 miles from the intersection.

Center Street in Kamas is UT 150, at the only real intersection in town. The Forest Service office is just after you turn onto UT 150, about half a block on the right. From here it is 32 miles to Mirror Lake and 72 miles to Evanston, Wyoming.

It is 2.5 miles from the outskirts of Kamas to Kamas Fish Hatchery (open daily, 8 A.M. to 4 P.M.) on the right, and another 2.8 miles to the entrance

The first week of July, near the high point of the Mirror Lake Scenic Byway.

Drive 21: Mirror Lake Scenic Byway
Kamas to the Wyoming line

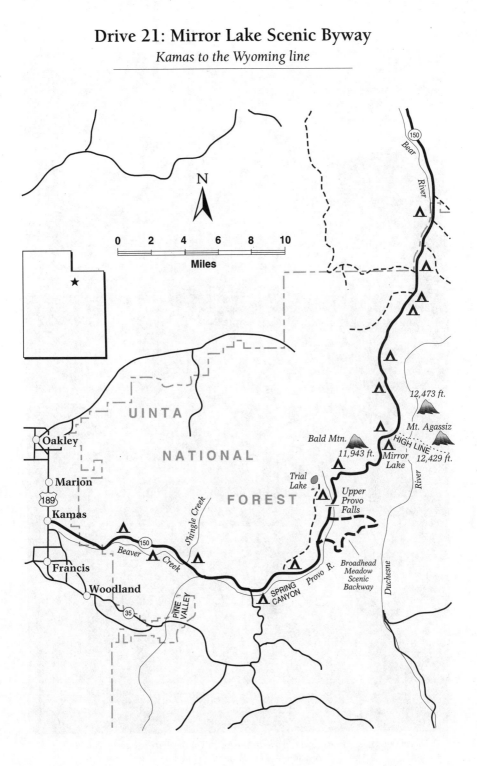

The snowy High Uintas tower above the north end of the Mirror Lake Scenic Byway, just south of the Wyoming state line.

to Wasatch National Forest. Just inside the forest boundary is Yellow Pine Campground. Beaver Creek, Taylor's Fork, and Shingle Creek campgrounds follow in rapid succession. At Shingle Creek Campground the byway leaves Beaver Creek and climbs steadily, crossing the North Fork of the Provo River.

A little more than 8 miles beyond Shingle Creek (just past mile marker 17), on the right, is a pullout at the west portal of the Duchesne River Tunnel. The 6-mile tunnel, completed in 1952, diverts 600 cubic feet of water per second from the east-flowing Duchesne River, augmenting the flow that irrigates the valleys behind the Wasatch Front. This is the first real indication of just how important the Uintas are in supplying water to the region. Four major rivers—the Weber, Bear, Duchesne, and Provo—originate in small mountain lakes in this corner of the Uintas.

Watch next for Slate Gorge Overlook about 5 miles past the Duchesne Tunnel. A short trail leads to a view of a 200-foot canyon created from overlapping layers of billion-year-old Precambrian shale (shale is not exactly slate, but pretty close).

About 2 miles farther is the turnoff on the right for the Broadhead Meadow Scenic Backway. This unsurfaced and rocky road (called Murdock Basin Road here) loops for 4.5 miles through lodgepole pine forests and past a large alpine meadow through which runs a crystal-clear creek. It returns to UT 150 just south of the Upper Provo River Falls. Near the start of this drive you can see a new forest regenerating after a large fire in 1980. This very scenic drive can be rather rough, and it is recommended for high-clearance vehicles only.

Be sure to stop at the Provo Falls Overlook and to hike the good trails down to see the lower falls; it's about 100 yards on well-maintained trail. The falls are about 0.5 mile after the signs indicating the Provo River crossing and the Provo River Campground on the right.

The byway continues to climb into a beautiful alpine world of glacial tarns and lovely meadows beyond the upper limit of the forest. You are now near the top of the Mirror Lake Byway and in one of Utah's finest outdoor recreation areas. Hiking and bicycling trails wind across the ridges, and high mountain trout lakes are scattered throughout this cool, breezy tundra.

It is 2.5 miles from Provo Falls Overlook to Lily Lake Campground, then 2.5 more miles of ascent from Lily Lake to Bald Mountain Pass, the high point of this drive. Be sure to stop at the Bald Mountain Overlook just below the pass. The 11,947-foot Bald Mountain is only a bit more than a thousand feet higher than the road. The views out over the surrounding river valleys toward the distant mountains of the Wasatch Range, however, seem most striking. The byway crosses Bald Mountain Pass at 10,687 feet. The two-mile Bald Mountain National Recreation Trail leads from the pass to the summit of Bald Mountain, where the views are terrific. Bring a sweater—it's cold up here!

On the north-side descent from the pass, it's 0.75 mile to Hayden Peak Overlook. A bit farther along, Mirror Lake, Moosehorn, and Butterfly campgrounds (all higher than 10,000 feet) are the highest campgrounds on this drive. Mirror Lake is especially attractive, shaded by fir trees in a beautiful meadow. Pass Lake is 0.25 mile north of the Mirror Lake turnoff. From Pass Lake, the road winds up for a few miles to its final high point, 10,347-foot Hayden Pass, before descending on the north side of the range. From Hayden Pass there is a nice trail to very pretty Ruth Lake less than a mile away. Just after crossing into Summit County, watch for the Forest Service sign on the right commemorating Richard Kletting, who helped to establish this forest reserve (Utah's first) in 1897.

The byway follows the Hayden Fork of the Bear River down through deep green spruce and fir forest. Watch for moose on the descent of the north slope of the Uintas, as this forest is home to the state's largest concentration of moose. Other animals abound as well, and it would be unusual not to see wildlife along this drive. Short trail walks along the Hayden Fork are likely to yield animal sightings, especially in the late afternoon and early evening. Beaver are plentiful in this stream.

Roadside fishing in the Uintas.

Bear River Ranger Station is open from the middle of May (though you will probably not reach it from the south that early) through October (closed Tuesday and Wednesday). The view back toward the south and east is especially fine early in the summer when the Uintas are still snow-covered.

Just north of the national forest boundary, on the right, is the turnoff for Forest Road 058, the North Slope Scenic Backway. This extremely scenic drive strikes due east along the north slope of the Uinta Range, passing China Meadows to its end at Stateline Reservoir. At the end of the backway, you will be as close to 13,528-foot King's Peak (Utah's highest) as you can get in a vehicle.

The 38-mile drive on partially improved dirt/gravel road involves a fair bit of ascent and descent and is liable to be impassable in any vehicle when wet. In good conditions, it is possible to use this route (continuing north from Stateline Reservoir) to reach Fort Bridger, Wyoming. You might want to check at Bear River Station for current road conditions and for a detailed description of this sometimes rough but very worthwhile drive.

The national forest boundary is the official end of the Mirror Lake Scenic Byway. If you absolutely loved the drive, you might consider retracing your route. Otherwise, the quickest route back to the Salt Lake Valley from here is via Evanston, Wyoming, where you can pick up I-80. The Wyoming state line is 6 miles north of the forest boundary; it's 23 miles farther to Evanston. The drive north is very enjoyable and remains scenic, coming out of the forest and continuing across high prairie and beautiful ranchland. There is a gas station and grocery store at the state line.

22

Provo Canyon Scenic Drives
Provo to Heber City, via American Fork

General description: A 32-mile alpine canyon drive, with an attractive branch drive to Cascade Springs and Timpanogos Cave.

Special attractions: Bridal Veil Falls, Heber Creeper Railroad, Sundance Resort, spectacular views of Mount Timpanogos, Timpanogos Cave National Monument, Cascade Springs, autumn colors on the Alpine Loop Scenic Backway.

Location: North-central Utah.

Drive route number and name: U.S. Highway 189, Provo Canyon Scenic Byway, Utah Highway 92, Alpine Scenic Loop Backway, Forest Road 114, Cascade Springs Scenic Backway.

Travel season: Provo Canyon is open year-round; the Alpine Scenic Loop and Cascade Springs roads are usually closed by snow from late October until late May.

Camping: Two state park campgrounds, numerous national forest campgrounds in American Fork Canyon, two national forest campgrounds in Provo Canyon, commercial campgrounds at Provo, Heber City, and Midway.

Services: All services in Provo and Heber City; limited services in American Fork.

Nearby attractions: Camp Floyd and Pony Express Trail, Utah Lake and Provo attractions, Park City and Deer Valley resorts, Mt. Nebo and Mirror Lake scenic drives.

 The drive

This drive combines the Provo Canyon Scenic Byway with two extremely beautiful scenic backways: the Alpine Scenic Loop and the Cascade Springs Scenic Backway. Taken together, these three short drives offer an extended look at the lovely alpine landscape and forests blanketing the foot of rugged Mount Timpanogos.

The 32-mile Provo Canyon Scenic Byway links Utah Valley with the higher alpine valley around Heber City. The byway follows US 189 along the Provo River in craggy Provo Canyon, past the famous Bridal Veil Falls, and through lovely trout-fishing flats on its way to Deer Creek Reservoir at the lower end of the Heber Valley.

Drive 22: Provo Canyon Scenic Drives

Provo to Heber City, via American Fork

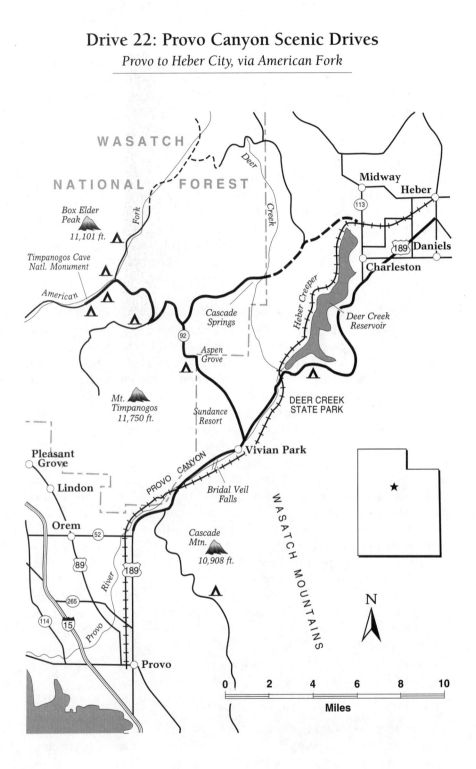

WASATCH

NATIONAL FOREST

Box Elder Peak
11,101 ft.

Timpanogos Cave Natl. Monument

American Fork

Deer Creek

Midway

Heber

113

189 Daniels

Charleston

Heber Creeper

Deer Creek Reservoir

Cascade Springs

92

Aspen Grove

DEER CREEK STATE PARK

Mt. Timpanogos
11,750 ft.

Sundance Resort

Pleasant Grove

Lindon

PROVO CANYON

Vivian Park

Bridal Veil Falls

Orem

52

89

River

189

Cascade Mtn.
10,908 ft.

WASATCH MOUNTAINS

265

114

15

Provo

Provo

N

| 0 | 2 | 4 | 6 | 8 | 10 |

Miles

The 20-mile Alpine Loop Scenic Backway runs between the Provo Canyon Scenic Byway and the mouth of American Fork Canyon, just below Timpanogos Cave National Monument. This paved (but steep and narrow) road presents outstanding views of 11,750-foot Mount Timpanogos and is a popular autumn colors drive. A paved branch road from the Alpine Loop leads to the limestone terraces and pools at Cascade Springs, then continues (upaved) down to the Heber Valley.

As might be expected of a drive with such complexity and diversity, there are a number of alternatives from which to choose, depending on your interests, your vehicle, and your time constraints. The entire Alpine Loop/ Cascade Springs segment of this drive may be closed by snows from October until late May, and these narrow, steep, twisting roads are always impractical for vehicles longer than 30 feet (trailers are *not allowed* on these roads), so drivers of large rigs (and wintertime travelers) will be limited to the Provo Canyon section.

A most-recommended route: Ascend the lower part of Provo Canyon, then the Alpine Loop Road past Sundance, drop down to Timpanogos Cave, then back over to Cascade Springs and on down to Heber. If you want to do a round-trip, you can descend back down Provo Canyon. Provo Canyon (US 189 past the UT 92 turnoff) is scenic enough, though certainly not as interesting or as scenic as the recommended Alpine Loop sidetrip.

This drive begins at the mouth of Provo Canyon at the northeast edge of the city of Provo. Provo is Utah's second largest city and the central community in Utah's second largest metropolitan area. The attractive and fertile position between fresh-water Utah Lake and the foot of the Wasatch Mountains was noted by the Dominguez-Escalante expedition in 1776, and it was singled out as a place for later colonization. Fifty years later, a French-Canadian fur trapper, Etienne Provost, had a serious run-in with a party of Snake Indians (eight of his men were killed) and moved on after first giving his name to the river that flows into Utah Lake.

When the Mormon pioneers made their way here in 1849 (just two years after establishing their first settlements in the Salt Lake Valley), they somehow passed over the names of sundry Book of Mormon prophets and church leaders in deciding on a shortened version of the fur-trapper's name for the new community. Today Provo is best known as the home of Brigham Young University, which was founded as Brigham Young Academy (high-school level) in 1875. The present institution of nearly 30,000 students is the nation's largest religiously affiliated university.

University Avenue in Provo, which runs past Brigham Young University, is U.S. Highway 89. Follow it north (signed for Heber City). As with other canyon drives along the Wasatch Front, you are in the mountains as soon as you enter the mouth of the canyon. Provo Canyon was the route used by the Timpanogos Utes who wintered around Utah Lake and also

Double-cataract Bridal Veil Falls is the most famous landmark in Provo Canyon.

used the Heber Valley as their summer hunting grounds. This was also the route followed by the first Mormon settlers of the Heber area, who took a surprisingly long time to establish themselves in that beautiful alpine valley in 1858.

Provo Canyon is surprisingly pristine, considering how close it is to a major urban area. This is, however, a very popular pleasure drive as well as a significant commuter corridor, so expect a fair amount of traffic.

A very small national forest campground, Rock Canyon Campground is about 5 miles up Squaw Peak Road (paved), 1.25 miles past the mouth of the canyon, on the right. At about mile 3 is the turnoff on the right for Bridal Veil Falls parking lot, tramway, trails, and base facilities. The extremely beautiful falls cascade 600 feet in two large steps. The tramway, said to be the steepest in the world, climbs 1,228 vertical feet to a ledge overlook just above the falls. If

The boardwalk trail at Cascade Springs is a great place to stretch your legs and to learn some things about how water interacts with the land.

you just want to view the falls, an excellent viewpoint about 0.25 mile farther along on the right gives a better look than from the base.

Two-and-a-half miles beyond the falls is Vivian Park, a very popular picnic spot that is also popular with fishermen; there is a very nice cafe here also. Vivian Park is the southern terminus for the "Heber Creeper" Railroad, properly called the Heber Valley Historic Railroad. The original version of this line, the Utah Eastern Railway, ran between Heber City and Provo from 1899 until the 1960s. It got its nickname from the slow pull up Provo Canyon. Today it runs as a scenic tourist attraction, with vintage railway coaches pulled by an authentic 1904 steam locomotive. There are usually two runs per day from Mother's Day through October. The 3.5-hour journey winds up Provo Canyon and around the west edge of Deer Creek Reservoir; you can buy tickets and board at Vivian Park. For schedule information call 1-800-982-3257.

About a mile beyond the park is the turnoff on the left for UT 92, clearly marked for Sundance. This is the start of the highly recommended Alpine Loop Backway. The continuation from here of the Provo Canyon Scenic Byway, east on US 189, is certainly scenic, but offers little of extraordinary interest. The rest of Provo Canyon continues as an alpine canyon drive to Deer Creek Reservoir, where the landscape turns into high sagebrush flat—no trees, just rolling hills and grass until Heber City. The state park at Deer Creek offers a modern campground (with showers). Deer Creek and nearby Jordanelle reservoirs are important recreational resources but rather uninspiring as scenic attractions.

The Alpine Loop Backway (UT 92) is entirely paved but too steep and too narrow for large RVs; **trailers are not permitted** on this road. The Alpine Scenic Loop and Cascade Springs roads are usually closed by snow above Sundance Resort from late October until late May. At mile 2.2 is the turnoff for the Sundance Resort and Institute parking.

Sundance is Robert Redford's pet project, a combination of environmentally responsible mountain resort development and an institute for advancement of the cinematic arts. Alas, for all its correctness and good intentions, it is *still* an imposition on the otherwise pristine landscape; unless you are looking for cafes or mountain bike rental, or just *like* the look of ski area development, this isn't particularly scenic or interesting. There are nice views of Mount Timpanogos from here, but nice views of Timpanogos are *everywhere* along this drive. As the road climbs past the Sundance base facilities, the views of Timpanogos increase in drama.

A little more than 2.5 miles past Sundance you will encounter more development in the form of a BYU alumni facility (campground and picnic area) and the trailhead for some of the popular Timpanogos hikes. You also enter Uinta National Forest here. The road becomes increasingly narrower as it winds up through lovely groves of aspen and pine. Do not park your vehicle along this road except at the designated pullouts (which are numerous).

At mile 6.2 from Sundance is the turnoff for Cascade Springs (described on return); about 0.25 mile farther along is a large pullout/parking area at the high point of the Alpine Loop Drive, a popular start point for hikes and mountain bike rides. At this point you must decide whether you will descend to Timpanogos Cave National Monument or head to Cascade Springs.

From here it is a long descent into American Fork Canyon. This road winds on down—much like on the uphill side—for about 5.5 miles to the canyon bottom, passing numerous roadside cascades. In the wooded canyon bottom there are several nice campgrounds and picnic spots for about 2 miles along the American Fork River. It is 2.5 miles from here to Timpanogos Cave.

At Timpanogos, three limestone caves display an impressive variety of stalagmites, stalactites, draperies, flowstones, and helictites, sometimes reflected in clear cavern pools. The first of these caves was discovered in 1887 by a rancher from nearby American Fork who, according to local legend, was tracking a mountain lion across ledges high on the south slope of the canyon.

Depending on snow conditions in the canyon, the caves are usually open from mid-May through September. The number of visitors to the caves is limited, and the process for visiting is somewhat constrained. First, you must secure a space on one of the scheduled tours. During May and September, tickets for the cave tours are sold between 8 A.M. and 2:30 P.M.; from Memorial Day until Labor Day between 7 A.M. and 4:30 P.M. There is usually a wait for available space, and tours for the day are often sold out by noon during the summer. If you want to do a cave tour, get there early and go *immediately* to the ticket window to reserve your spot. You do not ascend to the caves until your designated tour time, which might be hours from the time of your ticket purchase. So, if you want to tour the caves, come here *before* stopping for your picnic lunch. There is a fine nature trail on the opposite slope of the canyon—a good way to kill some waiting time.

It is a 1.5-mile hike to the caves from the visitor center/ticket office. The 0.5-mile tour through the caverns lasts about an hour, so count on about three hours for the round-trip. Prior to starting up to the caves, a read through the detailed informational brochure will make your visit more enjoyable.

It is 3 miles farther to the mouth of American Fork Canyon. Unless you are bailing out on this drive and want to get back to the Salt Lake/Provo areas, you may as well turn around at the cave; and if you are not interested in the cave, there is really no reason to descend on the American Fork side of the pass (except for the better picnic sites and abundant camping along the stream on this side of the pass).

Return to the high point of the Alpine Loop and FR 114 on the left, the road to Cascade Springs. This paved backway begins with a 2.5-mile descent from the Alpine Loop, then climbs for a mile before starting a long descent with grand, open views off to the south and east. Timpanogos and Mount Nebo loom grandly. There are nice pullouts from which to enjoy what are really the first "open" vistas you will have had along this drive.

At mile 6.8 you reach Cascade Springs, a very nice attraction and a good place to get out and stretch your legs. There are very easy walks along a 0.25-mile boardwalk and asphalt pathways that loop through the springs. These self-guided walks have lots of plaques describing the marsh grasses, birds, water flow, and the way the land is altered by water. This is an especially nice site for kids: they can get out on these nature trails and actually learn some things about the effects of water.

Beyond Cascade Springs the road does go through to the Heber Valley, if you do not want to return to Provo Canyon. Although the first 0.75 mile of this graded dirt road is rather steep and might be a tad rough, it is fine for family sedans and pickup/campers provided it is dry and you are not too

State high school rodeo finals at Heber City. Heber City is a service center for the mountain ranch country between the Wasatch Range and the Uintas.

heavily loaded. If conditions are poor, you will know within the first mile whether or not you can make it; after that, it is all downhill.

On the descent there are lovely views of the Heber Valley. After 1.5 miles you will catch a glimpse of Deer Creek Reservoir, and just past mile 5 you reach the farms of Midway. When you hit the "T" at the hard-surfaced road (mile 5.5), turn right. The road winds through attractive farmland and pastureland until it hits Utah Highway 113. Turn left here for Midway/Heber, right to return to Provo.

The well-watered Heber Valley is commonly referred to as "Utah's Switzerland," both for its dramatic alpine scenery and for the many Swiss immigrants who settled in Midway. Heber City has a very useful information center, on the left, at the north end of Main Street (US 189/U.S. Highway 40).

The nearby old mining town of Park City has been thoroughly transformed into Utah's largest ski resort, a popular and legitimate year-round attraction. Once you have penetrated the dense perimeter of condo development and tennis courts, there is a genuinely interesting remade old uptown area that offers some glimpses of its mining past.

The quickest return to the Salt Lake Valley from Heber City is north for 19 miles on US 40 (Heber City's Main Street) to Interstate 80, then 22 miles west.

23

Rush Valley/Skull Valley Drive

Fairfield to Tooele to Dugway to Interstate 80

General description: A long basin and range drive, revealing elements of Utah's mining history, the Pony Express trail, and the early Mormon settlement of Rush, Tooele, and Skull Valleys, as well as the dramatic alpine terrain of the Deseret Peaks Wilderness Area and the forbidding desert wilderness of the Great Basin.

Special attractions: Stagecoach Inn/Camp Floyd, Mercur/Ophir mining camps, Deseret Peak Wilderness Area, Stansbury Mountains, Skull Valley, Great Basin views, Iosepa.

Location: North-central Utah, just west of Salt Lake City.

Drive route number and name: Utah Highways 73, 36, 112, and 199; Middle Canyon Scenic Backway; South Willow Canyon Scenic Backway.

Travel season: Generally year-round. Both backways are closed in winter, while drifting snow can sometimes be a problem throughout this drive.

Camping: Fairly limited. Six national forest campgrounds on South Willow Road, one BLM campground at Johnsons Pass.

Services: All services at Tooele; most services at Grantsville; gas and food at Ophir and Stockton.

Nearby attractions: Pony Express Drive, Clipper Peak Overview, Great Basin drives, Great Salt Lake.

The drive

This 120-mile drive offers a combination of scenery and attractions designed to give an impression of the sparsely settled valleys on the edge of the Great Basin and to the immediate west of the Salt Lake Valley. The drive provides access to two highly recommended scenic backways, which are described as sidetrips: Middle Canyon Scenic Backway and South Willow Canyon Scenic Backway. Also accessible from this drive is the fascinating Pony Express Trail Scenic Backway.

Parts of this drive are almost "anti-scenic." The landscape south of Rush Valley and west of the Stansbury and Onaqui Mountains is harsh to the point of brutality but also extremely dramatic in its ruggedness. This drive is a very good (and relatively easy) introduction to the Great Basin region as a day excursion from Salt Lake. It is perhaps appropriate that two short sidetrips from this drive offer glimpses of both copper and gold mining operations: Utah ranks second in the nation in both.

There are several alternate ways to begin and end this drive. The drive organized here, a long, full-day excursion from the Salt Lake Valley, is designed to take advantage of the morning light on the east faces of the peaks of the Deseret Wilderness Area, and afternoon/evening light on its west side. Shorter versions of this drive might start at either Tooele or Grantsville (accessed quickly via Interstate 80 from Salt Lake), or might remain to the east of Deseret Peak with a possible return to Salt Lake over Middle Canyon Road. The exact configuration of this drive is, therefore, highly flexible to accommodate individual interests and time limitations. It would, however, be a shame to skip the final desert leg from Dugway north along the edge of desolate Skull Valley.

All of the valley roads, and up to Mercur and Ophir, are paved and suitable for all vehicles. Parts of the Middle Canyon and South Willow roads are unpaved and unsuitable for trailers and larger RVs.

The drive begins at Fairfield, reached easily from the Lehi/UT 73 exit on Interstate 15, a short drive south of Salt Lake City. As you drive west on UT 73, you are following the old Overland Stage and Pony Express route at the start of what was generally considered one of the most dangerous and difficult sections of the long trail across the western desert.

In 1858 General Albert Johnston arrived here with 3,000 federal troops out of government fears over a Mormon insurrection. Johnston established Camp Floyd, which was, at the time, the nation's largest single concentration of soldiers. The town of Fairfield grew prosperous on business generated by the troops, and it reportedly had seventeen saloons. The combined population of town and camp was more than seven thousand, making this the second largest community in the territory. The camp disbanded and the town depopulated in 1861 on the outbreak of Civil War hostilities back east.

The Central Overland Stage and the Pony Express had stops here, where John Carson built his popular inn. This inn has been restored as the centerpiece of a low-key historic site that also includes the Camp Floyd cemetery. It makes a nice picnic spot if you get a late start.

Continue west on UT 73 to where a good dirt road comes in on the left, well-marked as the Pony Express Scenic Backway. Take this left if you wish to continue on the fascinating Pony Express trail. This backway, on well-maintained gravel roads (suitable for all vehicles in dry conditions) runs through Faust, over Lookout Summit, to Simpson Springs and Fish Springs, then across Antelope Valley into Nevada. The drive traces the Pony Express trail across western Utah, one of the roughest stretches on its entire 1,900-mile route. Fish Springs is a true desert oasis, an 18,000-acre marshland

Drive 23: Rush Valley/Skull Valley Drive
Fairfield to Tooele to Dugway to I-80

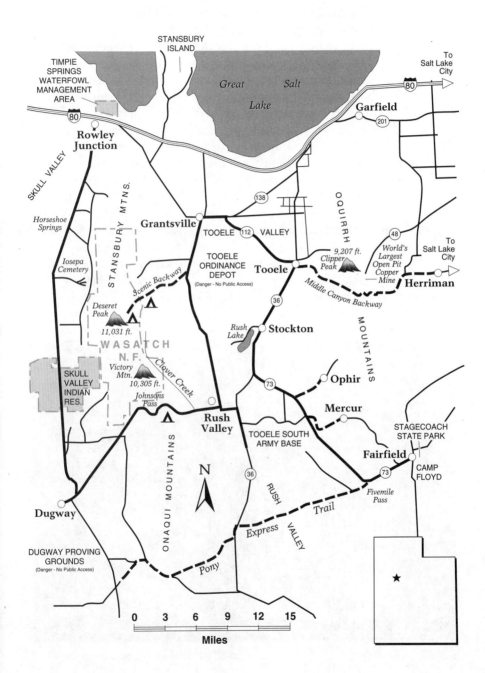

STANSBURY
ISLAND

TIMPIE
SPRINGS
WATERFOWL
MANAGEMENT
AREA

Great   Salt

Lake

To
Salt Lake
City

80

Garfield

201

Rowley
Junction

SKULL VALLEY

Horseshoe
Springs

STANSBURY MTNS.

138

Grantsville

TOOELE   112   VALLEY

OQUIRRH

9,207 ft.
Clipper
Peak

World's
Largest
Open Pit
Copper
Mine

48

To
Salt Lake
City

Iosepa
Cemetery

TOOELE
ORDINANCE
DEPOT
(Danger - No Public Access)

Tooele

Herriman

Scenic Backway

Middle Canyon Backway

Deseet
Peak

11,031 ft.

36

WASATCH
N. F.

Rush
Lake

Stockton

MOUNTAINS

Victory
Mtn.
10,305 ft.

Clover Creek

SKULL
VALLEY
INDIAN
RES.

Johnsons
Pass

Ophir

73

Mercur

Rush
Valley

ONAQUI MOUNTAINS

N

TOOELE SOUTH
ARMY BASE

STAGECOACH
STATE PARK

Fairfield

73

CAMP
FLOYD

36

RUSH

*Fivemile
Pass*

Dugway

Trail

VALLEY

Express

DUGWAY PROVING
GROUNDS
(Danger - No Public Access)

Pony

★

0   3   6   9   12   15

Miles

rich in waterfowl. The Pony Express trail is a much-recommended sidetrip if you have the time (and a full tank of gas—there are *no* services until Ibapah). The BLM distibutes a brochure describing historic sites en route, available at BLM offices in Salt Lake; it may also be found in Lehi or Fairfield.

UT 73, west of Fairfield and south of Mercur, gives a really good taste of Great Basin driving and a real sense of the immense desert expanses out here. The Oquirrh Mountains form the eastern boundary of Rush Valley, with the Stansbury and Onaqui mountains on the west. Back and to the left is the rough, empty terrain crossed by the Pony Express; it is still essentially unchanged today. In early light, the east face of Deseret Peak is especially dramatic from the east side of the valley.

UT 73 curves to the north just past the Pony Express turnoff, entering the well-watered Rush and Tooele valleys. The proximity of these desert valleys to the original Mormon Salt Lake Valley settlement made this an early choice for satellite settlements. Mormons herded livestock here shortly after their 1847 arrival in Utah, permanently settling the Tooele Valley by 1849.

About 9 miles from the Pony Express turnoff is the turn on the right for Barrick/Mercur Gold Mine. Utah's leading producer of gold (about 100,000 ounces yearly), Barrick has been operating round-the-clock since 1983.

View of the Bingham Copper Pit from Clipper Peak, with a backdrop of the Salt Lake Valley and Wasatch Front.

Rich silver ores were discovered in the area in the 1870s by prospecting soldiers from Fort Douglas (Salt Lake City). In 1879 a German prospector found gold in cinnabar, a form of mercury ore. He named his claim "Mercur." It was another twelve years before an effective chemical method was developed to extract gold from Mercur's ore, but by the turn of the century this was a major boom town. Mercur's population was at a peak of about six thousand when a disastrous fire destroyed most of the town in 1902. The mining at Mercur went into decline, the mill closed in 1914, and the place was a ghost town by 1917. There was a short-lived revival during the 1930s, but the Federal Mine Closure Act shut it all down again during World War II.

The astronomical rise in gold prices during the 1970s created this latest rebirth of "the town that can't stay dead." But the major players that have controlled Mercur during the past two decades, first Getty Oil, then Barrick, had no intention of reviving a town here. This is a modern, high-volume strip-mine operation. There is no quaint mine town to visit and none of the sort of boisterous, high-energy society that characterizes traditional mining communities.

A visit to Barrick/Mercur means a short stop at the small visitor center, where a few basic displays give some sense of both Mercur's history and of the nature of modern gold processing. The visitor center is open Thursday-Monday, 10 A.M. to 7 P.M., Memorial Day to Labor Day.

Just north of the Mercur road you get really excellent views of the Tooele South Army Base, formally named the Deseret Chemical Corps Depot, and you may wonder "gee, what sort of nastiness goes on down there?" This is, indeed, a chemical weapons storage depot, which might make the prospect of buying a lot with a view above the valley somewhat less attractive. It is a little more than 4 miles to the road to Ophir, on the right. Ophir is a pleasant 3.75-mile diversion, a quiet community of summer homes and satellite dishes. In the 1870s a mining boom put the population at nearly six thousand.

Just north of the Ophir turnoff you will see Rush Lake. Like the Great Salt Lake, this lake has no surface outflow, draining solely by underground seepage and evaporation. In wet years, Rush Lake can grow rather large and has become very popular with sail boarders. UT 73 ends 4.5 miles north of the Ophir road at the intersection with UT 36. A little more than 2.5 miles north of here, note on the left the marker topped with a red metallic pennant (nicely perforated with bullet holes). An early military camp was established here in 1854 by the first detachment of soldiers to enter the Rocky Mountain region. Access to Rush Lake is through tiny Stockton (with cafe and gas station), 4.5 miles north of the UT 73/UT 36 intersection.

It is 10 miles from here to Tooele, a proper little metropolis. Tooele is the modern version of the old community at Fairfield, economically tied to the local military ordnance depot. (It remains to be seen whether Tooele goes the way of old Fairfield as well, now that the Tooele Depot has been slated for closure.) The best suggestions for the source of the name Tooele is that it is a corrupt form of the name of an early Indian chief, *Tuilla*, or of the Spanish/Aztec word *tule*, for bullrush.

Drive north on Main Street to Vine Street, the main east-west street in the heart of Tooele. (There may or may not be a sign for Middle Canyon Scenic Backway, so just watch for Vine Street.) Just as you turn right (east) on Vine, note the very attractive stone building on the left, built in 1867 as the Tooele County Courthouse, now the museum of the DUP. A few blocks farther along is the very interesting Tooele County Museum. Continue east on Vine past the prominent Catholic Church on the right, then the road winds up and out of town. You will soon see wooded Middle Canyon looming ahead.

This road is too narrow to be much fun in a large RV. There are nice picnic spots on both sides of the road and it is obvious this is where the Tooelites go to escape the valley heat. At about mile 5.5 the canyon opens up a bit and this becomes an attractive mountain drive, still on good paved road. At mile 6.7 the hard surface ends and there is a sign declaring **no trailers or large motor homes beyond this point**. The road beyond here can be rough, so inquire in Tooele about conditions. At mile 8.2 you reach the high point on this main road, and it drops down on the other side into the Salt Lake Valley (making this a good alternative return to Salt Lake City). On the left is a good dirt road that goes up another 2.5 miles to an absolutely incredible viewpoint—in my opinion one of the most spectacular views in all of Utah. From the Clipper Peak viewpoint, the Bingham Copper Pit is right below, and across the valley is the Wasatch Front, with Salt Lake at its feet. From here you can see all the way north to Ogden and south to Provo and Mount Nebo. In 1995 you could conceivably drive a well-tuned, lightly loaded family sedan or mini-van all the way to the top (although I'm not sure I would want to be in the car with you when you did it).

The Middle Canyon Road is rougher and steeper on the Tooele side than to the east. On the east (Salt Lake) side of the pass are 4.2 miles of steep but good gravel road, descending through forests (and about 7,553 Kennecott Copper Co. "No Trespassing" signs) to the start of the pavement on the east side. At about mile 5.5 the top of the Bingham Pit comes into view on the left.

Back down in the Tooele Valley it is about 7 miles on UT 112 from the northwest suburbs of Tooele to the intersection with Utah Highway 138. Merge left here and UT 138 becomes Main Street, Grantsville, whose small downtown has gas stations, a motel, and a supermarket. Continue west on Main Street right through town until 400 West Street, on the left, very well marked for Wasatch National Forest Recreation Sites, North Willow Canyon and South Willow Canyon.

As you drive south, the big snowcapped peak to the south and east is Mount Nebo. It is about 4 miles from Grantsville to the Willow Creek Road, on the right. This highly recommended backway drive may or may not be marked, but it is the only hard-surfaced road leading off to the right. The road is narrow but paved and well maintained. It climbs gradually but steadily, with Willow Creek running far below and to the left. Soon you leave the scrubland behind and enter the pinyon/juniper forest. While still paved, the road deteriorates after a few miles. It is also very narrow, and because of the surrounding vegetation it is sometimes difficult to see other vehicles—of which there (fortunately) will not be many.

At just past mile 3 the pavement ends and you enter Wasatch National Forest on good graded gravel. You will pass Cottonwood Campground at mile 4, and Intake Campground 0.5 mile farther. Just past Intake is the ranger station; after that the road (still well maintained) begins to climb more steeply. This is probably about the limit for RVs and trailers unless you have good low gearing. At just past mile 5 you pass Boy Scout Campground, then the road proceeds through a very impressive narrow cut in the lime-stone walls. The road gets a little rougher after this narrow pasage, though still reasonably good—fine for most passenger vehicles.

At around mile 6 you reach Lower and Upper Narrows campgrounds, then another interesting narrow passage. From here the road climbs out of the canyon, the landscape becomes very alpine, and the views of Deseret Peak start getting really terrific. At mile 6.7 you reach Loop Campground. The road toward the end is rough but reasonable, perfectly manageable in anything but the largest RVs. It is definitely worth driving up here to expe-rience one of the more pristine forests accessible by car. The road ends just after mile 7.

There are very nice, uncrowded hiking trails above Loop Campground that take you up through gorgeous forest right to the snows of Deseret Peak. (If you happen to hear an occasional explosion, do not be alarmed; that will just be the folks down at the Tooele Ordnance Depot blowing off their big firecrackers.)

Twelve miles south of the Willow Canyon road you will reach the very spread-out community of Rush Valley. This road becomes Main Street, which doesn't look particularly "main." In fact, it looks no different than any of the other streets in this strictly residential community. There are no businesses here (no signs either), just well-spaced homes. Part of the reason for this sprawling aspect is that Rush Valley had originally been two separate towns, St. John and Clover. Main Street ends at UT 199, which may or may not be signed for Dugway, to the right.

Young buckaroo tests his mettle at a community rodeo in Rush Valley.

UT 199 begins to climb to a pass that marks the gap between the Stansbury and Onaqui mountains. After about 4 miles you reach Clover Springs Campground. This is a very nice—but very basic—campground, with outhouses and a spring of clear, sweet water. A good authority (a guard at Dugway Base) led me to the highest point of the stream (right where it issues from the ground), where I found the water to be wonderfully cold and sweet, despite the warning sign at the campground.

It is 2 miles from Clover Springs to Johnsons Pass. Above Clover Springs it gets cool and green as you climb higher into these truly beautiful desert mountains. The road here is extremely well maintained, with several scenic pullouts where you get a nice view of the somewhat ominous-looking bunkers of the Deseret Chemical Corps Depot to the southeast. Just on the start of the descent of the west side of the pass you will pass Willow Springs Lodge (a cafe, not really a lodge), then descend to the cluster of homes that constitute Terra. This is also approximately where the pine forests end, signaling your arrival in Skull Valley. Just ahead is the notorious, sinister, top-secret, you-don't-even-want-to-know-what-goes-on-here Dugway Proving Grounds.

About 7.5 miles from Terra you may notice ahead in the distance, like some sort of mirage, the biggest, most elaborate LDS church you would ever *not* expect to see out in the middle of nowhere. This church serves the Dugway Proving Grounds, which is actually quite a substantial community, even supporting its own high school (nicknamed the Mustangs, after the wild horses in the region). You cannot go on the military base, although the very friendly security officers at the entry post will let you patronize their pop machine and give you all the directions and information you need about the country outside the base.

Dugway is a bit of a mystery, and a somewhat shadowy one at that. Built in the 1940s as a chemical and biological warfare test center, the base ignited controversy in the 1970s when many area sheep mysteriously died. Today it seems safe enough to drive by with the windows down . . . probably.

Just between the intersection with the base road and the entry to the base is the good dirt road to the south that meets the Pony Express trail 10 miles south of here. The restored express station and campground at Simpson Springs is about 10 miles down this road, making this a reasonable over-night option.

The road north from Dugway to I-80 stretches out before you almost menacingly. The land out here is extremely desolate and forbidding. The bleak and desolate valley off to the left goes by the friendly name of Skull Valley, which seems appropriate enough. At this point you are parallel with the southern limit of the Cedar Mountains. Way off to the right, south of the Cedars, is one of the BLM wild horse areas.

Deseret Peak Wilderness Area marks the southern boundary of the Stansbury Mountains and is part of the Wasatch National Forest system. A few miles north of Dugway you begin to see the rugged outline of Deseret Peak, which, at 11,031 feet, retains snow for all but a few months of the year.

About 3 miles onto the small Skull Valley Gosiute Indian Reservation is the Pony Express gas station and convenience store, which may or may not be open. This is completely in the middle of nowhere (and rather north of the old Pony Express trail, which ran more than 20 miles south of here).

It is 8 miles from the reservation to the site of Iosepa. Not much remains of the old colony that existed here for nearly fifty years, a community of about a hundred Hawaiian colonists brought here by the church in the 1860s. The Mormon missionaries of the 1850s and 1860s found eager converts in the Hawaiian Islands, and it was decided to settle a community here in desolate Skull Valley. Iosepa was essentially a plantation owned by the LDS Church; the Hawaiians were little more than indentured servants, not owners of the land at which they scratched away. Despite their absolute, even blind, loyalty to the church, they were simply never considered equals to the European settlers.

A minor leprosy outbreak in 1896 gave Iosepa the distinction of having one of the only leper colonies on American soil, and further distanced the Islanders from the Euro-American Mormons. When the Mormon Temple on Oahu was finished, the colony of Iosepa was dissolved. The only Hawaiian who did not return to the islands was in the army.

It is a strange story set in a rather strange place. Not much remains of the patch of green that once clung to the rocky east bench of Skull Valley. Of the several hundred fruit and shade trees planted here, all but a handful have succumbed to Nature, which, once the irrigating hands of the tenants departed, turned the land inexorably back into desert.

You see the site of Iosepa a long time before reaching it, with the last remaining handful of beautiful old shade trees clearly visible for several miles. The townsite is a private ranch today, but you may still access the very interesting old cemetery, where there is an especially fine memorial and historical marker describing the settlement of the area. The cemetery can be seen from the road, about half a mile off to the right.

Just north of Iosepa, the valley on the left is well watered, supporting several small ranches with fields under irrigation. The land around here is a mix of private ranches and public land; the land remains pristine mainly because there is really not much to do out here and no reason to develop the land. There isn't enough water for homesites, and there are many other more "attractive" sites for new commuter communities. But it is certainly scenic in its own very rugged way. The sheer walls of Deseret Peak tower above the road on the right; the lower and drier Cedar Mountains form the western border of Skull Valley off to the left.

About 5 miles north of Iosepa is the turnoff on the left for Horseshoe Springs Wildlife Management Area, which is one of those places where water

This memorial and cemetery are all that remain of the Polynesian colony at Iosepa.

flows in the wilderness and everything is lush and green. Horseshoe Springs is worth a short stop, though there is not a lot to see besides a few pretty ponds, lush vegetation, and lots of birds. This is also a nice example of a local cooperative management project carried out on BLM-administered land. Local groups are in the process of developing a low-key interpretive site here, where there will eventually be a boardwalk path with interpretive signs.

There is no actual town of Rowley Junction, just a long-deserted truck stop and an interstate entrance. Wendover, and the famed Bonneville Salt Flats Race Track, are 75 miles to the west; Salt Lake City is 45 miles east.

24

The Two Cottonwood Drives
Salt Lake City to Brighton and Alta

General description: Two short alpine canyon drives from Salt Lake City up into the Wasatch Front.

Special attractions: Mount Olympus and Twin Peaks Wilderness Areas; Solitude, Brighton, Snowbird, and Alta ski resorts; excellent hiking trails and rock climbing.

Location: North-central Utah, at the southeastern edge of the Salt Lake City metropolitan area.

Drive route number and name: Utah Highways 152 and 210, Big Cottonwood Canyon/Little Cottonwood Canyon Scenic Byways.

Travel season: Year-round, though winter driving in the canyons can be slow and hazardous; snow tires or chains required November 1 to May 1. Even for non-skiers, these drives are worthwhile on clear winter days.

Camping: Two national forest campgrounds in each canyon, commercial campgrounds in Salt Lake City.

Services: All services in Salt Lake City; limited services (food and lodging) at the four ski resorts.

Nearby attractions: Guardsman Pass Scenic Backway, Salt Lake City attractions.

The drive

This drive combines two short designated scenic byways into one drive, still moderate in length. Both canyon drives can be completed in less than half a day, making this a reasonable excursion for Salt Lake City visitors who have but a few hours to spend exploring the area's scenic treasures. You might do one or the other of the two short canyon drives, or combine them.

The two canyons are similar in character: both lie primarily within the Wasatch National Forest, and each has two small pockets of development around ski resorts (though the Big Cottonwood Canyon resorts are considerably smaller than those of Little Cottonwood Canyon.) Both drives ascend narrow canyons with streams rushing beside the road. The roads in both canyons are paved (except for graded gravel from Alta to Albion Basin), excellent in condition, and driveable in all vehicles. Snows come early and remain late—the local ski resorts are justly proud of the 450 inches per year average snowfall—and winter driving can be difficult, especially in Little Cottonwood Canyon.

Both canyon drives nicely mask the reality of being in the backyard of a major metropolitan area, giving the traveler the impression of being far, far away from the urban grind, but within five minutes of driving. Given the aggressive real estate development in the Salt Lake Valley, the two canyons remain remarkably unspoiled. Due to their proximity to the city, both canyons are very popular with the locals for picnics and after-work excursions. Traffic can be high on both drives, especially on the weekend. Watch for cyclists in both canyons.

The start of the Big Cottonwood Canyon Scenic Byway is the mouth of the canyon, at approximately 7000 South, off Wasatch Boulevard (also designated as UT 210). Just watch for the signs for Brighton/Solitude ski areas. The route designation is UT 152, and the drive to Brighton is 15 miles.

As soon as you pass the water treatment plant at the mouth of the canyon, you are in the mountains. Just 4 miles into the canyon, an interpretive site describes the Storm Mountain Slide Area and the effect of the fault zone that lies beneath the Wasatch Front. Several geological interpretive signs along the lower part of this drive help explain the dramatic transitions of the earth that formed these rugged gorges in what is actually the extreme west bench of the Rocky Mountains.

At mile 10 you pass Spruce's Campground (97 sites), after which you encounter the mercifully light development buildup indicating you have reached Solitude, first of the canyon's two ski areas. At about this point you will notice that aspens have become the predominant roadside tree. Redman Campground (38 sites) is right above Solitude, at 8,300 feet.

Just past Redman, on the left, is the turnoff for Guardsman Pass Scenic Backway (Utah Highway 224). This maintained gravel road, passable for passenger cars in dry conditions, travels 20+ miles over the pass into the Heber Valley, with alternate finishes in either Park City or at the visitor center in Wasatch Mountain State Park. This drive offers some of the best roadside views of the Wasatch Front, but these twin factors of scenery and accessibility usually draw too much traffic on weekends to give the kind of solitude you would expect of a gravel road. The backway closes in winter.

Because Big Cottonwood Canyon is broader than Little Cottonwood, it offers more popular trails departing from the roadside. The Mill B South Fork Trail to Lake Blanche, departing the byway from just below Brighton, is one of the best of these.

Brighton was named for Scottish emigrant William Brighton, who came to Utah with his wife, Katherine, as part of a Mormon handcart company in 1857. In 1874 the Brightons opened a small hotel to accommodate the traffic crossing the high passes between the mining towns of Alta and Park City. The attractive mountain setting made this a popular summer excursion site

Drive 24: The Two Cottonwood Drives

Salt Lake City to Brighton and Alta

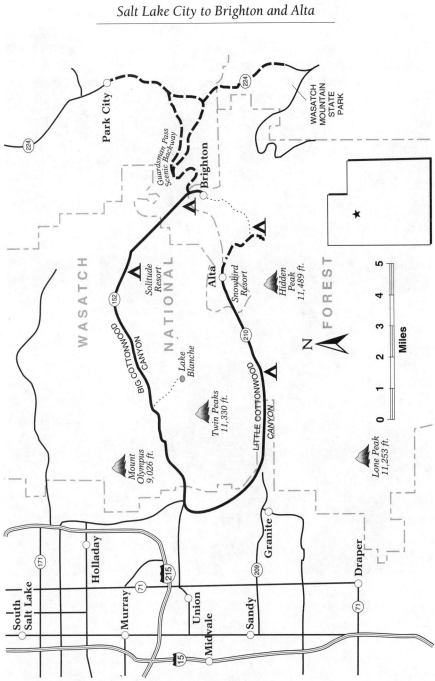

Big Cottonwood Canyon. Both Cottonwood Canyon drives feature pristine alpine scenery in dramatic narrow canyons just minutes from downtown Salt Lake City.

for Salt Lake Valley residents, so it developed as a folksy sort of Mormon alpine resort. Non-lift skiing started prior to the first World War. The first ski lift cranked up in 1939, making this the state's second oldest ski resort (after Alta).

The Brighton/Silver Lake Trail deserves mention as one of the finer handicap-accessible trails in the state. This 1-mile loop around Silver Lake, right at the base of 10,000-foot Mount Millicent, provides boardwalks that cross the meadow areas and paved pathways that run through forest groves. Fishing docks are easily accessible from the boardwalks.

From the road's end at Brighton, return to UT 210. On exiting the mouth of Big Cottonwood Canyon, turn left at the light and continue south on UT 210. It is an easy 3.5-mile drive to the mouth of Little Cottonwood Canyon.

As the name suggests, Little Cottonwood is narrower than Big Cottonwood and more closed-in. At a little more than 8 miles to its end at Alta, it is also considerably shorter. The canyon separates two wilderness areas: Twin Peaks Wilderness to the north and Lone Peaks to the south.

The sheer granite walls at the mouth of the canyon are also more dramatic than those of Big Cottonwood Canyon, and very popular with local climbers. While this canyon offers more climbing opportunities, there are fewer hiking trails. The cars pulled off the road in the lower part of this canyon more likely will belong to climbers than hikers. These granite walls were also the source of the stone used to build the Salt Lake Temple.

Just half a mile into the canyon, look up to the left and note the tunnel carved out of the granite, used to store geneological and LDS church records. When I was doing the ski-bum thing in Salt Lake City in the early 1970s there were all kinds of apochryphal stories floating around about weird rituals that supposedly took place up there. Visitors can't get near the place, so maybe those stories were true after all. . . . Half a mile farther along, on the left, is a particularly popular parking area for rock climbers—and for watching climbers, who you may very well see just above.

At mile 4.5, at Tanner's Flat, is perhaps the most attractive campground in the Salt Lake area, with thirty-nine sites. While there are no elaborate amenities here (no hookups or showers), Tanner's Flat is very nicely situated in a shady grove beside Little Cottonwood Creek.

At mile 6 is the lower entrance to Snowbird Ski Resort, the largest of the four ski areas in Salt Lake City's backyard. The main entrance for the lodge and summertime attractions is 0.5 mile farther up the canyon. Unlike the other Cottonwood ski resorts, Snowbird remains quite an active place through the summer (in fact, the lift-serviced skiing has been known to continue into July after particularly heavy snow years). Skiing aside, the resort maintains a fairly full slate of activities throughout the summer; for more information call 801-742-2222.

Snowbird's aerial tramway to the summit of 11,000-foot Hidden Peak presents terrific views of the Wasatch Front and Salt Lake Valley, with particularly fine perspectives on Mount Timpanagos just to the south. The tram runs regularly through the year, except for a two-week servicing at the end of October.

From here on up to Alta the canyon is pretty much massive condo development. Fortunately, the canyon's narrowness (and the constant threat of avalanches every winter) limits development somewhat.

An extensive mining camp once filled the end of this narrow canyon. Silver was discovered here in 1863, and over the next ten years the highly transient population rose to as much as 5,000. By 1873 there were 186 buildings here, 26 of them saloons. So much mineral wealth was being pulled out of these mountains that two years later a narrow-gauge rail line was opened to Alta. After the collapse of the silver market in 1893, Alta lay fairly dormant for the next forty years. Between the World Wars, the basin at the end of Little Cottonwood Canyon attracted a new sort of pioneer recreationist, who climbed up to ski the ridges and steep powder-filled bowls in numbers such that it was deemed worthwhile to open the second ski lift in the West (after Sun Valley) in 1938. Thus the booming Utah ski industry was born.

The end of the paved road is at mile 8.5, with Albion Basin Campground about 2.5 miles farther. Albion Basin, high and cool, is famous for its brilliant array of wildflowers, and is a delightful place for camping, picnics, or hiking.

Big Cottonwood Canyon has a long history as a recreational site for Salt Lake City residents.

The Snowbird tram is a year-round attraction in Little Cottonwood Canyon.

Several fine trails depart from Albion Basin. The Lake Mary Trail is an easy 3.5-mile hike over Katherine Pass to Brighton, at the head of neighboring Big Cottonwood Canyon. A short trail (just under 1 mile) leads to Cecret Lake, an absolute gem of a high-alpine glacial tarn.

25

Ogden River Scenic Byway
Ogden to Monte Cristo

General description: A 30-mile canyon/alpine drive with an optional 30-mile descent to Woodruff in the Bear River Valley.

Special attractions: Pineview Reservoir, Abbey of the Holy Trinity, Star Burgers at the Shooting Star Saloon, lovely mountain panoramas.

Location: North-central Utah. The byway travels east from Ogden to the eastern boundary of the Wasatch-Cache National Forest.

Drive route number and name: Utah Highway 39, Ogden River Scenic Byway.

Travel season: Year-round through Huntsville. The highest part of the byway, where it approaches Monte Cristo Summit, is closed during winter. Closure dates depend on snow conditions, usually from December through April. Dense and varied foliage makes this a popular autumn drive.

Camping: Ten national forest campgrounds.

Services: All services in Ogden; gas, food, and camping at Huntsville and Woodruff.

Nearby attractions: Trappers Loop Scenic Backway, Hardware Ranch Game Management Area.

The drive

Like other drives that run east from valley towns into the mountains, the Ogden River Scenic Byway follows a narrow canyon away from the urban center and up into spectacular alpine landscapes. Along the way to its high point of nearly 9,000 feet at Monte Cristo Summit, it passes through a complex quartzite gorge, a beautiful high valley, and some of the finest mountain meadows and forest in northern Utah. Also along the way are significant manmade attractions: a genuine monastery and prize-winning hamburgers. There's plenty of variety on this drive.

The road is paved the entire way and suitable for all vehicles. Weekend traffic in summer and during the ski season can be heavy between Ogden and Huntsville. Beyond Huntsville it is doubtful you will see much traffic along UT 39, especially beyond the high point at Monte Cristo. Expect snow anytime after September. The road through the canyon above Ogden can be very difficult when icy and most inconvenient for large RVs. East of Huntsville

Drive 25: Ogden River Scenic Byway
Ogden to Monte Cristo

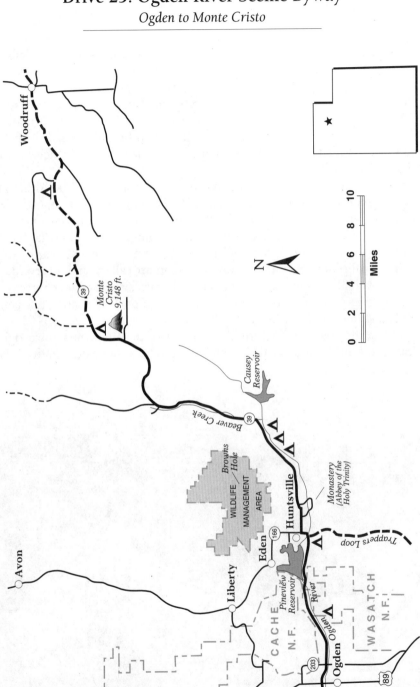

the byway is subject to winter snow closures. Inquire in Ogden as to the current status of this road.

Ogden is one of very few Utah communities founded and settled by pre-Mormon pioneers. American and British trappers were active in the area from the early 1800s. Miles Goodyear established a trading post at the present site of Ogden in 1845, the first white settlement in the entire Great Basin. When the Mormons arrived two years later, Brigham Young promptly bought Goodyear out and resettled the area with his faithful followers. The city is named for British trapper and explorer Peter Skene Ogden, who never actually visited the site.

The city's growth was also tied to non-Mormon interests. Although the transcontinental rail line was joined at Promontory Summit, 60 miles away, the primary rail yard and depot were established early-on at Ogden. The old Union Station (2501 North Wall Avenue) houses the Utah State Railroad Museum, Ogden Natural History Museum, Browning Firearms Museum, a collection of vintage automobiles, an art gallery, and a very complete travel information center, with all the books, maps, and brochures you will need to make the most of your visit. Make a point of visiting this jam-packed collection of Ogden-area exhibits.

Utah Highway 39 is 12th Street, north of the city center. Turn right (east) on UT 39. Because the Wasatch Range abuts the eastern limit of the

The Trappers Loop Scenic Backway runs south from Huntsville and offers fine views of the Wasatch Range.

city, within 3 miles of downtown Ogden you are in complete mountain wilderness in a very narrow canyon beside a fast-moving stream. The chief (and rather significant) difference between this canyon drive and those from other Wasatch Front towns is that Ogden Canyon is mostly private property, while the others are mainly national forest. That makes this the eastern "suburbs" of Ogden. In places the road is lined with the private residences of those fortunate enough to have homes in this extremely beautiful wooded canyon. Several attractive roadside restaurants might make nice stops.

In addition to resident traffic, this is a major conduit between Ogden and its lake and mountain recreation areas, so you might experience a fair amount of traffic in the canyon. The road is also rather narrow, with sharp curves, so large vehicles should exercise care and make use of the infrequent pullouts to allow faster traffic to pass.

At mile 7 you pass the city water treatment plant and immediately enter Wasatch-Cache National Forest. Just beyond, you reach the dam and lower end of Pineview Reservoir, the major recreational resource for the Ogden area. The two campgrounds (total of 105 sites) at the reservoir can fill up quickly on weekends. If you are looking for a place to picnic, there are actually nicer spots along the Ogden River and at Causey Reservoir east of Huntsville.

At mile 10 is the turnoff for Snow Basin, site of the 2002 Olympic downhill event. Just past the turnoff is Anderson Cove Campground on the left. In another 0.5 mile, on the right, is the turnoff for Utah Highway 167, the Trappers Loop Scenic Backway, clearly marked for Mountain Green.

Trappers Loop is recommended as a short sidetrip. It is named as the probable route followed by Peter Skene Ogden and his party of Hudson's Bay trappers. This is 9 miles of perfectly maintained paved road with really marvelous views to the south of the east faces of the northern segment of the Wasatch Front. The round-trip drive takes 30–45 minutes. There is gas and a convenience store in Mountain Green.

The land adjacent to the Trappers Loop drive is the most completely pristine, privately held land in the Wasatch Front. This is how the valley around Heber City and Deer Valley must have looked fifty years ago, before alpine-urban sprawl set in. One must wonder (and perhaps worry) how much the coming Olympic Games will affect this beautiful place.

At Mountain Green is a sign proclaiming:

"The only hostile encounter between American and British fur trappers, known to history as the encounter at Mountain Green or Deserter Point, occurred in this area between May 23-25, 1825. Peter Skene Ogden, one of the most capable and successful brigade leaders of the British Hudson's Bay Company, camped here after completing an extraordinarily successful six-day hunt in Ogden's

Hole, the mountain valley located approximately eight miles north of this site. During that hunt, Ogden's Brigade, consisting of 131 persons, including trappers, squaws and half-breed children, 268 horses and 352 traps, took over 80 prime beaver per day. The brigade's assignment to this area by Hudson's Bay officials was part of a determined British policy to make the Oregon Territory unattractive to American trappers by removing all the beaver. Camped within 100 yards of Ogden's camp was a rowdy bunch of American free trappers who resented the British trappers' presence on so-called American soil. Under the vocal leadership of Johnson Gardner, 25 Americans and 14 deserters from Ogden's Brigade, all well armed, rode into Ogden's camp, demanded the removal of the British from American territory, declared freedom and protection to Ogden's Brigade members who would like to join the Americans, and offered $3.58 per pound for their pelts, which happened to be eight times the price paid by Hudson's Bay Company. After two days of such attractive inducements, Ogden lost 23 of his free trappers and over 700 pelts to the Americans. To avoid a more extended mutiny and a possible shootout with the Americans, Ogden broke camp and returned north by the same route he had come. No Hudson's Bay trapper ever penetrated south of this point. The irony of this event, and the conflicting territorial claims of the American and British trappers, is that they were south of jointly-occupied Oregon Territory, which lay north of the 42 parallel. In 1825, all present at this site were trespassers on Mexican territory, which wouldn't become American until the Treaty of Guadalupe-Hidalgo in 1848."

Retrace the Trappers Loop backway to UT 39, where it is 1.5 miles to Huntsville. Most of this attractive community lies just off to the left of the highway, as the signs indicate.

An interesting short diversion at Huntsville is a visit to the Trappist monastery, the Abbey of the Holy Trinity. Turn right at the sign for the monastery, drive 2 miles through the rather nondescript southern suburbs of the greater Huntsville metropolitan area to a "T," and turn right. It is 0.5 mile to the entrance.

The abbey houses a community of twenty-five monks of the Cistercian Order, better known in America as "Trappists." This 900-year-old order is known for austerity and seclusion from worldly concerns, devoted to a simple life of prayer and manual labor. They remain in the abbey community for life.

The abbey, one of only twelve in the United States, was founded in 1947. This high valley must have seemed ideal for the Cistercian goals of seclusion and contemplation of God. And one must imagine that the Mormon residents of the Ogden Valley must have looked upon their new neighbors, with their long-standing Trappist traditions of hard work, simplicity, and absolute devotion to God, with a certain mixture of curiosity and admiration.

The abbey supports itself by selling honey and beef cattle. They sell their flavored creamed honey both by mail order and in a shop at the abbey reception room.

If you are expecting a stone gothic building, you are in for a surprise, but probably *not* a disappointment. The physical appearance of the abbey is one of its most interesting features. This is modern Quonset hut architecture on a grand scale. The buildings were, in fact, army-surplus Quonset huts, perfectly functional and probably a heck of a good deal in 1947. The exteriors have been sprayed with a urethane foam insulation, then painted an off-white with brown trim, giving it a distinctive *adobe-like* look.

In spite of their absolute devotion to work and prayer, Trappists are known for their hospitality. There is not a lot to see here, since the abbey does not give tours of the monastery or of its farm, but visitors are invited to the abbey reception room/shop and to attend any of the seven communal services in the abbey chapel—a unique opportunity to witness one of the most traditional forms of Catholic devotion. The schedule of services is:

6:00	to	6:20	A.M.	Lauds: the solemn morning prayer of praise.
6:20	to	7:00	A.M.	Mass
7:45	to	7:55	A.M.	Terce
12:15	to	12:25	P.M.	Sext
2:15	to	2:25	P.M.	None
5:30	to	5:50	P.M.	Vespers: solemn evening prayer of praise.
7:30	to	7:45	P.M.	Compline: the end of day. Abbey closes.

Now to move on from the sacred to the profane . . . well, perhaps not really *profane*, but tiny Huntsville's other major attraction is certainly of a much more *secular* nature. Actually, it's a barroom. If everyone in your party is over twenty-one years old (and heavily into beef), you really should stop in at the Shooting Star Saloon for a world-famous Star Burger. The fare is simple: beer and burgers. That's it. But their burgers are consistently judged among the nation's top ten, and they have several times been named number one by *USA Today*. The Shooting Star, a Huntsville institution since 1879, claims to be the oldest operating saloon in Utah, and it is packed with interesting artifacts. Do keep in mind that this is a bar, and in accordance with state laws they do not admit children.

If you can tear yourself away from Huntsville's indoor attractions, there is more fine scenery waiting down the road. Just past the turnoff to town on the left, and after the sign for the monastery, there is a sign indicating a right turn to stay on UT 39, headed east. Straight here goes to Eden. We will take the right to continue up to Monte Cristo.

Most of the land around the lake is private, but just east of Huntsville the road re-enters the national forest and you pass six national forest campgrounds in quick succession, with a total of 150 campsites. These campgrounds are all nicely shaded by old cottonwood trees on the banks of the fast-flowing Ogden River. Just past the last of these campgrounds is the turnoff on the right for Causey Reservoir and Weber County Memorial Park, a good place for a picnic or a swim.

Beyond the turnoff for Causey Reservoir, UT 39 turns north and follows Beaver Creek up into the forested mountains. The forest here is primarily aspen, making this a truly spectacular autumn drive. This region is rich in animal life and is a most-likely place to spot moose and porcupines beside the road and beavers in the creek that bears their name.

About 4.5 miles along Beaver Creek is a popular roadside stop for spring water, and 1.5 miles farther is the turnoff on the left for Hardware Ranch Game Management Area, 14 miles north on an unpaved and partly rough road. Hardware Ranch is primarily a winter elk preserve, though some of the animals remain through the summer and the visitor center and restaurant are open year-round. Check at the Monte Cristo guard station on current road conditions; you might be able to use Hardware Ranch as an interesting return option on this drive, provided you are driving a high-clearance vehicle.

After 23 miles (and what seems like a rather long climb from Huntsville) you come up to a prominent pass. In normal years there will be snow up here into June. The road climbs almost to the summit of 9,081-foot Mount McKinnon. The guard station and campground at Monte Cristo technically mark the end of the Ogden River Scenic Byway, but you might want to continue down to Woodruff in the Bear River Valley. This 30-mile continuation is every bit as scenic as the ascent to Monte Cristo. From Woodruff, it is but a half-hour drive to reach Interstate 80 (at Evanston, Wyoming) for the quickest return to the Salt Lake Valley.

One great attraction to the drive down to Woodruff is the near total absence of traffic. (If you see more than a dozen cars between here and Woodruff, you can consider it a crowd.) Toward the end of the long descent to Woodruff, the road pases through some absolutely beautiful ranchland.

Woodruff was settled in 1870 by pioneers from the present town of Bountiful. As is usual with these old LDS towns, there are a few nice old brick buildings, but there is nothing extraordinary about the town. There is a gas station, convenience store, a nice little park with picnic area, and a cute little rodeo arena. As expected, the most substantial building in town is the LDS church. Woodruff is a cold spot, averaging only fifty-seven frost-

North of Causey Reservoir, the drive follows swift-flowing Beaver Creek.

A ranch-country tradition in remote, rural Woodruff.

free days per year. The state record low temperature was set here in 1899: a chilly -50° F.

The region surrounding Woodruff is undeveloped, unspoiled, and relatively unvisited. It is 11 miles to the Wyoming state line and 14 more to Evanston, through pretty ranchland with nice views of the Uinta Mountains to the south.

26

Bear River Bird Refuge Drive
Brigham City to the Refuge

General description: A 22-mile drive through lush marshlands and across impoundment pools at the mouth of the Bear River.
Special attractions: The Great Salt Lake, myriad varieties of marsh-dependent birds.
Location: North-central Utah, at the mouth of the Bear River, where it flows into the northeast corner of the Great Salt Lake.
Drive route number and name: Forest Street to Bird Refuge Road.
Travel season: The refuge usually closes in January and reopens in March or April. Call the refuge manager during this period to check on status. Otherwise, the refuge is open daily from sunrise until sunset. Heavy spring rains may make the gravel roads impassable.
Camping: Public camping in the area is scarce. No camping is allowed at present on the refuge. Willard Bay State Park is 10 miles south of Brigham City; Mantua Reservoir, 6 miles east of Brigham City, has primitive campsites.
Services: All services are available at Brigham City; absolutely no services on the refuge itself.
Nearby attractions: Ogden River Scenic Byway, Willard Peak Scenic Backway, Antelope Island/Great Salt Lake State Park, Harold Crane Waterfowl Management Area.

The drive

Utah sits right on a migratory path called the Pacific Flyway. Each fall and spring hundreds of thousands of waterfowl congregate in the marshlands formed where fresh water flows into the Great Salt Lake. This drive focuses on the most extensive of several waterfowl refuges established to protect migrating birds, which have also become year-round homes to a great variety of wildlife.

In terms of miles driven, this is a very short outing. It is a 44-mile round-trip from Brigham City; the refuge loop drive itself is but 12 miles. But you can spend lots of time on this drive because convenient pullouts allow you to park and study the incredible variety of life lurking in the pools and marsh grasses.

In terms of scenery, this drive may seem rather limited when compared to drives that sweep the traveler past an ever-changing spectacle of alpine vistas or redrock panoramas. Views generally change more slowly in the broad basin that occupies the western third of the state. Here on this small corner of the Great Salt Lake, we are looking at a fairly encapsulated, confined space of water, marsh grass, and sky. It is, perhaps, an odd sort of scenic drive, and one in which you must focus in close on small spaces, rather than cast your view across the broad, expansive landscapes for which Utah is so well known. The reward, however, is an experience that few other drives can provide. You will see things of great beauty and fascination.

There is another, equally compelling reason for including this drive: the Great Salt Lake. This is one of the most interesting bodies of water in the world, and one of the most famous lakes on the continent. And yet, as visually striking and as topographically and historically interesting as the lake is, it receives surprisingly little tourist attention. Famous it may be, but *well known* it certainly is not.

While everyone seems fascinated by the *idea* of the lake, and by its *statistics*, not much physical attention is paid to it. This is at least partly due to the lack of convenient, up-close viewpoints. The old lakeside resorts close to Salt Lake City are largely gone. The attraction called *Saltaire* is attempting to revive the old tradition of actually using the lake for recreation, and the new causeway and state park at Antelope Island provide an excellent opportunity for lake-oriented outings; but for the most part the lake is largely unapproachable and sadly ignored. This drive will bring you up very close to Bear River Bay, a prominent lake feature, and will give you some idea of the vastness and beauty of this unique body of water.

The Bear River Migratory Bird Refuge lies about 16 miles west of Brigham City, where the Bear River enters the Great Salt Lake. The scenic part of this drive begins about 6 miles west of Brigham City on the long country road leading out to the refuge. It continues through a small corner of the refuge on a road graded along the top of a containment dike built out into the lake.

The last 10 miles out to the refuge, as well as the roads on the refuge, are well-maintained gravel, perfectly level and presenting no problems for any vehicle. Occasionally the gravel roads become difficult during heavy rain or (infrequent) snow. The 12-mile route along the dike, though narrow, is one-way.

Try to do this drive in the early evening, when the light on the mountains east of Brigham City is lovely and you can catch the sunset over the lake—a very special visual experience. Weekends often draw crowds to the refuge, while weekdays find the place remarkably empty. The birds are most active mornings and evenings. A pair of binoculars will be most useful. This is also a tremendous place for wildlife photography.

Drive 26: Bear River Bird Refuge Drive
Brigham City to the Refuge

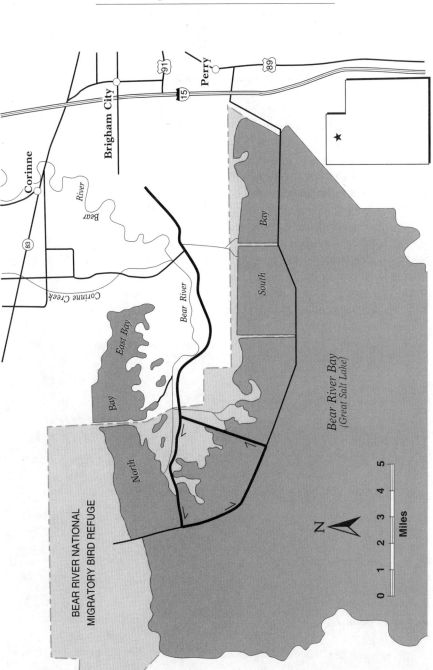

There is at present no interstate exit for the refuge (one is planned), so you will have to start from Brigham City, which is a nice town to visit. Since there is as yet no visitor center at the refuge, you may also want to stop in at the refuge office in town (866 South Main, in the Breitenbecker Plaza) for whatever literature they might provide.

The two most prominent landmarks in downtown Brigham City are the extremely ornate and picturesque Mormon Tabernacle and a sign that some of you may recognize from a well-known and very humorous beer commercial: the big "Welcome to Brigham" sign that spans Main Street and proclaims this *Gateway - World's Greatest Game Bird Refuge*. Brigham City is an interesting town to just poke around in: a quiet, unassuming community with some of the finest nineteenth-century homes and commercial buildings in the state. The Box Elder County Courthouse, a block or two north of the famous sign, is especially attractive. Stop in at the Brigham City visitor center, just north of the famous sign, on the right, for tour information.

From early summer into fall, the 15-mile stretch of U.S. Highway 89 south of Brigham City is a good place to find old-fashioned fruit stands selling local produce. The peach harvest (around Labor Day) is an especially important one, and it is celebrated in Brigham City with a Peach Festival, usually the weekend after Labor Day.

Brigham City's famous welcome sign.

216

To get to the refuge, take Main Street to Forest Street, just north of the "Welcome" sign. Turn left/west on Forest and follow this road under the interstate and onto country roads leading to the refuge. The first 6 miles or so are fairly mundane until you get far enough out onto the flats along the edge of the lake for the views to open up. As you get farther from Brigham City, the views back toward the northern section of the Wasatch Range become more impressive. You will know you are getting close when you come up alongside the slow-moving Bear River.

The Bear is the most confused river in America. It really doesn't seem to know for sure which way it's headed or where it will end up. Its source in the High Uintas is not so very far from where it ends here at the Great Salt Lake—less than 90 air miles southeast. Along the way it wanders northward up through Wyoming and into Idaho, where it suddenly changes its mind and does an about-face, flowing south into Utah. In Utah it meanders aimlessly for a ways across the bed of what used to be ancient Lake Bonneville before finally finding its way here. All together this vagrant stream wanders 350 miles, only to end up almost back where it started. It seems appropriate that the wayward Bear is the longest river in America that does not ultimately reach an ocean (though Utah's Sevier, which runs north from the Markagunt and Paunsaugunt plateaus, then west to die in the wastelands of the Great Basin, is nearly as long). Of course, the reasons for the river's erratic course have to do with the dramatic geologic forces that formed this complex land of uptilt faults, dropped valleys, and barrier ranges—yet another geology lesson read upon the land.

This area *outside* the refuge, before the Bear River enters the lake and as it flows through about 10 miles of marshland, is just as good for bird watching as the refuge itself; in certain conditions it is actually the best place to view certain kinds of birds. John C. Fremont, one of Utah's earliest and most enthusiastic tourists, passed through this area in 1843 and was especially impressed by the abundance and variety of the waterfowl he discovered in the marshes of the Bear River. Fremont wrote in his journal: "The whole morass was animated with multitudes of waterfowl . . . with a noise like distant thunder."

Between April and October, one of the most commonly seen birds in the Bear River marshes is the white-faced ibis. Seventy-nine percent of the entire population of North American white-faced ibis breeds in the marshlands of the Great Salt Lake.

The single best time to see large concentrations of birds is in the early fall, although exact months vary according to species. The fall migration of ducks and geese numbers as much as half a million. Large concentrations of whistling swans occur here in the fall as well; in 1969 their count reached forty thousand. The refuge management office in Brigham City has a very useful pamphlet showing the statistics (as graphs) for eighty-one varieties of birds common to the refuge, indicating average monthly abundance. Hopefully, the planned visitor center will keep the latest updates on current attractions.

Here are a few examples of what you might see on the refuge:

Bird Species	Highest Month	Average Peak Number
white pelican	August	4,600
black-crowned night heron	August	600
great blue heron	August	780
snowy egret	July	2,800
whistling swan	Nov/Dec	16,000
mallard	October	27,000
redhead duck	Sept/Oct	28,000
pintail	September	180,000
green-winged teal	October	120,000
blue-winged teal	September	490
cinnamon teal	September	33,000
ruddy duck	April/May	20,000
American widgeon	Sept/Oct	67,000
marsh hawk	November	26
short-eared owl	July	12
golden eagle	March	9
bald eagle	March	33

All that greets you at the refuge boundary is a sign and an open area containing a small pavilion, a simple information board, toilets, and a handful of benches. There is no water, and no camping is allowed on the refuge. There is also no charge for entering the refuge.

The dramatic rise in the level of the Great Salt Lake in 1983 created massive destruction of the few manmade facilities that stood on the edge of the lake. The same flooding and damage that closed the bathing and amusement center of Saltaire inflicted severe damage on the bird refuge. Most of the marshland habitat and virtually all of the structures were destroyed.

A new facility has been planned that will include a large visitor center with interpretive exhibits, and a research unit that will help monitor the area's birdlife and continue the search for cures for the severe diseases that afflict waterfowl. For now the refuge is meant strictly for day visits (technically, it is open from sunrise to sunset), and all is strictly independent, with no personnel on the site.

The Bear River Migratory Bird Refuge was established by an act of Congress in 1928, out of concern over the loss of marsh habitat and the alarming increase in waterfowl deaths due to disease and unrestricted hunting.

During the period of Mormon settlement of the Salt Lake Valley, migratory waterfowl became a prime source of market income. From 1877 until 1900, 200,000 ducks were harvested each year, mostly for eastern restaurants. After the turn of the century, a virulent strain of avian botulism killed more than half of the migrating birds that stopped to rest here, leaving the marshes clogged with their dead bodies. At about this same time, widespread diversion of water from the mouth of the Bear River for farming in the valley caused the marshes to dry up. By 1920, only 2,000 to 3,000 acres of the original 45,000 acres remained. It was a classic example of "use-it-upedness" combined with an extremely devastating aviary epizootic.

Today's Bear River Refuge is the result of efforts to counter and repair the destructive circumstances of the past. It is a facility born of sheer ecological necessity. The refuge currently consists of 73,000 carefully managed acres of marsh, open water, and mudflats. A system of dikes and other water-control features maintain five 5,000-acre water impoundments in order to slow the flow of the fresh water into the Great Salt Lake. While the mysteries of avian botulism have not yet been solved, important research continues on the refuge, and advances have been made in controlling the disease.

The refuge drive is organized to follow around the top of the dikes of one of the impoundment ponds. The route is well marked and obvious:

Bear River Bay, where the Bear River empties into the Great Salt Lake.

there is no way to miss it. Once started along the narrow dikes, it is impossible to go astray—if you do, you'll end up in the lake. Just remember to continue in the same direction and not reverse your route. When you've completed the loop, you will go back out the way you came in.

Along the 12-mile drive are periodic interpretive boards describing various features of the marsh habitat and its inhabitants. But the real attractions along here are the birds themselves. More than two hundred species are regularly sighted here; of these, sixty-two are known to nest and breed in these marshes, making the refuge important for production as well. In addition to the many varieties of birds that frequent the refuge, this is home to 29 species of mammals, 12 species of fish, 5 species of reptiles/amphibians, and 177 species of plants.

This manmade causeway jutting out into the Great Salt Lake is also a good place to study Utah's version of the Biblical Dead Sea. Is it scenic? You be the judge. *Pretty*, it certainly is *not*. But it no doubt deserves the title *Great*. Directly across the water, the long barren ridge of the Promontory Mountains defines the western horizon. To the south stretches fifty miles of briney water baking in the sun. With a salt content as high as twenty-seven percent, the lake is eight times as salty as the ocean. Of all the bodies of water on earth, only the Dead Sea is saltier than the Great Salt Lake.

The bird refuge at the mouth of the Bear River is a haven for many varieties of waterfowl.

The cause of the lake's salinity is fairly obvious if you look at a map. The lake receives water from numerous streams and rivers, yet it has no outlet. It is, in effect, a broad evaporation pond. Although it is, on average, seventy miles long and thirty miles across, it averages only thirteen feet in depth and is only thirty-four feet at its deepest. As moisture is lost to evaporation, the mineral salts washed into the lake remain. This process has been going on since at least the last Ice Age, when most of western Utah and parts of Idaho and Nevada were covered by prehistoric Lake Bonneville, of which the Great Salt Lake is a remnant.

Due to the high salt content, nothing lives in the lake except for a tiny sort of brine shrimp that is harvested as fish food. So what do all the waterfowl who live here permanently and visit annually eat? The marsh grasses and mudflats here are a great breeding ground for a wide variety of insects, which the birds consume with gusto. The mudflats at the edge of the water are also popular with frogs, a favorite food for herons and egrets. And there are plenty of fish in the mouth of the Bear River to keep the pelicans and other fish-eaters happy.

In fact, there is a waterfowl management area at each point where a large source of fresh water flows into the salty lake: at the mouths of the Bear, Weber, Ogden, and Jordan rivers. These must have long ago been established as prime "buffet spots" for the migratory birds. The large inflow of fresh river water also supports the large variety of marsh grasses that grow in these places, on a lake that is otherwise conspicuous for its lack of vegetation.

Ducks banded at the Bear River Refuge have been found in thirty-one states and five foreign countries, from Siberia to Colombia, from Maryland to Palmyra Island. One of the most interesting stories regarding the refuge's temporary winged visitors is of a pintail duck, banded and treated for botulism in 1942, who was found 83 days later on Palmyra Island—3,500 miles from here. The bird was described as being in an exhausted state. I guess I would be too.

27

Logan Canyon/Bear Lake Drive

From Logan to Bear Lake

General description: A 55-mile canyon and alpine drive from Logan to scenic Bear Lake.

Special attractions: Wasatch-Cache National Forest, dramatic canyon scenery, Jardine Juniper, Rick's Spring, Bear Lake, rock climbing, raspberry milkshakes.

Location: Northeast Utah, primarily in the Wasatch National Forest. The drive starts at Logan, east of Interstate 15, and runs to the southern tip of Bear Lake, on the Utah/Idaho state line.

Drive route number and name: U.S. Highway 89/Utah Highway 30, Logan Canyon Scenic Byway/UT 30 Scenic Byway.

Travel season: Year-round, though roads may be slick during winter. Autumn colors can be extremely attractive in Logan Canyon.

Camping: Ten national forest campgrounds along the Logan Canyon Byway, four state park campgounds around Bear Lake.

Services: All services in Logan; most services in Garden City.

Nearby attractions: Mount Naomi Wilderness Area, Old Ephraim's Grave, Hardware Ranch Scenic Backway.

The drive

This drive combines two designated scenic byways in a single excursion. The entire drive can be completed (one-way) in just an hour and a half, though more time is recommended for stops and sidetrips in the car or on foot.

The Logan Canyon Scenic Byway runs east along US 89, from the backyard of Utah State University in Logan, up the narrow gorge of Logan Canyon, and over the Bear River Mountains to the resort town of Garden City on the banks of scenic Bear Lake. This 40-mile alpine/canyon drive passes beneath imposing limestone cliffs carved by the Logan River and through lush green forest on its 3,000-foot climb to Bear Lake Summit. A second designated scenic byway continues for 15 miles from Garden City to Laketown, at the southern end of the lake.

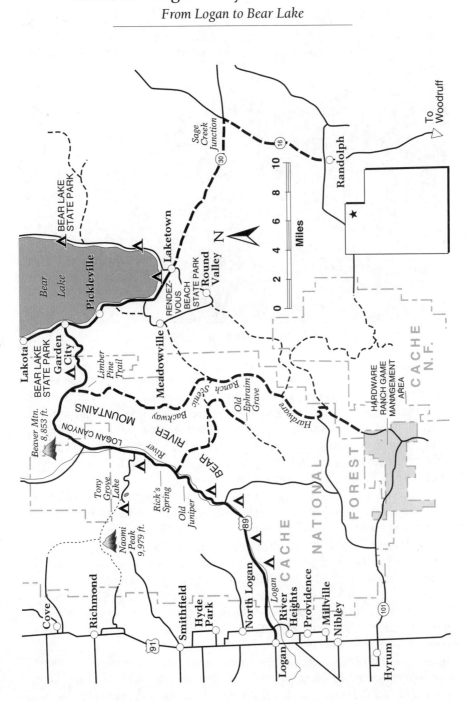

Wasatch National Forest resident, Logan Canyon.

The roads on this drive are in excellent condition, and there are no inordinately steep grades. The upper part of Logan Canyon and the road over the summit receive heavy snow in winter; snow tires or chains will be helpful. This is also known to be the coldest part of the state. Definitely bring more clothes than you think you'll need, even in summer, and carry emergency gear—warm clothes, spare food and water, even sleeping bags—if driving in this region during winter.

The drive begins in Logan, a university town and the regional center for northern Utah. Worth viewing in town are the Logan LDS Temple (200 North 200 East) and nearby Logan Tabernacle. The modified gothic-style Logan Temple, built between 1877 and 1884, is the second-oldest temple in Utah (after St. George) and justifiably considered one of the most beautiful religious buildings in the West. Logan's main claim to fame today is Utah State University, which sits practically at the mouth of Logan Canyon.

From downtown Logan, 400 North is US 89. Once east of the university you are pretty much out of town. As with the drives farther south, as soon as you enter the mouth of the canyon, just past the Forest Service information office, you are in the mountains. You might want to visit the Forest Service office on your way out of town, especially if you plan on returning via the unpaved Hardware Ranch Backway. This is also the best place to pick up information on hikes from Logan Canyon trailheads.

As with other canyons within commuting distance of Utah's larger urban areas (Ogden Canyon and the Cottonwoods), there are a number of private homes here, although much better hidden than in nearby Ogden Canyon. Most are tucked away in the trees, and you will barely catch a glimpse of them. Keep in mind that this is the backyard of Utah State University, so watch for bicyclists. If you are driving slowly, use the pullouts to let backed-up traffic pass.

Slightly more than 3 miles from the mouth of the canyon is Zanavoo Lodge Restaurant, followed by Bridger and Spring Hollow campgrounds. At about mile 4 the canyon opens up a little and some nice fishing ponds have formed along the Logan River. Also here is Malibu-Guinavah Campground. The campgounds, as well as several picnic areas, are all on the right, beside the river. Logan Canyon is popular with rock climbers, and particularly between miles 9-12 you might see folks climbing right beside the road.

At around mile 11 watch on the left for Wood Camp Campground, which is also the start of the trail leading to the 1,500-year-old Jardine Juniper. This ancient tree is thought to be the oldest juniper in the Rocky Mountains. The trail gains nearly 2,000 feet in just under 5 miles and leads through a beautiful alpine landscape.

Another mile or two up the canyon is the turnoff on the right (Forest Road 007) for Old Ephraim's Grave. Ephraim was the name given to a huge grizzly bear (some say nine feet tall, some say eleven) who lived in the Cache National Forest, and who had a rather large appetite for cattle and sheep from around 1911 until he was shot in 1923. Local boy scouts erected the present marker to the legendary beast, whose skull can be viewed at the Bridgerland Travel Office in Logan. It's a 6-mile drive on unpaved road to the grave site.

Just up the canyon, watch for well-marked Rick's Spring, a flow of crystal clear water that issues from a cave on the left of the road. This is a *must stop*. A nice pathway less than 20 yards from the road leads to the cave. Note the pioneer signatures on the rock, just above the point where the water issues forth.

Beyond Rick's Spring, the road runs up and out of the well-defined canyon and takes on the aspect of a mountain drive. The stream still flows on the right, but the canyon has widened greatly, the views are more open, and the predominant tree is now aspen. About 4 miles beyond Rick's Spring is the turnoff on the left for Tony Grove Lake Recreation Area. Paved Forest Road 003 leads 6 miles up to the lake, at 8,500 feet. On a weekday, you might find a space in the lovely campground here, set in an aspen grove beside this extremely beautiful glacial lake. This is also a good starting point for hikes into the Mount Naomi Wilderness Area. If the campground is full, there are two other campgrounds near the intersection of FR 003 and US 89.

Rick's Spring issues from a cave beside the road, near the top of Logan Canyon.

The turnoff for Beaver Mountain Ski Area is about 5 miles farther up the canyon. Six miles past Beaver Mountain is Limber Pine Trail, on the right, which is about the high point of this drive. The turnoff for the Hardware Ranch Scenic Backway is 0.25 mile west of Limber Pine. The first 7 miles of this 25-mile mountain backway, from US 89 to Hardware Ranch Wildlife Management Area, are unpaved and impassable when wet. From Hardware Ranch to Hyrum, the road is paved. Because of unique atmospheric conditions, some of the coldest winter temperatures ever recorded in the lower forty-eight have been at Middle Sinks, between here and Hardware Ranch (unofficially, -65° in 1888; officially, -49° in 1979). This would make an interesting return route to Logan, in good weather and in a suitable vehicle. Call the district ranger in Logan or check in Garden City for current conditions.

Half a mile in descent from the summit is Sunrise Campground and a fine scenic overlook with a great view of Bear Lake. From this height you get some idea of why the lake has been called "the Caribbean of the Rockies," for it really is a remarkable shade of blue, ringed with sandy beaches. This color is sometimes attributed to limestone particles carried into the lake from the surrounding hills, or to the lake's sandy white bottom and relative shallowness—208 feet at its deepest. The lake is twenty miles long, eight miles wide, and it sits in a *graben* (a valley depression created by two faults). Like the Great Salt Lake, Bear Lake has no surface outlet. But unlike the briney Great Salt Lake, Bear Lake loses most of its waters through percolation or subsurface flow through the earth itself. These waters later resurface as springs.

Descend (steeply) to Garden City, the main resort community on Bear Lake. Once you leave the national forest and as you approach town, you pass through fairly significant property development. The steepness of this descent might suggest a different return route for drivers of large vehicles: either through Woodruff to reach I-80 at Evanston, Wyoming, or via Utah Highway 39 from Woodruff to Ogden (reversing Drive #25 from this guide).

In 1827 and 1828 Bear Lake was the site of the annual rendezvous held by regional fur trappers. The lake basin had been a popular Shoshone Indian gathering place for many years before Donald Mackenzie, a Scottish-Canadian trapper, first saw it in 1819 and named it Black Bear Lake.

Although early maps of the Oregon Trail indicate it passed considerably north of here, there is some evidence that at least some of the earlier emigrants (circa 1830) passed along the south shore of Bear Lake and then went up through canyons to the northwest. There are old wagon ruts from this period, and stories of early settlers and Indians support this claim. This seems to make logistical sense, since the important rendezvous held here in 1827 and 1828 would have made Bear Lake well known to all early travelers through the region.

Despite the lake's notoriety among early trappers and explorers, no year-round settlement occurred until the mid 1860s, when cabins were built at present Garden City. The old settlement has since spread up and down the west side of the lake in typical resort development fashion.

Bear Lake is a watersports center for northern Utah, southeastern Idaho, and southwestern Wyoming. While this may sound like it draws an awful lot of people, these sparsely populated regions don't have that many folks even when combined. Summer weekends are fairly busy, but this is hardly a destination resort, so weekdays are nice and slow. Facilities (including boat rentals) are located all around the lake. Boating, camping, and picnicking facilities are provided at four state-run parks: Bear Lake Marina, Rendezvous Beach, Eastside State Park, and North Beach State Park.

The state highway map indicates the designated Logan Canyon Scenic Byway continuing north from Garden City to the Idaho state line (about 4 miles). This part of the lakefront probably *was* scenic before it was all sectioned off and developed. There is no real reason to drive north of town unless you wish to visit the historic LDS towns of Paris and Montpelier, in Idaho. Otherwise, I recommend turning south here or returning to Logan.

Before leaving Garden City, don't fail to partake of the raspberry treats for which this place is famous. The town probably has more drive-ins per capita than anywhere in the West, and they all specialize in fresh raspberry shakes.

Aspens near Limber Pine Trail, the high point of the Logan Canyon Scenic Byway.

About 3 miles south of Garden City is the resort town of Pickleville, with its summertime theater specializing in Western melodrama. This is also the site of some truly atrocious rabbit-warren condominium development. Just past Pickleville the lakefront development ends abruptly and the drive actually becomes scenic again, with the big lake to the left and scrub-covered hills on the right. This is private land; there's no telling how long it will remain open and undeveloped.

Eight miles south of Garden City is Rendezvous Beach State Recreation Area. It is 1.5 miles farther to the rustic village of Laketown (which isn't quite on the lake at all), where you have several options. You can return via the same route to Logan. You can continue on to Woodruff, where you may either head to Evanston, Wyoming, and hop on the interstate back to the Salt Lake Valley, or you can do Drive #25 in reverse back to Ogden. If you want to make this a multi-day excursion, you might even consider driving south from Evanston and doing the Mirror Lake Drive (#21) in reverse.

Laketown to Woodruff is a very pleasant drive: 30 miles of virtual wilderness punctuated by just one real settlement at Randolph. The landscape here is not terribly scenic; in fact, it is rather rough but primitive and unspoiled. At Sage Creek Junction, 12 miles past Lakeside, turn right on Utah Highway 16 and drive 9 miles south to Randolph. With a population of just five hundred, Randolph must surely be one of the nation's smaller county seats. The town does have a cute little courthouse, a nice pink brick LDS church, several gas stations, a mechanic, a grocery store, and two fast-food restaurants.

Woodruff (gas station/convenience store) is 10 miles south; Evanston, Wyoming, is 25 miles farther.

28

Northwest
Corner Expedition
Snowville - Grouse Creek - Golden Spike - Corinne

General description: A long excursion into the desert and grasslands of Utah's neglected northwest corner.
Special attractions: Great Basin views, remote ranching communities, old Central Pacific rail line, Golden Spike National Historic Site, rocket display at Thiokol, old Corinne.
Location: Northwestern Utah.
Drive route number and name: Utah Highway 30, Utah Highway 83, Central Pacific Railroad Trail Scenic Backway.
Travel season: Year-round, though drifting snow can be a winter problem.
Camping: Limited. There are no developed campsites along this route.
Services: Basic services at Snowville and Corinne; gas and groceries at Grouse Creek and Montello, Nevada; gas and cafe at Park Valley. There are *no* services along the 88-mile Central Pacific Railroad Trail.
Nearby attractions: City of Rocks, Sawtooth National Forest, Spiral Jetty and Sun Tunnels, Bear River Bird Refuge (Drive #26).

The drive

While God may not necessarily have foresaken this corner of Utah, Man certainly has. Apart from a handful of isolated ranch communities, the entire northwest corner of the state, from the Great Salt Lake to the Idaho and Nevada borders, is a vast, empty quarter.

For about forty years, from 1869 until just after the turn of the century, the main track of the transcontinental rail line passed through this remote desert grassland. In a peculiar way, the lifeline of the railroad, with as many as ten trains per day and several important railtowns, meant this empty land was more populous, more lively, and much less lonely one hundred years ago than it is today. Today only the landscape remains, along with a few relics of yet another abandoned project.

The two regional attractions for the modern traveler focus on these key elements of railroad history and wide-open spaces. This is a big area, and the drive is potentially very long; some serious decisions need to be made regarding itinerary. Snowville to Grouse Creek is 104 miles. The

Drive 28: Northwest Corner Expedition
Snowville - Grouse Creek - Golden Spike - Corinne

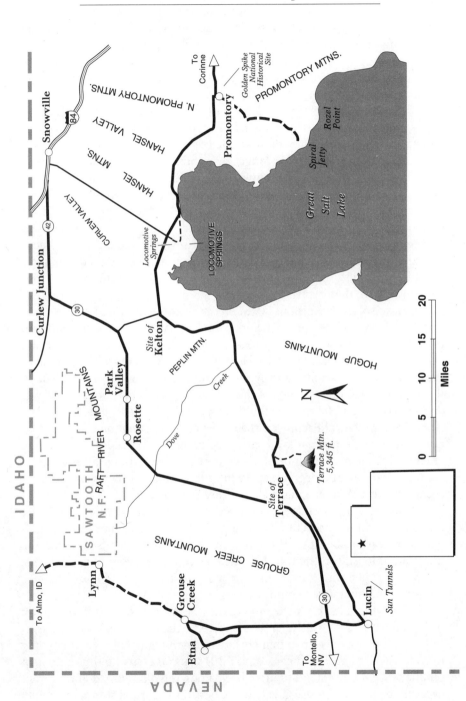

backway return along the old railroad bed from Lucin to Golden Spike is 88 (very slow) miles, then another 25 miles to Corinne. If you intend to do the entire loop, it is *technically* possible to do this in a single marathon day, presuming an early start from Snowville and no dawdling. The problem with extending this into a slower, more relaxed overnight trip is that, except for a small motel at Park Valley, there is no place to overnight, apart from camping on the abundant BLM-administered public lands.

The old railroad grade is suitable for most, but not all, passenger vehicles, but it is a slow drive in any rig. The roadway is narrow, often rutted, and has no shoulders. Though driveable (slowly) in conventional vehicles, the BLM recommends nothing longer than thirty feet. Vehicle limitations or time constraints may suggest against the four-hour (or more) rail-bed drive. You may opt to skip this backway, or to drive just a short stretch of it. There are two reasonable options for getting a sense of the nature of the drive without committing to its entire length: either start east from Lucin, then escape back north to paved UT 30 on one of several good dirt roads (mentioned in the route description); or drive west along the old grade for a few miles from Golden Spike, perhaps as far as Locomotive Springs or the Cemetery at Kelton, then return to Promontory.

These sorts of decisions will determine the length and character of this drive for you. The start of the drive, on UT 30, is in excellent condition, as is the well-maintained gravel road up to Grouse Creek. These roads are suitable for all vehicles. The drive back along the old rail bed, from Lucin to Promontory, is a fascinating experience and a good way to get up close to the wild desert and grasslands of this remote region. This part of the drive, designated a BLM National Back Country Byway in 1994, follows the last stretch of the Central Pacific Railroad line before meeting the Union Pacific at Promontory Summit. It is a *highly* recommended excursion, but anyone attempting this drive must be prepared for desert conditions. Summer temperatures can top 100 degrees, and winter lows can drop below zero. Carry plenty of extra food and water and *at least* one spare tire.

This drive begins at the Snowville exit on Interstate 84. Even along the interstate drive to Snowville you will get a pretty good sense of this area's grand desolation. Because of the detachment from the landscape that the interstate imposes on the traveler, this may not promise to be particularly "scenic," but just wait: this is land you must get close to, and you will, once you leave the interstate behind.

Snowville is a truck-stop town and the best place to fill your tank before embarking on this long desert drive. A final logistical warning is in order here: if you have an extremely large capacity tank (or if you plan only to go to Grouse Creek and back on UT 30) you can easily do this entire trip on one tank. If you intend to drive back along the old railroad grade, however, fill the tank at Grouse Creek just to be safe. The truck stop at Snowville

Utah Highway 30 cuts across the state's deserted northwest corner.

is open all night, and there is a small motel. Snowville also has a classic western cafe: Molly's Cafe is just past the couple of gas stations that make up the Greater Snowville Commercial District.

From Snowville, follow I-84 west about 2 miles to the first exit, marked UT 30 and signed for Park Valley. You cross back over the highway on the two-lane, signed here also for Elko, and you are on your way to a driving adventure.

The road runs west, straight as an arrow, toward the Raft River Mountains. The first 10 miles pass through fairly monotonous irrigated farmland

Old brick house, Grouse Creek.

that gradually turns to dry sagebrush prairie. At this point the drive becomes interesting. It is fascinating to contemplate the vastness of this land and the scarcity of people here. About 15 miles from the interstate, you will reach the point shown on the map as Curlew Junction. There is no town here, just a fork in the road. Straight ahead is Utah Highway 42; left is the continuation of UT 30. Take this left, signed for Park Valley, Montello, and Elko.

Here the road strikes out to the southwest, and the land becomes increasingly more remote. At this point, something quite interesting happens to increase this sense of remoteness: you leave the power line behind, so only the sparse traffic along this road reminds you of civilization.

This is Great Basin desert—much rougher and less "scenic" in conventional terms than the sandstone plateau country and rugged alpine terrain to the south and east. The land here has a hard, unfriendly look. It is, in fact, inhospitable, resistant to Man's attempts to subdue it. This is one of the most pristine and unspoiled regions in America, precisely because the land is so uninviting.

The few folks who inhabit the region are, however, anything but inhospitable. As in other remote ranching districts of the American West, passing motorists still wave to one another out here, a tradition that hopefully will endure. There are many things about this corner of Utah that suggest times past, reinforcing the sense that this place is still tied to pioneer traditions, where people are friendly enough, but in that very independent *cowboy* way.

A few miles past the major direction change at Curlew Junction, if you look off ahead and to the left you may just catch a glimpse of the sun glinting off the Great Salt Lake. Also note that off to the left/south is approximately the route of the return option along the old railroad bed. About 10 miles past Curlew Junction is the turnoff on the left for Kelton, a good dirt road leading down to the ghost town described in the rail-bed return option. (If you plan on missing the rail line return, you may want to make a sidetrip here to see the site of Kelton.) In another few miles, note the occasional field under cultivation, indicating that you are approaching the ranching community of Park Valley. Park Valley has a gas station, a motel, a cafe that appears not to be open on Sunday, and not much else other than the ubiquitous LDS church (quite a cute little LDS church, in fact).

It is 4 more miles to the tiny hamlet of Rosette, home to more horses than people and without services. Other than Park Valley and Rosette, there are no real communities out here; most of the road signs at the side roads are for private family ranches rather than for towns. As you drive south/southwest from Rosette, look straight ahead in the distance to see the extremely remote Silver Island Mountains, far to the south near the Bonneville Salt Flats. A designated scenic backway (on dirt roads) encircles these fascinating peaks, but this drive is best accessed from Interstate 80, west from Salt Lake, just before the Nevada state line at Wendover. Driving south from Lucin is not advised unless you are prepared for rough conditions.

About 25 miles past Park Valley, note on the left what must surely be the only two fully grown trees within 20 miles or more. You cannot miss them, standing all alone on the featureless plain. At the pullout here you can see *why* these trees have grown so robustly: at the base of the larger tree, a pipe sunk into the ground accesses spring water that flows beneath the surface. Apparently a plaque once stood here (which may be replaced in the future), marking what had been a stage stop in past times.

About 13 miles farther along, note the concrete structure on the right (the work of those clever folks at ATT), the first manmade edifice since Rosette. Five miles farther, note the picturesque old United States Department of Interior sign for Rabbit Spring, on the left, indicating the use of these springs by grazing livestock. Forty-six miles west of Park Valley is the obvious intersection with the good gravel road: north to Grouse Creek, south to Lucin.

It is 20 miles of good gravel road to Grouse Creek. It may be useful to know that the land to the east of this road is mostly public (at least for the first 12 miles), where you may camp, provided you are self-sufficient and practice no-impact camping techniques. The land on the west side of the road is almost entirely private property.

Mudflats, west of Kelton along the old railroad line.

Grouse Creek is an attractive, prosperous-looking town, well watered, in an extremely beautiful valley. In addition to all basic services (but no motel), there is an imposing stone elementary school and, of course, a large LDS church. Grouse Creek also has one of the most picturesque little rodeo arenas in all of Utah, with the old-style (and soon to be extinct) wooden bucking chutes. If you happen to be here the weekend prior to July 4th, they put on a community rodeo that has a long tradition in this very traditional ranch country.

From Grouse Creek, the drive up to Almo, Idaho, is extremely scenic and gives the opportunity to visit City of Rocks. Ask in Grouse Creek about the condition of the road, which can be difficult when wet. To return to the intersection with UT 30, a good option is the loop through Etna from Grouse Creek. While well maintained, this gravel road is fairly narrow, so RVs and trailers should probably return south on the main gravel road. This alternate return doesn't provide sights much different from the main road (Etna is not an actual town, just a handful of ranches and a closed school), but it does give a slight change of scenery.

At the intersection with UT 30, you must decide whether to do the rail-bed drive or return to Snowville on UT 30. A third option—the quickest way back to the Salt Lake Valley—is to continue **west** on UT 30 to Montello, Nevada, then 24 miles southwest to intersect with I-80, 59 miles west of Wendover. If you do return to Snowville on UT 30, by all means rejoin this drive at Golden Spike National Historic Site. The easiest way to do this from Snowville is to take I-84 to exit 26 (Howell/UT 83) and follow UT 83 south for 14 miles to the well-marked turn on the right (just past the Thiokol rocket display).

For those of you game to drive the rail line, cross the highway and drive 4.5 miles south to the start of the Central Pacific Railroad Trail Scenic Backway. Set your odometer to zero: mileages here are from the start of the backway.

One of the most significant events in the history of American transportation took place on May 10, 1869, 88 miles east of here at Promontory, when the driving of the Golden Spike joined the Union Pacific and Central Pacific railroads, completing the transcontinental line. It was, at the time, an event of the same magnitude and public interest as that which took place almost exactly a century later: the landing of a man on the moon.

This drive runs pretty much right along the old railroad grade, the final stretch of the Central Pacific's 800-mile line from California. You may wonder why there is no longer a rail line here today (nor is there a town of Lucin, for that matter). In 1904, the Lucin Cutoff (the line currently in use) was completed south of here, crossing the lake by trestle. This shortened the route to Ogden by forty miles and eliminated some of the difficult grades you will see later along the old line.

Following the completion of the cutoff, traffic along the original Promontory line dwindled to just local residents and livestock. As soon as the main line shifted south, the old towns along the original line began to die, and many buildings were taken down and moved to more important sites in the lumber-poor desert. Regular traffic ceased completely in 1938, and in 1942 the rails were removed so the steel could be used in the war effort.

That pretty well tells it all. At one time there were large and vibrant railroad towns strung along this now-abandoned line. Today nothing remains from that epic era but desert and a very few building foundations. That, and one more thing: the old trace of the railroad bed, which gives us this fine graded surface on which to drive across the desert.

The deserted (even ignored) character of this region made it a perfect setting for two monumental art pieces created by two prominent figures in the 1970s arts movement sometimes referred to as *earthworks*. These artists created large pieces in outdoor settings in an attempt to *engage* the landscape and to comment on our relationship to physical environments. It is an interesting coincidence that one of these grand-scale pieces lies at the very western end of the old railroad grade, the other close to the eastern terminus. It is also of some interest that each was produced, separately, by husband and wife.

"Sun Tunnels" was created between 1973 and 1976 by Nancy Holt on the barren desert floor 4 miles from Lucin. The "tunnels" are actually four huge concrete pipes laid out to mark sunrises and sunsets at the winter and summer solstices. To find the desert artwork (hard to miss in this empty plain), cross the rail line at the deceased town of Lucin and follow the good dirt road 4 miles to the southeast. You can see the piece from the site of Lucin.

The site is sure to inspire some viewers to contemplate such things as the complexity of these open, empty spaces; others may find these terse concrete pipes as evocative and interesting as highway construction debris. If you have kids, they will no doubt want to run around inside the gigantic tubes. Tear them away from the desert playground and return to Lucin. At the far end of the rail line, you will have the opportunity to see the somewhat more famous piece created by Holt's deceased husband, Robert Smithson, called "Spiral Jetty."

This is not exactly a sandy desert. Depending on how much moisture there has been, this landscape can be quite luxuriant with desert grasses. Spaced along the old rail bed are many very nice brown BLM historical markers describing important places along the old line. It is impossible to miss these markers in this treeless landscape. There are more than thirty interpretive sites. Please heed the frequent written warnings not to collect souvenirs or vandalize the few remaining ruins and artifacts, or soon nothing will be left for future visitors. The BLM requests that anyone witnessing the disturbance of any site here contact them at 1-800-722-3998. Get a license number and vehicle description if you can.

Watch your speed along the old grade: 25 mph is about right for most vehicles, 30 mph maximum. The road is smooth enough in places that you may want to increase speed—but you will be sorry when you hit the inevitable rut. Keep your eyes on the road. Old rail spikes occasionally surface. There are also numerous creek beds to cross on old wooden bridges and many small deviations around bridges deemed too weak to support vehicle traffic.

Apart from the hazards and slowness of the rough surface, this is an extremely interesting and enjoyable driving experience. The old rail line, just barely wider than your vehicle, is elevated slightly above the surrounding desert, giving you a heightened sense of being out in the middle of the desert—which, in fact, you are. No-impact camping is permitted along the railroad grade, though no facilities or water are available anywhere.

At mile 22 you reach the site of the former community of Terrace, which lasted from 1869 until around 1910. Terrace was the largest of the Central Pacific towns built in Utah. The town had a sixteen-stall roundhouse and an eight-track switching yard and boasted many businesses, a school, a library, a Wells-Fargo office, a public bath, and even a justice of the peace. The most reasonable estimates for the former population of Terrace are around one thousand. Most of the commercial buildings were north of the tracks; residential neighborhoods were to the south. There was a nice town square and the streets were lined with trees all watered with water brought in by train. With the completion of the Lucin Cutoff, most of buildings were transported to Carlin, Nevada, and the town of Terrace died.

Not much remains of the town, but if you stroll around you can find foundations of brick buildings and traces of the old railyard. To think that for over thirty years a substantial community existed out here in this desert wilderness is rather odd. From the townsite, note on the right that the old ties (without the track) are still in place. The cemetery site is well marked about half a mile farther along. A sign explains that the cemetery was in pretty good condition until 1986, when vandals stole most of the remaining headstones.

At mile 25 is a good escape route up to UT 30 (8 miles north), at a well-marked intersection. At just under mile 27 the road begins to climb up into the hills, becoming a little rocky but posing no real problem. To this point the road has been perfectly fine for anything but large RVs and trailers. Conventional passenger vehicles will just have to take it slowly.

At about mile 40 there is a view off to the left and down onto the place where Dove Creek forms either a pond or a mudflat, depending on the season. Also here is the rough road on the right to the very remote Hogup Mountains (in a cave in the Hogup area, artifacts from the Desert Archaic period of proto-Indian culture date back ten thousand years). At just under mile 45 there is a nice view ahead and to the right of the lake, which has been rather elusive to this point.

At just past mile 45 the railroad grade takes a jog to the left. Here there are a couple of the by-now familiar signs for deviations from the grade. There is also here a very prominent road descending on the right, signed for Kelton. Take this road, as the road along the grade dies shortly past here. It should be obvious what is happening with the route. The dirt road drops down onto the desert flat, while the rail line clings to the rocky hillside, clearly visible above and to the left. Drive slowly down on these flats, as there may be occasional washed-out sections. At just under mile 49 you will intersect a major dirt road, signed for Kelton, to the left. Take this obvious left, continuing in the same general northeast direction as the rail line.

Again, looking up toward the hillside on your left, you can see the very obvious line of the old grade. At just past mile 50 you will re-cross the old grade and you can see how the grade has actually been closed off. At mile 52, intersect another good dirt road and trend to the right (northeast), signed for Kelton. Two-and-a-half miles farther, note on the right the Kelton cemetery, which, according to the sign: "served the residents of Kelton until it was abandoned in 1942." Sadly, this extremely picturesque old graveyard has been badly vandalized.

Continue on to the prominent historic markers for the town of Kelton, clearly visible to the northeast. Kelton (also known as Indian Creek) survived until 1942, partly due to its importance as a transportation hub. There was evidently a very substantial town here (about seven hundred), where the stage from Oregon Territory to the north made the rail connection. This northern stage line was reportedly the most often-robbed stage in the West, usually robbed weekly, sometimes daily.

At this point you can rejoin the railroad grade, which is nicely maintained from here east and signed for Golden Spike National Historic Site. If you are completely tired of the desert driving, you can also follow the good road north to rejoin UT 30, although at this point that option provides no real advantage, as the route from here east is so well maintained. In fact, the route east from Kelton has been so heavily traveled (this is obviously a popular excursion from the east) that it barely resembles a rail line; it seems more like a normal desert road.

At mile 65 is the important intersection with the good road north to Snowville (again, no point taking this unless your tank is empty). Also here is Locomotive Springs, which is actually a series of springs and ponds, and serves as a bird refuge. It makes a decent place to camp, provided you need no facilities and the bugs aren't too vicious.

The railroad bed continues to Golden Spike (mileages from here are taken from Locomotive Springs). East of Locomotive Springs, it can be pretty rough; at any rate, at mile 3.5 you will have to exit to the good dirt road on the left. I suggest getting on this road right from Locomotive Springs: it runs parallel to the rail line, about 30 yards to its left. At just under 8 miles from Locomotive Springs take the prominent right fork (signs around here may be missing or badly shot-up, but the route is obvious—just stay on the main road, avoiding deviations to the left).

At mile 13 is a good opportunity to return to the railroad grade. A BLM sign indicates Golden Spike 11 miles ahead and the old railroad grade to the right. The only real advantages to driving the old grade from here are the better views of the lake, off to the right, along with a few more historical markers.

A prominent BLM back country drive sign indicates your arrival at Golden Spike. At this sign, go left about 10 yards, then turn right to drive along the designated West Grade Auto Tour. It is about 5 miles from here to the visitor center.

Exhibits, films, and literature at the visitor center describe both the momentous Goldon Spike event and its profound impact on the subsequent history of the American West. A short section of track has been re-laid at precisely the spot where the two lines met, and exact replicas of the Central Pacific's "Jupiter" and the Union Pacific's "119" make scheduled appearances during the summer season. There is also a very nice 9-mile driving tour with interpretive signs—which will probably seem rather tame to those who have just finished the old rail-bed drive from Lucin. Of course, for those who opted *not* to drive east along the old rail bed, this is a fine opportunity for an abbreviated introduction to this fascinating and important slice of American history.

The visitor center is open 8 A.M. until 6 P.M. daily, Memorial Day to Labor Day; 8 A.M. until 4:30 P.M. for the rest of the year (closed Thanksgiving, Christmas, and New Year's Day). Appearances by the locomotives are at 9:30 A.M., and at 1:30 and 4 P.M., with additional summer demonstrations at 11:30 A.M. and 3:30 P.M. No camping or services are available at Golden Spike.

Now for the *second* installment on the Northwest Utah Post-Modern Arts Tour. "Spiral Jetty," Robert Smithson's odd embellishment of the salty shores of the Great Salt Lake, is a 15-mile drive on good dirt roads from Golden Spike. It is definitely worth a visit, but check first with the folks at Golden Spike on the status of the road into the site. "Spiral Jetty" has a genuinely *archaeological* look to it, as if it somehow belongs there, or might have performed some arcane function, either nautical or spiritual, in the distant past. Constructed in 1970, it disappeared under the rising waters of the lake two years later. It remained submerged in the briny depths until 1994, when the lake receded.

It is precisely what the name suggests: a grand spiral jetty winding its way offshore. Built of earth and rock, like some sort of monumental hippy-era hallucinogenic road-building scheme, it will surely cause you to ponder deeply significant questions like: Why? One thing seems certain. If it belongs anywhere, to quote Brigham one final time: *Surely, this is the place.*

To continue on to Corinne from Golden Spike, follow the paved road about 8 miles to the intersection with UT 83. As you near the intersection, note the extensive research, testing, and production facilities of the Thiokol Corporation. To visit their very nice rocket display, you must turn left/north and drive just under 2 miles. This is definitely worth the two-minute detour, especially if you have kids with you (alas, when they see these real-live rockets they will no doubt forget all about concrete pipes and earthen causeways). It does seem appropriate that a company that builds space exploration vehicles should choose to do its testing and development here in this rather extra-terrestial landscape.

It is 17 miles from the UT 83 intersection to Corinne. This is a very attractive and interesting rough landscape: alkali salt flats to the south/right, rough scrub hills to the left. This stretch of road serves as a final reminder that this is land upon which humanity cannot impose its will—partly because changing it has been deemed not worth the time and energy required, and partly because nature here resists change. There are large tracts of marshland along the road home to myriad forms of bird life. The final 6 miles to Corinne pass through attractive, productive farmland.

Golden Spike National Historic Monument, at Promontory, is the site of the meeting of the Union Pacific and Central Pacific railroads.

The story of old Corinne is one of the more interesting tales of Utah's early history, and the peaceful demeanor of the present farm town belies its rather roughneck past. As the two rail lines pushed toward this area from east and west, non-Mormon speculators rushed in to promote the rowdy shanty town and freight relay station of Corinne as the future transportation hub of the Intermountain West. They assumed that the joining of the rails, along with the important freighting needs of the new Montana and Idaho mining districts to the north and the newly formed Tintic District to the south, would make Corinne's crossroads position ideal. The town grew to a very boisterous and decidedly anti-Mormon 1,500, with boosters claiming Corinne would eclipse Salt Lake City and become the new territorial capital.

Corinne's first disappointment came when Promontory was selected for the joining of the lines, and her bubble ultimately burst when Ogden was chosen for the regional rail center. The boosters slinked off, the community gradually dissolved, and Corinne was finally "resettled" as a conventional Mormon town. Though at one time there were twenty-nine saloons and two dance halls here, not much remains of Corinne's heyday. One lasting reminder of its non-Mormon character is the old Methodist/Episcopal Church (dedicated in 1870), the oldest existing Protestant church building in Utah.

It is 2.5 miles from Corinne to Interstate 15, and another 4 miles to Brigham City.

Appendix
Sources of more information

For more information on lands and events, please
contact the following agencies and organizations.

Drive 1

Washington County Travel and
  Convention Bureau
425 South 70 East
St. George, UT 84770
1-800-869-6635

Color Country Travel
  Information
906 North 1400 West
P.O. Box 1550
St. George, UT 84771-1550
1-800-233-8824

Drive 2

Color Country Travel
  Information
906 North 1400 West
P.O. Box 1550
St. George, UT 84771-1550
1-800-233-8824

Superintendent, Zion
  National Park
Springdale, UT 84767
801-772-3256

Drive 3

Kolob Canyons Visitor Center
801-586-9548

Color Country Travel
  Information
906 North 1400 West
P.O. Box 1550
St. George, UT 84771-1550
1-800-233-8824

Drive 4

Kane County
  Information Center
41 South 100 East
Kanab, UT 84741
801-644-5033

Color Country Travel
  Information
906 North 1400 West
P.O. Box 1550
St. George, UT 84771-1550
1-800-233-8824

Drive 5

Dixie National Forest,
  Cedar Breaks Ranger District
82 North 100 East
P.O. Box 580
Cedar City, UT 84721-0580
801-865-3700/865-3200

Dixie National Forest,
  Powell Ranger District
225 East Center Street
Panguitch, UT 84759
801-676-8815

Color Country Travel
  Information
906 North 1400 West
P.O. Box 1550
St. George, UT 84771-1550
1-800-233-8824

Drive 6

Color Country Travel
 Information
906 North 1400 West
P.O. Box 1550
St. George, UT 84771-1550
1-800-233-8824

Superintendent, Bryce Canyon
 National Park
Bryce Canyon, UT 84717
801-834-5322

Dixie National Forest,
 Escalante Ranger District
270 West Main Street
Escalante, UT 84726
801-826-4221

Drive 7

Dixie National Forest,
 Escalante Ranger District
270 West Main Street
Escalante, UT 84726
801-826-4221

Dixie National Forest,
 Teasdale Ranger District
P.O. Box 99
Teasdale, UT 84773
801-425-3702

Drive 8

Panoramaland Travel
 Information
250 North Main Street
Richfield, UT 84701
1-800-748-4361

Capitol Reef National Park
Torrey, UT 84775
801-425-3791

Dixie National Forest,
 Teasdale Ranger District
P.O. Box 99
Teasdale, UT 84773
801-425-3702

Hanksville Area BLM Office
406 South 100 West
Hanksville, UT 84734
801-542-3461

Drive 9

Hanksville Area BLM Office
406 South 100 West
Hanksville, UT 84734
801-542-3461

Superintendent, Natural Bridges
 National Monument
Box 1
Lake Powell, UT 84533
801-259-5174

San Juan Travel Information
117 South Main Street
Monticello, UT 84535
1-800-575-4FUN

Drive 10

Canyonlands Travel Information
117 South Main
Monticello, UT 84535
1-800-574-4FUN

Monument Valley Visitors Center
520-727-3287

Drive 11

Monticello Multi-Agency
 Visitor Center
Box 490
Monticello, UT 84535
1-800-574-4386/801-587-3235

Superintendent, Canyonlands
  National Park
125 West 200 South
Moab, UT 84532
801-259-7164

Drive 12

Canyonlands Travel Information
Center and Main Streets
Moab, UT 84532
1-800-635-6622

Drive 13

Canyonlands Travel Information
Center and Main Streets
Moab, UT 84532
1-800-635-6622

Bureau of Land Management,
  Moab District Office
82 East Dogwood
Moab, UT 8453
801-259-6111
(Please review the BLM's "Canyon
Country Minimum Impact Practices"
brochure while visiting this area.)

Drive 14

Loa Ranger District
150 South Main Street
Loa, UT 84747
801-836-2811/836-2800

Panoramaland Travel
  Information
250 North Main
P.O. Box 820
Richfield, UT 84701
1-800-748-4361

Drive 15

USDA Forest Service,
  Beaver Ranger District
190 North 100 East
Beaver, UT 84713
801-438-2436

Beaver County Travel Council
Box 272
Beaver, UT 84713
801-438-2975/438-2808

USDA Forest Service,
  Richfield Ranger District
115 East 900 North
Richfield, UT 84701
801-896-9233

Sevier Travel Council
220 North 600 West
Richfield, UT 84701
1-800-662-8898

Drive 16

Panoramaland Travel Information
250 North Main Street
Richfield, UT 84701
1-800-748-4361

Delta Visitor Information
328 West 100 North
Delta, UT 84624
801-864-5013

Drive 17

Spanish Fork Ranger District
44 West 400 North
Spanish Fork, UT 84660
801-798-3571

Uinta National Forest
740 South Main
Nephi, UT 84648
801-623-2735

Drive 18

Sanpete Ranger District
150 South Main
Ephraim, UT 84627
801-283-4151

Castle Country Travel Information
155 East Main
P.O. Box 1037
Price, UT 84501
1-800-842-0789

Drive 19

Castle Country Travel Council
155 East Main
Price, UT 84501
801-637-1930

Duchesne Ranger District
801-738-2482

Drive 20

Ashley National Forest
355 North Vernal Avenue
Vernal, UT 84078
801-789-1181

Dinosaurland Regional
  Travel Office
25 East Main Street
Vernal, UT 84078
1-800-477-5558

Drive 21

Kamas Ranger District
Kamas, UT 84036
801-783-4338

Evanston Ranger District
Evanston, WY 82980
307-789-3194

Mountainland Travel Information
2545 North Canyon Road
Provo, UT 84604
801-377-2262

Drive 22

Mountainland Travel Information
2545 North Canyon Road
Provo, UT 84604
801-377-2262

Drive 23

Great Salt Lake Country
  Travel Information
180 South West Temple
Salt Lake City, UT 84101-1493
801-521-2822

BLM Salt Lake District Office
2370 South 2300 West
Salt Lake City, UT 84119
801-977-3300

Drive 24

Salt Lake Ranger District
6944 South 3000 East
Salt Lake City, UT 84121
801-524-5042

Salt Lake Convention and Visitors
Bureau and Information Center
180 South West Temple
Salt Lake City, UT 84101
1-800-541-4955

Bridgerland Travel and
Tourism Office
160 North Main Street
Logan, UT 84321
1-800-882-4433

Drive 25

Ogden Ranger District
507 25th Street
Suite 103
Ogden, UT 84402
801-625-5112

Golden Spike Empire
Travel Office
2501 Wall Avenue
Ogden, UT 84401
1-800-255-8824

Drive 28

Golden Spike Empire
Travel Information
2501 Wall Avenue
Ogden, UT 84401
1-800-255-8824

Drive 26

Refuge Manager, Bear River
Migratory Bird Refuge
866 South Main
Brigham City, UT 84302
801-723-5887

Brigham City Area Chamber of
Commerce Visitor Center
6 North Main Street
Brigham City, UT 84302
801-723-3937

Drive 27

District Ranger,
Logan Ranger District
860 North 1200 East
Logan, UT 84321
801-753-2772

Index

FALCON GUIDES® Leading the Way™

FALCON GUIDES® are available for where-to-go hiking, mountain biking, rock climbing, walking, scenic driving, fishing, rockhounding, paddling, birding, wildlife viewing, and camping. We also have FalconGuides on essential outdoor skills and subjects and field identification. The following titles are currently available, but this list grows every year. For a free catalog with a complete list of titles, call FALCON toll-free at 1-800-582-2665.

SCENIC DRIVING GUIDES

Scenic Driving Alaska and the Yukon
Scenic Driving Arizona
Scenic Driving the Beartooth Highway
Scenic Driving California
Scenic Driving Colorado
Scenic Driving Florida
Scenic Driving Georgia
Scenic Driving Hawaii
Scenic Driving Idaho
Scenic Driving Michigan
Scenic Driving Minnesota
Scenic Driving Montana
Scenic Driving New England
Scenic Driving New Mexico
Scenic Driving North Carolina
Scenic Driving Oregon
Scenic Driving the Ozarks
Scenic Driving Pennsylvania
Scenic Driving Texas
Scenic Driving Utah
Scenic Driving Washington
Scenic Driving Wisconsin
Scenic Driving Wyoming
Scenic Driving Yellowstone and
   the Grand Teton National Parks
Scenic Byways East
Scenic Byways Far West
Scenic Byways Rocky Mountains
Back Country Byways

HISTORIC TRAIL GUIDES

Traveling California's Gold Rush Country
Traveling the Lewis & Clark Trail
Traveling the Oregon Trail
Traveler's Guide to the Pony Express Trail

WILDLIFE VIEWING GUIDES

Alaska Wildlife Viewing Guide
Arizona Wildlife Viewing Guide
California Wildlife Viewing Guide
Colorado Wildlife Viewing Guide
Florida Wildlife Viewing Guide
Indiana Wildlife Vewing Guide
Iowa Wildlife Viewing Guide
Kentucky Wildlife Viewing Guide
Massachusetts Wildlife Viewing Guide
Montana Wildlife Viewing Guide
Nebraska Wildlife Viewing Guide
Nevada Wildlife Viewing Guide
New Hampshire Wildlife Viewing Guide
New Jersey Wildlife Viewing Guide
New Mexico Wildlife Viewing Guide
New York Wildlife Viewing Guide
North Carolina Wildlife Viewing Guide
North Dakota Wildlife Viewing Guide
Ohio Wildlife Viewing Guide
Oregon Wildlife Viewing Guide
Puerto Rico & the Virgin Islands
   Wildlife Viewing Guide
Tennessee Wildlife Viewing Guide
Texas Wildlife Viewing Guide
Utah Wildlife Viewing Guide
Vermont Wildlife Viewing Guide
Virginia Wildlife Viewing Guide
Washington Wildlife Viewing Guide
West Virginia Wildlife Viewing Guide
Wisconsin Wildlife Viewing Guide

■ *To order any of these books, check with your local bookseller*
or call FALCON ® *at 1-800-582-2665.*
Visit us on the world wide web at:
www.FalconOutdoors.com

FALCON®